JIHADI TERRORISM AND THE RADICALISATION CHALLENGE IN EUROPE

Jihadi Terrorism and the Radicalisation Challenge in Europe

Edited by

RIK COOLSAET
Ghent University, Belgium

ASHGATE

Published by
Ashgate Publishing Limited
Gower House
Croft Road
Aldershot
Hampshire GU11 3HR
England

Ashgate Publishing Company
Suite 420
101 Cherry Street
Burlington, VT 05401-4405
USA

Ashgate website: http://www.ashgate.com

British Library Cataloguing in Publication Data
Jihadi Terrorism and the radicalisation challenge in Europe
   1. Terrorism - Religious aspects - Islam 2. Jihad
   3. Terrorism - Europe, Western - Prevention 4. Radicalism -
   Europe, Western 5. Islamic fundamentalism - Europe, Western
   I. Coolsaet, R.
   303.6'25'088297'094

Library of Congress Cataloging-in-Publication Data
Jihadi terrorism and the radicalisation challenge in Europe / by Rik Coolsaet.
     p. cm.
   Includes index.
   ISBN 978-0-7546-7217-3
   1. Terrorism--Europe. 2. Jihad. 3. Radicalism--Europe. 4. Islamic fundamentalism--Europe.
5. Terrorism--Europe--Prevention.

   HV6433.E85J54 2007
   363.325094--dc22

                         2007025290

ISBN 978 0 7546 7217 3

Printed and bound in Great Britain by MPG Books Ltd, Bodmin, Cornwall.

Contents

List of Figures and Tables

Figures

Tables

Notes on Contributors

Glenn Audenaert

Glenn Audenaert is Judicial Director of the Federal Judicial Police, Brussels and as such head of the anti-Terrorist Unit of the Belgian Federal Police. He is master in training at universities in Ghent, Antwerp, Brussels and Leuven. He has been visiting teacher at, among others, Winston Park College (UK Home Office), Police Staff College (Turkey) and NATO Defence College (Rome). He has performed many international police missions.

Edwin Bakker

Edwin Bakker is a political geographer by training and received his doctorate at the University of Groningen (1997). As a lecturer at the Center for International Conflict Analysis & Management (CICAM) of Nijmegen University (1997–2003) his research area shifted towards conflict management and the role of security organisations, in particular the Organisation for Security and Co-operation in Europe. At the Netherlands Institute Clingendael, he researches jihadi terrorism in Europe and counterterrorism policies. Recent projects on terrorism and non-proliferation include various publications in English and Dutch as well as (contributions to) reports for various ministries, non-governmental organisations and the media.

Jocelyne Cesari

Jocelyne Cesari has been a research associate at the Center for Middle Eastern Studies at Harvard University since spring 2001 and has also held teaching positions in the anthropology department and at Harvard Divinity School (where she teaches on Islam in America and Global Islam). Before coming to Harvard, she served as an Associate Research Scholar and Adjunct Professor at Columbia University's School of International and Public Affairs. At Harvard she is coordinating the Provost Interfaculty Program on Islam in the West. Her most recent books are: *When Islam and Democracy Meet: Muslims in Europe and in the United States* (Palgrave, 2004) and *European Muslims and the Secular State* (Ashgate, 2005).

Rik Coolsaet

Rik Coolsaet is Professor of International Relations at Ghent University (Belgium). He is Chair of the Department of Political Science at Ghent University and serves as Director of the Security & Global Governance Program at Egmont-Royal Institute for International Relations (Brussels). Between 1988 and 1995 he held several high-ranking positions at the (Belgian) Ministry of Defence and the Ministry of Foreign Affairs. His most recent publication in English is *Al-Qaeda: The Myth. The Root Causes of International Terrorism and How to Tackle Them* (Ghent: Academia Press, 2005; also translated into French and Dutch). He has been appointed to the European Commission's Expert Group on Violent Radicalisation (established in 2006).

Martha Crenshaw

Martha Crenshaw is the Colin and Nancy Campbell Professor of Global Issues and Democratic Thought and Professor of Government at Wesleyan University in Middletown (Connecticut, USA), where she has taught since 1974. She has written extensively on the issue of political terrorism. She has served on the Council of the APSA and is a former President and Councillor of the International Society of Political Psychology (ISPP). Her current research focuses on why the United States is the target of terrorism and the distinction between 'old' and 'new' terrorism, as well as how campaigns of terrorism come to an end.

Tarik Fraihi

Tarik Fraihi is a philosopher at the research institute of the Flemish Socialist Party (Belgium) and assistant professor at EHSAL-Institute for Higher Education (Brussels). He severely criticises minority policies in numerous essays and in his Dutch-language book *De smaak van ongelijkheid* (*The Taste of Inequity*).

Alain Grignard

Alain Grignard has been assigned to the anti-terrorist unit of the Gendarmerie (now the Federal Police) since 1980. Since 2000 he has served as Superintendent, Assistant Director at the anti-terrorist division of the Federal Police in Brussels. In addition to his police assignments, he has compiled a distinguished academic career as an expert on Islam. He is notably Master of Conference at the University of Liège, teaching courses on political Islam and the Muslim-Arab world. He is also in charge of education at the ESCLA and IHESI (Paris). He has published extensively on Islamism, Islamic armed groups and Islamic propaganda.

Noor Huda Ismail

Noor Huda Ismail has recently completed his studies at the International Security Studies programme of the University of St Andrews (United Kingdom). From April to September 2005 he worked in International Defence and Security Studies (Nanyang Technological University, Singapore) and before that (September 2003 to April 2005) he served as Special Correspondent for the Washington Post's Southeast Asia Bureau, Jakarta office. Noor Huda Ismail holds a BA in Arabic Language and Literature from an Islamic State Institute 'Sunan Kalijaga' (Jogjakarta, Indonesia) and a Diploma in Communication Studies from Gadjah Mada University (Jogjakarta, Indonesia).

Gilles de Kerchove d'Ousselghem

Gilles de Kerchove d'Ousselghem is the EU Counter-terrorism coordinator since 2007. He teaches at the Catholic University of Louvain-la-Neuve, the Institute of European Studies of the Free University Brussels (ULB) and the Facultés Universitaires Saint Louis (Brussels). He is also Assistant Professor at the Ecole Nationale d'Administration of Strasbourg. With A. Weyembergh he has published several books on EU law, including: *Sécurité et justice: enjeu de la politique extérieure de l'Union européenne* (Editions de l'Université de Bruxelles, 2003); *La confiance mutuelle dans l'espace pénal européen* (Editions de l'Université de Bruxelles, 2005).

Rudolph (Ruud) Peters

Ruud Peters is an expert in modern Islam, Islamic law and radical Islam in Europe. He holds degrees in law and Islamic languages (Arabic and Turkish) from the Universities of Amsterdam and Leiden and a PhD in Islamic studies from the University of Amsterdam. He has recently published *Jihad in Classical and Modern Islam* (Princeton, NJ: Markus Wiener, 2005; first ed. 1996); and *Crime and Punishment in Islamic Law* (Cambridge University Press, 2005), as well as various articles. He is a professor of Islamic studies and Islamic law at the University of Amsterdam.

Paul R. Pillar

Paul R. Pillar is Visiting Professor of Security Studies at the Georgetown University. From 1977 to 2005 he was intelligence officer with the Central Intelligence Agency and the National Intelligence Council. He has notably published *Terrorism and U.S. Foreign Policy* (Brookings Institution Press, 2001); *Negotiating Peace: War Termination as a Bargaining Process* (Princeton University Press, 1983), as well as several articles and chapters in edited volumes.

Hugh Roberts

Dr Hugh Roberts is the Director of the North Africa Project for the International Crisis Group. From 1997 to 2002 he was a Senior Research Fellow of the Development Studies Institute at the London School of Economics and Political Science, and he remains a Senior Visiting Research Fellow of DESTIN's Development Research Centre. Between 1976 and 1997 he lectured in the School of Development Studies at the University of East Anglia, the Institute of Development Studies at the University of Sussex, the Department of Political Science at the University of California, Berkeley and the Department of History at the School of Oriental and African Studies in the University of London. His book, *The Battlefield: Algeria, 1988–2002: Studies in a Broken Polity*, was published by Verso in March 2003.

Olivier Roy

Olivier Roy is Director of Studies at the Ecole des Hautes Etudes en Sciences Sociales as well as Director of Research at the French CNRS. He has published extensively on global and political Islam and terrorism including: *L'Afghanistan, Islam et modernité politique* (Le Seuil, 1985); *L'Echec de l'Islam politique* (Le Seuil, 1992); *La nouvelle Asie centrale, ou la fabrication des nations* (Le Seuil, 1997); *Iran: comment sortir d'une révolution religieuse?* (with Farhad Khosrokhavar) (Le Seuil, 1999); *Les illusions du 11 septembre* (Le Seuil, 2002); *Globalized Islam* (Columbia University Press, 2006); *La Turquie aujourd'hui: Un pays européen?* (Paris: Universalis, 2004); *Secularism Confronts Islam* (Columbia University Press, 2007).

Tanguy Struye de Swielande

Tanguy Struye de Swielande has a PhD in Political Sciences from the Catholic University of Louvain-la-Neuve and is Senior Researcher at the Centre for Studies on Conflicts and Crises (CECRI-UCL). He teaches at the Royal Military Academy (Brussels) and at the University of Mons. He joined the Egmont Institute as Research Fellow in the Security & Global Governance Department in February 2007. His publications include: *La politique étrangère américaine après la guerre froide et les défis asymétriques* (Presses Universitaires de Louvain, 2003); *La politique étrangère sous l'Administration Bush: Analyse de la prise de décision* (Bruxelles: P.IE.-Peter Lang, 2007).

Teun Van de Voorde

Teun Van de Voorde is Research Fellow at the Department of Political Science (Ghent University). She is preparing a PhD on 'The Root Causes of International Terrorism: A Longitudinal Study into the Rise and Demise of Successive Waves of Major Terrorist Activities'.

Ran van Reedt Dortland

Ran van Reedt Dortland works as a seconded national expert at the General Secretariat of the Council of the European Union.

Gijs de Vries

From 2004 to 2007 Gijs de Vries served as the European Union's Counter-Terrorism Coordinator. He is a former member of the Government of the Netherlands (Deputy Minister of the Interior, 1998–2002) and a former Member of the European Parliament (Leader of the Liberal and Democratic Group, 1994–98). He was the representative of the Dutch Government in the European Convention, which drew up the European Union's draft constitutional treaty (2002–2003). In April 2007 he joined the Netherlands Institute of International Relations 'Clingendael' as a Senior Fellow. Gijs de Vries is a Member of the World Economic Forum's Council for West–Islamic World Dialogue (C-100).

Foreword

Al-Qaeda's unprecedented attack on the United States and America's subsequent reaction have radically reshaped international relations. The world's pre-eminent superpower has elevated the 'war on terror' to the top of its agenda. Although the war paradigm may have proven controversial legally as well as politically, it is the prism through which America has come to see and deal with much of the world.

More than six years after 9/11 it is clear that Osama bin Laden and his followers have failed to realise some of their strategic objectives. Western countries have not fundamentally altered their foreign and security policies. There have been no Islamist revolutions in majority-Muslim countries. Nor has the notion of a Caliphate been embraced by most Muslims. On the contrary, opinion surveys show that support for universal values of freedom and democracy among Muslims remains strong. Governments across the world have successfully improved their capacity to prevent and combat terrorism.

Yet the fight against al-Qaeda and its legacy has not been won. Al-Qaeda itself has been diminished but not defeated. Its suicide operations have been emulated widely: four out of five incidents of suicide terrorism perpetrated worldwide between 1968 and 2004 have occurred since 9/11. Intermittent counter-measures by the Pakistani authorities notwithstanding, al-Qaeda has managed to reconstitute an operational capacity in Waziristan and other regions bordering Afghanistan. Its strategic focus remains to inflict maximum harm on the United States and its allies. It has honed its ideological capacity into a potent and deadly instrument – one which its opponents still struggle to counter effectively. Half of its struggle, al-Qaeda has indicated, is waged through the media. In what Bin Laden and Zawahiri might count as their most important achievement to date, al-Qaeda's record and its ideology continue to inspire individuals and networks on several continents. Many countries accordingly remain at high risk of new terrorist attacks. The threat of further attacks in Europe also remains acute. In France, for example, at least three major Islamist plots have been thwarted in the past two years. They included initiatives to bomb the Paris Metro and Orly Airport. The North Africa-based *Groupe Salafiste pour la Prédication et le Combat* (GSPC), which has linked up with al-Qaeda, has identified France as its prime target. Since the attacks in London in July 2005 the British authorities have disrupted five major conspiracies. In 2006 British intelligence services declared they were monitoring some 200 networks, totalling over 1,600 identified individuals who were actively engaged in plotting or facilitating terrorist acts in the United Kingdom or elsewhere in the world. Islamist terrorists have been tried and convicted in courts across Europe, from Ireland to Italy.

Islamist terrorism poses a threat to societies not only because of the casualties caused. Statistics alone do not tell the whole story. Among the most insidious consequences of jihadi terrorism is a climate of suspicion and fear both between Muslims and non-Muslims and among Muslims themselves. In democratic countries terrorism deepens ethnic and religious divisions. In non-democratic states it bolsters the forces of authoritarianism. Everywhere, governments are at risk of over-reacting in the fight against terrorism and of compromising the very rights and liberties they have pledged to uphold. Terrorism in the name of Islam thus tears at the very fabric of society. To counter terrorism effectively governments must address its root causes. Poverty does not, as such, appear to rank among these causes, though relative deprivation and sensitivity to discriminatory or other unequal treatment may well at times play a role as a contributing cause. However, in the mechanisms of radicalisation, recruitment, and active participation in acts of terrorism there is much which remains to be fully understood. Different dynamics of time, place and circumstances need to be taken into account. Explanations applicable to Indonesia or the Philippines, for example, may not be equally relevant to Algeria or Morocco. Even within Europe patterns of radicalisation differ from country to country. Nevertheless, some patterns can be said to be of wider significance. In the processes of radicalisation, political grievances rooted in an interpretation of relations between the West and the Islamic world generally play a dominant role. Since 2003 the war in Iraq has enabled Islamist ideologues to proffer their narrative of victimhood with renewed vigour and notable success. Of course Muslim grievances against the United States and its allies predate the war in Iraq. But by fuelling Muslim radicalisation and terrorism this war has been a serious setback to counter-terrorism in Europe and elsewhere in the world.

Many expect the phenomenon of jihadi terrorism to last for a considerable number of years, possibly a generation. All the more reason, therefore, to assess carefully the nature and the causes of this type of terrorism and to examine to what extent our experience with other types of terrorism holds lessons which might prove relevant. This is what the authors of this publication have set out to do. Their insights and analyses constitute a welcome contribution to our understanding of one of the most important and complex phenomena of our time.

Gijs de Vries
European Union Counter-Terrorism Coordinator
2007

Introduction

Rik Coolsaet

In early 2003 the Belgian Egmont-Royal Institute for International Relations organised a major conference in Brussels on international terrorism, under the heading 'Root Causes of International Terrorism'. At that moment the very notion that there existed underlying forces that shaped the context and causes that led to 9/11 looked self-evident to academics, but was still very much a taboo concept in policy circles. One of the main conclusions of the conference was that these 'root causes' were numerous. No single root cause can explain all forms and modes of terrorism. Digging deeper, even today's 'jihadi' terrorism could not be reduced to one single factor. Depending upon the continent and the countries involved, jihadi terrorism is influenced and boosted by very different sources of discontent – but thriving on an enabling global environment.

Today's terrorism is still often labelled as a 'global threat'. By now most European observers, however, view the terrorist threat rather in terms of a 'patchwork of self-radicalising local groups with international contacts, but without any central engine and any central organisational design', as one of the contributors to this book, Glenn Audenaert, the leading Belgian police official in charge of counter-terrorism, once observed. Jihadi terrorism today is a 'glocal' phenomenon: a cloak patched from different sources of local discontent, stitched together by a puritanical and radical interpretation of Islam, and thriving on a global momentum.

The title of this book merits some clarification. Media and officials in the West still routinely declare that terrorists are primarily after 'us', and that Western civilisation is the main target of 'Islamic/Islamist/Muslim terrorism'. Framing today's main terrorist threat in these terms shows a lack of empathy with the many victims of terrorism in Muslim countries. For indeed, how do these words sound when heard in Algiers, Casablanca, Baghdad or Riyadh? Western rhetoric often fails to notice that neither Americans nor Europeans are the prime victims of these attacks. The Western public does not fully realize that the earliest victims of jihadi terror groups did not fall on September 11, 2001. Long before the first victims fell in New York and Washington tens of thousands of Muslims and Arab citizens had been murdered in a wave of terrorist attacks in Arab countries. A very rough estimate puts the number of victims in Muslim countries since the start of jihadi terrorism in the early 1990s as high as forty times the number of victims in Western countries. This pattern has not altered since. Muslims are the ones to suffer the most under these attacks: intellectuals, civil servants, ordinary citizens and security agents in Algeria, Egypt, Yemen, Saudi Arabia, Turkey, Morocco and, now, Iraq.

In 2004 Peter Clarke of the anti-terrorism branch of the London Metropolitan Police was probably amongst the first officials to warn against labelling today's main terrorist threat as 'Islamic', since this is both offensive and misleading. *Al-Salafiyya al-Jihadiyya* being the closest denomination to describe the terrorists' discourse and ideology, it is appropriate to call them simply 'jihadis' and their brand of terrorism 'jihadi terrorism' – thus emphasising that we are not confronted with a clash between the West and Islam, but with a common threat and challenge for Western and Muslim countries alike. Calling it by this name, we avoid labelling as potential suspects those who already bear the largest share of the burden of terrorism.

Research within the Egmont-Royal Institute for International Relations has largely revolved around two questions: first, how exactly the global environment boosts local and regional terrorism, and, second, how does this relate to the radicalisation process, which is occurring within Europe too. This book tries to give answers to both questions. It grew out of a series of public conferences, seminars and informal brainstormings with many stakeholders from diverse horizons involved.

This book is articulated around these two themes. First, it will attempt to establish the state of jihadi terrorism today, almost two decades after it started in the early 1990s. Second, zooming in on Europe, it asks, what do we know about radicalisation as the main root cause of potential jihadi terrorism in this part of the world?

The specificity of the jihadi threat to Europe has been made clear by the attacks in London and Madrid as well as by the murder of Dutch film-maker Theo van Gogh. These events drew attention to an ongoing process of self-recruitment and self-radicalisation. This is now viewed by many as being the main engine behind the threat within Europe. This home-grown, bottom-up dynamic of the radicalisation process has now become a more important source of potential jihadi recruitment than any top-down internationally organised network of recruiters. This, then, goes to the heart of the European strategy for combating radicalisation and recruitment. European countries and the European Union (EU) are increasingly aware of this phenomenon. A number of governments and the EU itself have elaborated national strategies for countering radicalisation, considering that victory will not be achieved as long as the circumstances are not addressed by which specific individuals turn into terrorists, both in Europe and elsewhere. We therefore tend to believe that this collective work – providing both a precise assessment of the state of the threat as well as a thorough analysis of the radicalisation process – is timely. Aiming at an audience of policy-makers, academia and think-tanks, as well as, last but certainly not least, civil society at large, the chapters in this book combine theoretical approaches with novel thinking and practical steps at de-radicalisation.

This book comprises four parts. Part 1 will provide a worldwide assessment of the jihadi threat in the post al-Qaeda era, an analysis of the figures of jihadi terrorism's lethality and an historical perspective on jihadi terrorism. In Chapter 1 Paul Pillar describes the strength of radical Islamism today. He judges that radicals, in particular the 'descendants' of al-Qaeda, although completely decentralised are still at least as robust as before. For the author the strength of the jihadi movement probably has not yet peaked, but its course over the next several years will depend heavily on events extraneous to terrorism itself. The quantitative assessment in Chapter 2, by Teun Van de Voorde and myself, indicates that international terrorism is more of a challenge than of an existential threat and that Muslims, and not the West, bear by far the heaviest burden of terrorist attacks in the name of Islam. In the third chapter, Martha Crenshaw assesses the widespread belief that terrorism is associated with religion and particularly with Islam. She questions the novelty of today's brand of terrorism, and compares it with other and older forms of terrorism. Although terrorism has changed over time, the differences represent an evolution of the phenomenon and not a radical break between the past and the future of terrorism.

Part 2 will compare jihadism in Europe and elsewhere, with specific focus on South East Asia, North Africa, Europe and Belgium. In Chapter 4 Hugh Roberts analyses the history of jihadi movements in North Africa. He argues that the local context – and not ideology – explains what people actually do. More particularly, he emphasises that jihadi terrorism in the Maghreb occurred only since the onset of the 'global war on terror' and has been primarily an emanation of the Muslim diaspora in Europe. Noor Huda Ismail, in Chapter 5, deals with Jamaah Islamiyah (JI). The author argues that JI has survived partly because it is held together by an intricate pattern of kinship – an observation that is worth keeping in mind when analysing the situation in Europe. Generally, people do not gravitate to JI due to some individual pathology. Most recruits look, dress and behave like normal individuals, at least until they are given a deadly mission or are deeply engaged with the JI ideology and group. Once inside the group, JI members tend to cement ideological and other bonds by marrying the sisters and daughters of their comrades-in-arms. This is a unique tool utilised for recruitment and for further engagement in the JI cause, thus limiting disengagement options for JI members and blocking effective counter-terrorism tactics. In Chapter 6 Edwin Bakker aims at contributing to a better understanding of jihadi terrorism in Europe by investigating the characteristics of the individuals that have been behind jihadi terrorist activities in Europe and by comparing them with the characteristics of jihadi terrorists elsewhere. For this comparison the chapter focuses on the research by the American psychiatrist Marc Sageman, who studied the profiles of global jihadis. In the concluding chapter of Part 2, Alain Grignard sketches how police forces witnessed the evolution of this particular brand of terrorism from its original 'islamo-nationalist' nature in the 1980s to today's post-Iraq jihadi networks. He uses Belgium as a case-study for assessing a development that occurred elsewhere in Europe too.

Part 3 will then turn to the root causes of radicalisation in European Muslims and immigrant communities with a Muslim background by analysing the identity-building processes in these communities and the spread of jihadi ideology among the children and grandchildren of immigrants. In Chapter 8 Jocelyne Cesari assesses the reality of the jihadi threat and presents the main factors contributing to a potential radicalisation of Muslim communities, such as socio-economic and political status. She also gauges the influence of salafi and jihadi Islam and of transnational networks in the building of religious communities in Europe. Olivier Roy (Chapter 9) emphasises, for his part, the importance of converts in the jihadi movement. Through a series of examples he presents some characteristics of these 'born again' jihadis and the links or associations amongst them. Ruud Peters (Chapter 10) sketches the ideological development and the radicalisation process of Mohamed Bouyeri, the murderer of the Dutch filmmaker Theo van Gogh. Among the digital material found on the computers of Mohamed Bouyeri and the so-called 'Hofstad Group', there were about sixty documents written or translated by Mohamed Bouyeri. On the basis of the documents' properties, these could be dated and thus the chronology of his radicalisation could be established.

Part 4 will finally put forward policy proposals to de-escalate the radicalisation process, as seen from within immigrant communities, the police and the EU. Tarik Fraihi (Chapter 11) examines why it is so difficult to publicly discuss radicalisation tendencies within Muslim communities themselves. Glenn Audenaert (Chapter 12) addresses two apparent contradictions. The first is the ongoing evolution towards the community policing approach versus the hard-line multidisciplinary fight against extremism and terrorism. The second opposes the role of the police as the armed component of the government policy with regard to radicalisation of the Muslim community and eventual terrorist organisations and the possible task of the police in the process of de-radicalisation. These two contradictions are, for the author, merely apparent, since they form the two law enforcement elements of a multidisciplinary and customised approach to radicalisation. In the final chapter of Part 4 Gilles de Kerchove and Ran van Reedt Dortland provide for an overview of European initiatives addressing the factors that contribute to radicalisation and recruitment and subsequently demonstrate the increasing role of the European Union in the implementation of a global strategy. The concluding epilogue, wrapping it all up, surveys some differences of analysis among the contributions and summarises the catalogue of initiatives and proposals aimed at stemming the radicalisation process.

No book can succeed without the help of many people. The Egmont-Royal Institute for International Relations has had the pleasure to convene at numerous instances the contributors to this book. I also want to thank the Fund for Scientific Research-Flanders that supported terrorism research at Ghent University through a four year project. My sincere thanks also go to Tanguy Struye de Swielande for the editorial and research support in preparing the manuscript. A last expression of warm gratitude goes of course to the contributors to this volume: Glenn Audenaert, Edwin Bakker, Jocelyne Cesari, Martha Crenshaw, Tarik Fraihi, Alain Grignard, Noor Huda Ismail, Gilles de Kerchove d'Ousselghem, Ruud Peters, Paul R. Pillar, Hugh Roberts, Olivier Roy, Teun Van de Voorde and Ran van Reedt Dortland, and Gijs de Vries, who kindly agreed to contribute a foreword. They represent a fine group of distinguished officials, academics and astute observers that share a common concern of avoiding stereotypes when dealing with such complex issues as terrorism and radicalisation.

Rik Coolsaet
June 2007

PART 1
The State of the Threat

Chapter 1

Jihadi Terrorism: A Global Assessment of the Threat in the Post al-Qaeda Era

Paul R. Pillar

The extent of the threat from international terrorism in general, or jihadi terrorism in particular, is the subject of frequent questioning. Is such terrorism the most serious menace of our time, or has the threat been exaggerated? Is the real threat as great as the fears and attention focused on it, especially since the attacks on the United States in 2001? Is the phenomenon currently growing or fading? This essay presents a sketch of the state and shape of jihadi terrorism today, with a summary of the reasons for why it presents the threat that it does. It is intended to provide a baseline for the chapters that follow. It will say a few things about future changes, but more in the nature of posing questions and highlighting relevant variables, rather than making specific forecasts.

Jihadi terrorism is the variety of international terrorism that draws on extreme interpretations of Islam for its rationale, its ideology and, to varying degrees, its motivation, and whose focus is not limited to any one national or ethnic milieu. It does not revolve around any one national conflict or campaign. So defined, it is a diverse phenomenon that is taking many different forms. But it also is not to be equated with all Islamist terrorism. There are major differences between, say, Osama bin Laden's al-Qaeda, which is the best known exemplar of jihadi terrorism, and the Palestinian group Hamas, which certainly is Islamist but whose objectives are focused not on aspirations, such as those of bin Laden, to re-establish a Caliphate, but instead on issues of political power in Palestine.

Strength of Jihadism

Two general propositions sum up the current state of the threat from jihadi terrorism. The first is that jihadi terrorism is the pre-eminent type of terrorist threat today, by several measures. It certainly is the variety of terrorism against which more Western security services devote more of their counter-terrorist efforts than against any other variety. It is the brand of terrorism about which more western publics evince concern. And those efforts and concerns are not misplaced. The jihadi phenomenon comprises terrorist capabilities that have touched interests, and touched them recently, not only in the West but elsewhere around the globe.

The objectives of jihadi terrorists are, by their nature, not subject to being quelled or satisfied through negotiations or agreements. They involve, instead, objectives too extreme or far-reaching to leave anything to negotiate or are aimed ultimately at political change in countries other than those that are the immediate targets of the terrorist attacks. The motivations of some jihadis – at least rank-and-file adherents, if not the leadership – are at least as much a matter of emotion and hatred as of political calculation.

The other general proposition is that jihadi terrorism is at least as robust today as it has ever been. This proposition is consistent with the judgments of, among others, the US intelligence community, which released in 2006 its assessment that jihadis were increasing in both number and geographic dispersion (DNI 2006). Any attempt to measure the strength of a terrorist group or movement is admittedly fraught with difficulty, even though there are constant demands, from the press and others, to make such measurements, as if the endeavours of terrorists and of counter-terrorist elements that oppose them were some kind of athletic contest with a scoreboard that tallies points. In the United States the question is often asked whether the so-called 'war on terrorism' is being 'won'. That question is too oversimplified for any answer in direct response to it to be useful.

A common and obvious measurement is terrorist attacks themselves. That measurement has its limitations and statistics on terrorist incidents are slippery enough that they can be manipulated to demonstrate just about any proposition that the user of the statistics wants to demonstrate. Among other problems, terrorist attacks, at least significant ones, are rare events – in the mathematician's sense – that punctuate our history at odd intervals in staccato fashion but do not lend themselves very well to trend analysis, at least not without a greater passage of time and more of the perspective of history.

Another question asked frequently is why there has not been another major terrorist attack by jihadis in the United States in the years since the attacks of September 2001, or an attack anywhere in the world comparable to 9/11. That question deserves to be deflected as well, because the very premise of the question conveys a misplaced sense of security. There are some valid answers to that question, but none that should leave one at all surprised if another major jihadi attack were to occur in the United States or Europe tomorrow. Enhanced security countermeasures have been a factor, of course. At least as important is the long time-frame of terrorists, in which planning for individual terrorist operations has been known to take a couple of years, and the process of adapting tactics and strategy to new security measures takes even longer.

The point is that something like an absence of further major attacks on US soil since 9/11 should not be taken as a sign of weakness or weakening in jihadi terrorism. The proposition about the current robustness of that phenomenon rests on several other, admittedly nonsystematic, nonquantitative indicators. One is the pattern, especially geographic, of jihadi terrorist attacks since 9/11, which have covered much of the globe, from Western Europe to Southeast Asia. Another is indications of widening participation, extending to more nationalities, in this brand of terrorism, as exemplified by the British subjects who perpetrated bombings in London. Another is the jihadi colouration assumed by much of the violence in conflicts that may have arisen for largely non-jihadi reasons, such as in Iraq or Chechnya. And yet another is indications of a wider resonance that some jihadi themes have among broader populations, despite the ultimate bankruptcy of jihadism in ameliorating the problems that most concern those populations.

To note the strength and robustness of the overall jihadi phenomenon does not say anything about the status of any individual jihadi terrorist group. The group with which jihadi terrorism often is loosely identified, or even misleadingly equated – *viz.* Osama bin Laden's al-Qaeda – is almost certainly not as capable as it was at the time of the 9/11 attacks. Any such statement must immediately be accompanied by the caveat that the group is nonetheless still capable enough to inflict significant damage. Reports of ties that the perpetrators of several jihadi attacks in Europe have back to South Asia suggest that al-Qaeda has had at least a hand in some of those incidents. But bin Laden and his deputy Ayman Zawahiri are on the run and less able than they once were to direct operations, even if they are conspicuously able to mock with video and audio tapes the inability of their pursuers to catch them. Pressure and diligence by security services in the West as well as in the Muslim world have struck major blows against the infrastructure of bin Laden's group. A large proportion of the senior and mid-level operatives who were at large in the months immediately following 9/11 are now incarcerated or dead. The principal jihadi terrorist threats today come not from al-Qaeda but from the children or cousins of al-Qaeda.

Sources of Strength

Three complementary explanations, or sets of explanations, help to account for the current strength and persistence of jihadi terrorism.

One is that jihadi terrorism is the most extreme manifestation of a far larger, and overwhelmingly peaceful, phenomenon known as political Islam, which in turn is the most significant variety of political expression – especially, political opposition – in much of the Muslim world. Whenever a particular ideology or vocabulary or perspective (and political Islam is not a single ideology), becomes a dominant mode of political discourse, so too can the more extreme variants of that perspective be expected to dominate the sub-world of political extremism. That would be true if, say, leftist or communist perspectives were still as prevalent as they were 20 or 30 years ago. And it is true today of the political Islamist perspective. That perspective may have come to acquire pre-eminence in large part by default, because other perspectives and ideologies, such as the secular Arab nationalism of Nasser, have been tried and found wanting, but until a more promising and attractive alternative comes along, and until political Islam itself has been more thoroughly tried and found wanting, it can be expected to continue to prevail as a major form of discourse on much of the globe.

A second and related explanation is that jihadi terrorism derives energy from friction along the fault line between the Muslim world and the West. One does not have to accept totally hypotheses about clashes of civilisation to see how much friction, based partly on differences of culture and of religion, is occurring along that line, or how that friction plays into some jihadi themes, including notions of cultural imperialism, oppression of Muslims, and lack of respect for religion. The specific points of friction along that line range from things as insubstantial as satirical cartoons of the Prophet in Western publications to matters as major and deadly as the US-initiated war in Iraq. That war, which – among other facets of what is a complicated and multifaceted conflict – has become the latest and most prominent jihad, has given a substantial boost to the jihadi movement. The US intelligence community has assessed that the war has become a *cause célèbre* for jihadis, is 'shaping a new generation of terrorist leaders and operatives', is being exploited by al-Qaeda 'to attract new recruits and donors', and is one of the major factors fuelling the spread of the global jihadi movement (DNI 2006).

The third set of explanations concerns the social, economic and political conditions in much of the Muslim world, especially the Arab heartland in the Middle East, that constitute roots of terrorism. There has been a good deal of commentary aimed at debunking some of the links between such conditions and terrorism, chiefly using arguments by counter-example. One hears, for example, that economic hardship must not be a root cause of jihadi terrorism because terrorists such as the 9/11 hijackers were not conspicuously poor, and the most prominent jihadist of all, bin Laden, is conspicuously wealthy. And we hear that authoritarian politics must not have much to do with it either because jihadi terrorism takes place at least as often as anywhere else within liberal democracies, in places such as New York, Madrid or London.

But the economic arguments tend to erase important distinctions between abject poverty, which may not be associated with proclivity for terrorism, and frustration of ambitions for economic and social advancement, which is. The arguments also tend to blur distinctions between the backgrounds of prominent leaders or practitioners and conditions that can affect broader patterns of sympathy and support for terrorism, and sometimes low-level participation in it. The statistics commonly adduced in the political arguments say less about the roots of terrorism than about the practical fact that terrorist operations tend to be easier to execute in open societies than in tightly controlled police states. The closed and confining economic and social structures that prevail in much of the Middle East, combined with closed political systems that severely curtail opportunities for peaceful expression of the grievances that such societies are bound to generate, have much to do with sustaining jihadi terrorism.

A Decentralised Movement

The combination of the strength of the overall jihadi phenomenon, with the significant weakening of bin Laden's al-Qaeda group, have made jihadi terrorism a more decentralised phenomenon than it was just a few years ago (see Pillar 2004, 101–13). It is decentralised organisationally, with the next major jihadi attack in the West not likely to be conceived and directed by the likes of bin Laden and Zawahiri hiding somewhere in South Asia. It is decentralised geographically, with the perpetrators and not just the selected sites for operations being more worldwide than ever before. And with organisational and geographic breadth come a greater variety of motivations and ideological variants, with truly transnational jihadi goals being mixed in various proportions with more parochial national concerns.

Besides al-Qaeda, jihadi terrorism today includes offshoots, splinters or fragments of al-Qaeda. It includes groups, such as the one established by the late Abu Musab al

Zarqawi in Iraq, that have found it advantageous to benefit from the al-Qaeda brand name even though they are largely autonomous. It includes groups with other names, such as the Southeast Asian organisation Jamaah Islamiyah, having a transnational jihadi ideology melded with regional or country-oriented concerns. And it includes many nameless cells, as well as individuals, many no doubt yet unknown to security services, that believe in the jihadi message and are candidates for, if not yet outright participants in, terrorist behaviour. The picture of the overall jihadi movement is immensely complicated, with innumerable links that are difficult to untangle, and lines of influence that are unclear.

The breadth of potential targets for terrorist attacks reflects the worldwide breadth of the jihadi movement itself. There is a tendency to overanalyse terrorist target selection, which as often as not is more a matter of operational opportunities than of any specific message that the terrorists are attempting to send. Western Europe may be one region where both the operational opportunities (given the openness of the societies and uncertain loyalties of some resident Muslim populations) and possible intended messages (given animosity over such issues as the cartoons of the Prophet) suggest it will be a location for increased numbers of jihadi attacks in the years ahead.

Future Trends

What is the overall trend of jihadi terrorism – up or down? That question is subject to debate, and with good reason, for there is not a definite answer. History suggests that – while terrorism is a timeless tactic that has been used, and will continue to be used, by many different groups for many different purposes operating under many different ideological banners – no particular brand of terrorism is timeless. The American scholar David Rapoport has written of 'waves' of different varieties of terrorism, each of which has lasted for about forty years, and has died out largely for reasons other than the counter-terrorist efforts mounted directly against it (see Rapoport 2004, 46–73).

The current wave of jihadi and other Islamist terrorism could be said to have begun around 1979, with the Iranian revolution and the Soviet invasion of Afghanistan that led to the jihad in Afghanistan. By that calendar, it has been going on for over 25 years and there is reason to hope that its decline is within sight if not already underway. But from another perspective, the radical Sunni variety of jihadi terrorism that is the main worry for most of the West did not really emerge until early in the 1990s, after the Soviet occupation of Afghanistan had ended. Taking that view, maybe the phenomenon still has substantially longer to run.

Probably jihadi terrorism has not yet peaked, although some of the trend lines in the strength of the movement itself may be masked by the effects of heightened counter-terrorist measures taken against it. Even if it has peaked and already is on a downward slope, there still may be a lot of slope, with many attacks and much bloodshed, before reaching the bottom of the hill. Part of what makes this kind of prognostication so uncertain is that the course of jihadi terrorism over the next several years will depend heavily on events extraneous to terrorism itself. Particularly important will be political change in the Middle East, including anything affecting what is described above as roots of terrorism. Even if such change has no effect on terrorist leaders such as bin Laden, it will have an effect on followers and sympathisers. The policies of Western governments, especially the United States, will have effects, both insofar as they affect the roots and as a direct shaper of jihadi attitudes toward the Western Powers themselves. The course of certain salient conflicts, particularly those over Palestine and Iraq, also will have effects, even if jihadi interest in them is mostly a matter of exploiting operational and propaganda opportunities, rather than being at the core of their objectives. And outside the Middle East, there will be many things shaping the attitudes, and proclivity for extremism of Muslim populations in Europe and South and Southeast Asia.

Two concluding thoughts pertain to larger issues of how to think about countering current international terrorism. One is the need to avoid the tendency, all too common in popular discussions of terrorism in the United States, to equate jihadi terrorism with terrorism in general. That was one of the mistakes the 9/11 Commission in the United States made, in devising and promoting an intelligence organisation that it billed as having the mission of countering the jihadi movement but that will have to be relied upon to catch whatever is the next wave of terrorism. The other thought is that countering jihadi terrorism is not only a matter of programmes, including intelligence, and military and security measures that bear the label of 'counter-terrorism'. It includes as well a large number of political, diplomatic and economic policies that affect the roots and rationales of jihadi terrorism and will have a large effect on its future.

Chapter 2

Jihadi Terrorism: Perception and Reality in Perspective

Rik Coolsaet and Teun Van de Voorde

Three quarters of the world population believes terrorism is a threat to their country. According to the Voice of the People 2006 survey, in the United States this figure climbs as high as 92 per cent. The survey furthermore indicates that the public in other continents is almost as fearful of terrorism as Americans, with figures ranging from 72 to 78 per cent. Africa stands out: only slightly more than half of the respondents subscribes to this view. Commenting on the results of this study, Meril James, Secretary General of Gallup International said: 'There is a paradox in terrorism, as much as it divides the world, it also unites it in the fear towards it; all over the globe, people are worried they will become victims of terrorism, our Voice of the People edition shows.'[1] However, this is far from being the most conspicuous paradox of terrorism today. How can one indeed explain that such an overwhelming majority on all continents shares this fear and that such a huge amount of public expenditure is being devoted to protect against this threat, when the risk of being killed in a terror attack is tinier than being killed in a deer collision or drowning in a bathtub – save for people in a very limited number of countries?[2] When launching its new terrorism website in April 2004, the British MI5 said that the number of terrorist-related deaths in the UK since the late 1960s represented less than three per cent of the number of road accident deaths during the same period (and the great majority of these victims were in Northern Ireland). While reflecting upon this paradox, today's observer of terrorism should bear in mind the pertinent observation by Walter Laqueur, author of the standard work *Terrorism* (1977). He observed in 1985:

> [Historians] will note that presidents and other leaders frequently referred to terrorism as one of the greatest dangers facing mankind. For days and weeks on end, television networks devoted most of their prime-time news to covering terrorist operations. Publicists referred to terrorism as the cancer of the world, growing inexorably until it poisoned and engulfed the society on which it fed. ... In countless articles and books, our historian will read about the constantly rising number of terrorist attacks. Being a conscientious researcher he will analyse the statistics, which are bound to increase his confusion, for he will find that more American civilians were killed in 1974 (22) than in 1984 (16). (Laqueur 1986, 86–7)

---

1 <http://extranet.gallup-international.com/uploads/internetVOP%20TOLERANCE%20 DAY.pdf>.

2 This comparison is taken from Mueller (2006, 2 and 13).

Confronted with terrorism, numbers are of course only part of a broader picture. Behind each and every figure is human suffering and subsequent fear. This fear cannot be explained by the number of incidents or the number of fatalities alone. For terrorism to be successful in terms of its proclaimed aims, attacks by themselves would never suffice. It [terrorism] can only aim at obtaining a response that will achieve those goals for it, according to David Fromkin, the former head of the foreign policy team of Hubert Humphrey in the 1972 presidential campaign (Fromkin 1975, 683–98). Terrorists seek to foster a pervasive atmosphere of insecurity. One defining characteristic of terrorism is the intention of manipulating the polity by playing with people's emotions. Because terrorists use the weapon of fear in a very specific and complex manner, acute feelings such as anger, fear or sadness are inherently part of the phenomenon. Some aspects of terrorism are only subjectively felt and therefore difficult to track down empirically or to measure. Put differently, the dominating perception and subjective aspects of any terrorist campaign always constitute a crucial dimension of the phenomenon. These considerations obviously have far ranging implications for the study and interpretation of terrorism. As Paul Pillar observes in the previous chapter, measuring terrorism is fraught with difficulty. Suffice to say here that we should acknowledge the limits of a purely statistical and empirical approach. A quantitative analysis of terrorism nonetheless provides a reality check by helping to equate perception to reality. One might hope that this will help to avoid hasty generalisations and, especially, to reduce the possibilities for terrorists of exploiting the acute fear that disproportionably inflates their strength.

Quantifying Terrorism

It is not fortuitous that the quotations above date from the 1970s and the '80s. Most of contemporary terrorism analyses are devoid of a long-term perspective. Even if one is aware of the fact that terrorism occurred in the past too, terrorism is often exclusively portrayed as a radical new phenomenon of unknown dimensions, thus enhancing within public opinion the very angst terrorists try to arouse. The methodological confusion of the official US statistics on terrorism incidents increases the complexity of judging the rise and eventual fall of the threat. From the 1980s onwards, researchers could rely on two major open source instruments to quantify trends in terrorism.[3] The first was the *Patterns of Global Terrorism*. These annual reports were drawn up by the US Department of State at the request of Congress. Since 1981 the report has offered an overview of major trends in international terrorism. A statistical summary has been included, specifying amongst others the number of terrorist attacks and fatalities. Using the successive reports it was possible to make annual comparisons of the evolution of international terrorism from 1977 onwards.[4] Adhering to a more or less consistent methodology with findings that were comprehensive, the annual report was the closest approximation of any government

---

3 Two supplementary, but lesser used databases are Iterate and PGIS. For an overview, see: Gary LaFree, Laura Dugan, Heather V. Fogg, Jeffrey Scott, *Building a Global Terrorism Database*, University of Maryland, 27 April 2006.

4 <http://www.state.gov/s/ct/rls/crt/>.

effort to provide information in an objective and consistent manner.[5] The second instrument started with the RAND Corporation. It began researching terrorism as a separate domain in the wake of the murder of Olympic athletes in Munich (1972). The tools RAND developed for this purpose included databases and chronologies that are more sophisticated and detailed than the statistical analyses of the State Department. By 1995 RAND had developed a close collaborative relationship with the National Memorial Institute for the Prevention of Terrorism (MIPT). Finally, in 2004 the existing databases were integrated into a unique database, the MIPT Terrorism Knowledge Base (TKB) that incorporates all existing RAND data, together with additional sources.[6]

Many critical remarks have been formulated as to the methodology used in both instances. A recurrent theme was why some incidents were recorded and others apparently failed to appear in the statistics. Figures on terrorism will always be open for discussion and attacked for a number of reasons. As mentioned before, there are a variety of barriers to account for terrorism in a systematic and empirical manner. Especially the weight of subjective factors makes it a difficult phenomenon to measure. As a consequence, it should be borne in mind that any data on terrorism will be to some extent arbitrary. Closely related with this is the ambiguous nature of any definition of terrorism itself. As all experts and observers are aware, a generally satisfactory definition as to what exactly constitutes terrorism has never been agreed upon. Predictably, experts do not even concur on whether a particular incident should be accounted for as terrorism, or as another form of political violence. A general agreement about the numbers of incidents qualified as 'terrorism' will never be reached. Another serious impediment to a statistical analysis of terrorism is the quality of the data. Collecting data on the phenomenon of terrorism is a thorny matter. Field research is no option, survey techniques have proven to be flawed and accessibility to data is severely constrained. Take for instance the Terrorism Knowledge Base, which we will use extensively for the purpose of this chapter. Even though it is stated that 'every effort is made to verify the accuracy of the information in the reports',[7] accuracy of this type of material should be questioned. All information is taken from open source materials such as media coverage. At all times, we must remember that TKB makes no use of primary sources and that it does not offer independent data. The rules and procedures for data-collection are quite vague, so a certain amount of systematic bias should be assumed.

Taken together, these concerns add to our observation that the phenomenon of terrorism should not be reduced to figures alone. We thus acknowledge that interpreting the figures is fraught with dangers and problems. It should also be stressed that we consider the data of both State Department and RAND merely as

---

5 *Terrorism Statistics Flawed*, Center for Defense Information, 12 April 2006.

6 The MIPT Terrorism Knowledge Base integrates the data from the RAND Terrorism Chronology (1968–97) and the RAND–MIPT Terrorism Incident databases (1998–present), the Terrorism Indictment Database, and the DFI International's research on terrorists organisations (<www.tkb.org>).

7 See: Purpose and Description of Information Found in the Incident Database, <http://tkb.org/RandSummary.jsp?page=method>.

an indication of an overall and general trend, not so much as exact empirical proof of whichever argument or hypothesis. For the purpose of examining the rise and fall of terrorism, perfect agreement about absolute numbers is less important than establishing relative trends. The main advantage of using the data series of both the State Department and RAND Corporation thus lies in the internal consistency of the methodology they respectively use over a rather long period of time. Put differently, even if yardsticks and definitions vary between both data sets, they both have an internal consistency that enables the researcher to draw conclusions based upon one or the other's yardstick. In a 2004 study, we compared the trends derived from both data sets (see Figure 2.1).[8]

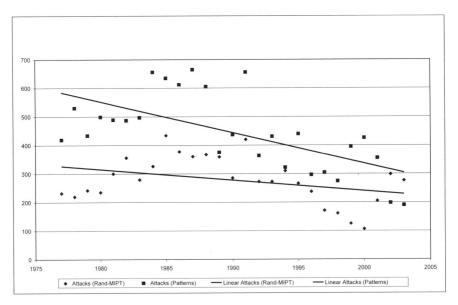

Figure 2.1   Number of International Terrorist Attacks (1977–2003)

Although definitions of terrorism diverged – RAND using a narrower definition of terrorism than State – both data series showed a similar trend line of declining numbers of international terrorist attacks over the period 1977–2003. In other words, whichever definition is used for international terrorism, the statistical analysis shows the same downward trend line for the period studied. The numbers of incidents in the *Patterns* reports indicated that the number of attacks for 2002 and 2003 represented an all-time low since 1977, with respectively 198 and 190 attacks. But as referred to in the introduction of *Patterns 2003*, we can even trace back to 1969 as a marker instead of 1977. This implies that 2002 and 2003 were the most 'terror free' years

---

8 Coolsaet and Van de Voorde (2004). The numbers mentioned in this chapter can be different from the original research paper and the 2006 follow-on paper, due to alterations in the number of reported incidents.

of the past 32 years (US Department of State 2004). The RAND data show the same downward trend line. Accounted for in absolute terms, 1997–2000 ranks as the most 'terror free' period, followed by an increase between 2000 and 2002, but ending with a decline in 2003 down to the – relatively low – levels of 1977–1980. This conclusion clearly stands in opposition to the general feeling of an increased global terrorist threat. This should come as no surprise. The dramatic and unexpected nature of 9/11 could not but arouse such feelings of anxiety. But as Figure 2.1 shows, over the past two decades, the use of international terrorism as a political tool has declined gradually but in a sustained manner, notwithstanding 9/11.

Lies, Damned Lies and Statistics

As Paul Pillar argues in the preceding chapter, statistics on terrorist incidents are slippery enough that they can be manipulated to demonstrate just about any proposition that the user of the statistics wants to demonstrate. An alternative interpretation to the preceding one is indeed possible. The figure above starts in 1977, since that year was the departure point for the *Patterns* reporting on terrorist incidents. It made it possible to compare for exactly the same period two databases that used different definitions of terrorism. If we limit ourselves to the RAND statistics, we can return even further in the past, until 1968. When drawing a trend line based solely on these statistics, a slightly upward trend line appears, instead of the aforementioned downward line (see Figure 2.2).

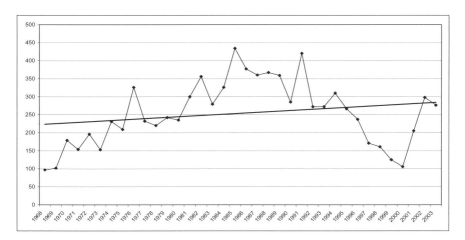

Figure 2.2   Number of International Terrorist Incidents (1968–2003)

When viewing the 1968–2003 trend line based solely upon the RAND database, we thus cannot concur with the earlier assessment of a gradual waning of international terrorism as a political tool. What we can conclude, however, is that after gradually increasing in the 1970s, the 1980s clearly represent a high tide of international terrorist activity. The ensuing 1990s represented a low tide in international terrorism, which then started to increase for two consecutive years after 2000. Looking at the curve we are still a long way from the peaks of the 1980s however. Simple looking at the statistics, the overall conclusion thus stands that we do not witness an extraordinary, novel phenomenon of unknown dimensions.

Methodological Confusion

Unfortunately, the year 2004 was the final year that a comparison between the two data sets was possible. Published in April 2004, the State Department's *Patterns of Global Terrorism 2003* became the subject of widespread controversy, both politically and methodologically. Since 9/11 terrorism had become the major topic in US politics. Statistics on terrorist attacks became as important as the unemployment rate or the GDP (Krueger and Laitin 2005). Many new agencies were competing to assure their place in the Global War on Terror and bureaucratic confusion and in-fighting ensued. Ultimately this brought to an end the analytical consistency of the US Government's terrorism accounting practices via the *Patterns of Global Terrorism* reports. Terror statistics turned into a major political hurdle indeed. At the heart of the controversy was the highly politicised question of whether the Bush administration was winning the War on Terror. The responsibility for obtaining and analysing the terror statistics was passed from one agency to another and was finally entrusted to the newly created National Counterterrorism Center (NCTC). The customary *Patterns* were discontinued and renamed *Country Reports on Terrorism*. The State Department remained in charge of the analyses of regions and countries, but the statistical annexes became the exclusive responsibility of the NCTC. This, however, was not the end of the saga of official American terrorism accounting. Numbers were retracted, counting methods were changed. Finally, in April 2006 the State Department's *Country Report 2005* and NCTC's *Report on Terrorist Incidents* were simultaneously released.[9] The most noticeable methodological change from the old *Patterns* statistics was the renunciation of any distinction between domestic and international terrorism, resulting in a much broader definition of terrorism. This new methodology, so it was confirmed at the launch of both reports, would henceforth become the 'benchmark' of all consecutive reports. But at the same time this more inclusive definition of terrorism made it all but impossible to compare the new data with the statistics in the old *Patterns* reports (US Department of State 2005).

The Evolution of Terrorism since 9/11

While the evolution of terrorism could up until 2005 be extracted both from the figures released by the US State Department and the TKB database, we can now only build our time series upon the latter source. In particular the 'analytical tools' that TKB puts at the researcher's disposal are now indispensable for studying the long

---

9 <http://www.state.gov/s/ct/rls/crt/c17689.htm> (*Country Report on Terrorism 2005*); <http://wits.nctc.gov/reports/crot2005nctcannexfinal.pdf> (*NCTC Report on Incidents of Terrorism 2005*).

term evolution of terrorism. Contrary to the NCTC database, the TKB database allows for filtering 'domestic' and 'international' terrorism. The former is understood as 'incidents perpetrated by local nationals against a purely domestic target'. The latter is defined as 'incidents in which terrorists go abroad to strike their targets, select domestic targets associated with a foreign state, or create an international incident by attacking airline passengers, personnel or equipment'. Distinguishing between both forms of terrorism remains arbitrary in a number of cases. TKB acknowledges this difficulty and partly tries to compensate by offering as much specific information as possible for each terrorist incident (day, country, group). Two major conclusions emerge from the TKB data. The first is international terrorism is not a large scale threat. It should therefore be characterised as a (political and intelligence) challenge rather than as a (military) threat. The second conclusion is that the West is not the prime victim of terrorism in the name of Islam.

International Terrorism is a Challenge; Domestic Terrorism a Threat – to Some Countries

The year 2006 showed a further overall decline of international terrorism, both in number of victims and attacks. The number of attacks dropped by a quarter and the number of casualties was almost halved. Taking into account the number of victims (551 casualties in 2005 and 294 in 2006), the assertion that international terrorism represents a major existential threat to the world or to human civilisation is not tenable. This perception is simply not corroborated by reality (see Table 2.1).

Table 2.1   International Terrorism, Number of Incidents and Fatalities

International terrorism	2006	2005	2004
Number of incidents	233	309	395
Number of fatalities	294	551	732

Constantly referring to international terrorism as an existential threat to society inflates the global character of the threat and at the same time ignores the local nature and root causes of most of today's terrorist violence. Indeed, international terrorism pales when compared with domestic terrorism. In 2006 the overall level of domestic terrorism substantiates the claim that it is a persistent and serious threat. These high figures (6,355 incidents and 11,733 fatalities) are in line with the roaring levels of 2005, when the amount of domestic terrorist activity had already dramatically increased as compared to 2004 (see Table 2.2).

Table 2.2   Domestic Terrorism, Number of Incidents and Fatalities

Domestic terrorism	2006	2005	2004
Number of incidents	6,355	4,654	2,251
Number of fatalities	11,733	7,641	4,334

In conclusion, whereas *international* terrorism was halved between 2004 and 2006 and the number of fatalities it caused dropped by 60 per cent, for the same period *domestic* terrorism increased by 175 per cent and the number of victims in domestic terrorist acts by almost the same percentage.

Not the West, but Muslims are the Primary Victims of Attacks in the Name of Islam

These statistics might be misleading though. Western opinion makers and officials often refer to jihadi terrorism as a deadly threat to Western civilisation and values. Such rhetoric obscures the very fact that citizens in Muslim countries bear by far the largest share of the burden of terrorist attacks in the name of Islam. As in the preceding year, in 2006 too most victims of international terrorism fell in Muslim countries. Iraq alone represented almost 60 per cent of the total number of victims of international terrorism (see Table 2.3).

Table 2.3   International Terrorism, Fatalities by Region

International terrorism	2006	2005	2004	2003	2002
Fatalities, of which:	294	551	732	470	970
in the Middle East,	168	416	403	327	375
of which:in Iraq	160	342	350	172	NA
in South Asia	81	53	72	30	102
in South East Asia / Oceania	NA	0	12	42	217
in North-America	NA	0	NA	NA	3
in Western Europe	0	0	192*	1	0

*Attacks in Madrid, March 2004
NA: not available

The numbers concerning domestic terrorism show the same gross discrepancy between victims in the West and victims in Muslim countries. Increasingly, the victims of terrorism are concentrated in the Middle East, and especially in Iraq, transforming terrorism from a global into a specific regional threat. Looking at the figures from 2002 until 2006, the conclusion that the Iraq war drastically boosted (domestic) terrorism is inescapable (see Table 2.4).

Table 2.4   Domestic Terrorism, Fatalities by Region

Domestic terrorism	2006	2005	2004	2003	2002
Fatalities, of which:	11,733	7,641	4,334	1,876	1,793
in the Middle East, of which:	9,432	6,056	2,291	555	189
in Iraq	9,337	5,904	2,121	367	3
in South Asia, of which:	1,796	959	729	773	904
in Afghanistan/Pakistan	942	395	396	248	159
in South East Asia/Oceania	229	240	266	31	151
in North America	1	0	0	0	0
in Western Europe	6	56*	2	6	15

*Attacks London, July 2005

Putting Terrorism in a Long-Term Perspective

When inserting the data on terrorist incidents in 2005 and 2006 into the RAND data of Figure 2.2 (*Patterns* being discontinued), it results in an upward trend line. What is most striking though is the clear pattern of successive waves in international terrorism (see Figure 2.3). As concluded earlier, the 1980s clearly represented a high tide of international terrorist activity. Figure 2.3 indicates that the number of attacks in the 1980s remained almost uninterruptedly above the trend line for many consecutive years. This justifies calling the 1980s the 'terrorism decade' par excellence. Today's wave of jihadi terrorism however – starting in the beginning of the 1990s with the return of the Afghan veterans to their countries of origin – is much less marked as a climax of international terrorist activity. Indeed, during most of the 1990s, the number of terrorist attacks remained under the trend line. Only in 2002 the number of terrorist incidents again crossed the line, without, however, continuing at that level as in the 1980s. It is too early to tell if the contemporary wave of international terrorism that started in 2000 will show the same resilience as the preceding one in the 1980s. The graph rather suggests that this is not the case, as the curve starts to go down from 2004 onwards, after only four years of increasing numbers of terrorist incidents. These figures point to the conclusion that contrary to widespread belief, contemporary international terrorism represents less of a challenge than it did in the 1980s.

A second, and from a human point of view, the most important assessment, concerns the number of victims. 9/11 caused the death of almost three thousand victims. The scale of the attack is often referred to as the major novelty in today's terrorism. As Martha Crenshaw points out in the following chapter, however, in the past, too, terrorist movements could be as ferocious as today's jihadi terrorists. The TKB-data make it possible to put the high death toll in 2001 into perspective. When looking back from 1977 onwards, one can indeed detect a pattern of increased lethality (see Figure 2.4). A closer look, however, reveals a great variation in the number of fatalities, which is clearly the result of single-digit, but spectacular attacks

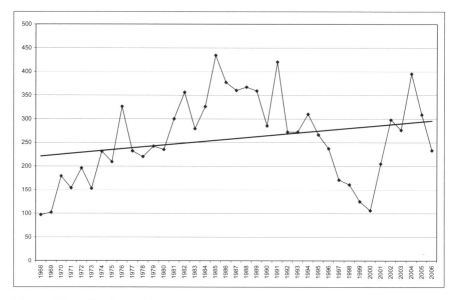

Figure 2.3   Number of International Terrorist Incidents (1968–2006)

with a high number of casualties: for example the series of bombs in Lebanon against American targets in 1983 with dozens of victims for each attack, the 329 victims on Air India Flight 182 brought down in 1985 between Montreal and London by a bomb planted by Sikh militants, the 270 victims on the PanAm 103 Flight that crashed in Lockerbie (Scotland) in 1988, the bombs in Bombay in 1993 that resulted in 317

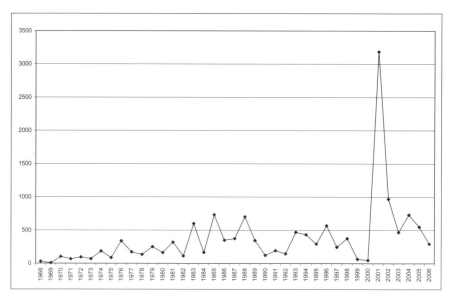

Figure 2.4   Number of Victims of International Terrorism (1968–2006)

deaths, the attack in Colombo (Sri Lanka) by the Tamil Tigers in 1996, and of course the attacks on September 11, 2001. Such attacks explain the peaks of higher numbers of casualties even if the number of terrorist attacks shows a downward trend. Due to these vast variations in the annual numbers of victims, we consider it as problematic to generalise about the emergence of a so-called new 'catastrophic mass terrorism', spectacular attacks such as 9/11 being 'low probability, high consequence' events.[10]

Conclusions

One of the reasons why international terrorism has continued to decline as a threat in recent years has been the dismantlement of al-Qaeda as an operational international network. Analysts, both governmental and academic, now largely share the assessment that the once hierarchical, disciplined and centralised al-Qaeda structure is more akin to a broken thermometer whose mercury has shattered into a multitude of small blobs, all highly toxic, but not specifically related to one another. Jihadi terrorism has largely turned into a grassroots phenomenon, a patchwork of home-grown, self-radicalising terror groups and freelance jihadis, each going their own way without central command, unified only into a common view of the world.

The broken thermometer image helps to explain why international terrorist activity has decreased, and why domestic terrorism could increase sharply, as highlighted by the TKB data. Terrorism, including its jihadi brand, is largely boosted by local root causes and grievances, and is undertaken almost exclusively by local groups. These autonomously operating small groups or individuals lack the resources and expertise of a structured organisation. Being rather novice sympathisers than highly trained terrorist operatives, they are less capable of inflicting global large-scale damage (US Department of State 2006). But they cause large-scale suffering in specific countries, largely populated by Muslims. Muslims are the principle target and victims of terrorism perpetrated in the name of Islam. This helps to explain the decreasing sympathy in Muslim countries and in Muslim communities in the West for jihadi terrorism and for Osama bin Laden in particular.[11]

More often than not, terrorist's actions are lone acts by small groups and individuals, reflecting a general mood of anger and deprivation that is boosted by an enabling global environment, as will be spelled out throughout this book, especially in its epilogue. The Iraq war has become part and parcel of this global environment. This war has drastically boosted terrorism, instead of lessening it – although this was the official rationale for going to war. The US National Intelligence Estimate '*Trends*

---

10 This concept is taken from Hoffman, B., 'Change and Continuity in Terrorism', *Studies in Conflict and Terrorism*, 24 (2001): 428. RAND analyst Bruce Hoffman used this concept to refer to the current narrow focus on the terrorist's use of weapons of mass destruction that does not reflect the realities of contemporary terrorist behaviour and operations.

11 *Conflicting Views in a Divided World*, Washington, DC, Pew, 2006; *Islamic Terrorism: Common Concern for Muslim and Western Publics*, Washington, DC, Pew, 14 July 2005 (<http://pewglobal.org/reports/pdf/248.pdf>). Ipsos-Stat conducted a survey in Jordan after the November 2005 Amman attacks. For results see: <http://www.alghad.jo/index.php?news=56817>.

in Global Terrorism', partially released in September 2006, now also subscribes to this assessment, once judged to be improper: 'The Iraq conflict has become the "cause celebre" for jihadists, breeding a deep resentment of US involvement in the Muslim world and cultivating supporters for the global jihadist movement.'[12] Considering the soaring level of terrorist attacks and fatalities in Iraq itself, one can only conclude that 9/11 and the ensuing War on Terror have above all contributed to a 'clash within one civilisation'. The Iraq war, being presented as part of the War on Terror, has contributed to turning Iraq into an epicentre of terrorism.

---

12 <http://www.dni.gov/press_releases/Declassified_NIE_Key_Judgments.pdf>. *The 2006 Country Reports on Terrorism*, published by the State Department in April 2007, makes a similar, but somewhat more edulcorated point, when observing that the war in Iraq 'has been used by terrorists as a rallying cry for radicalization and extremist activity that has contributed to instability in neighbouring countries'.

Chapter 3

'New' vs. 'Old' Terrorism: A Critical Appraisal[1]

Martha Crenshaw

The idea that the world confronts a 'new' terrorism completely unlike the terrorism of the past has taken hold in the minds of American policy makers, journalists, consultants and academics (examples include Hoffman 1998; Benjamin and Simon 2003; Laqueur 1999; Lesser et al. 1999; Bremer 2001; Morgan 2004; Giddens 2004). The government and policy elites have been blamed for not recognising the danger of the 'new' terrorism in the 1990s and thus failing to prevent the disaster of 9/11 (see for example Simon and Benjamin 2003, 381; 9/11 Commission Report, chapter 2). Our knowledge of the 'old' or traditional terrorism is considered irrelevant, obsolete and anachronistic, even harmful; the old paradigms should be discarded and replaced with a new reframed understanding (see Hoffman 1998, 196 and 205; Simon and Benjamin 2003, 221 and 384; Lesser et al. 1999, 2; Laqueur 1999, 7).

However, these claims should be systematically examined rather than accepted in their totality as self-evident (for other critical views Tucker 2001; Coolsaet 2005; Zimmerman 2003; Burnett and Whyte 2005, Aldrich 2005; Roy 2004, 41–54).

The point is not that there has been no change in terrorism but that changes need to be precisely identified and that they are not necessarily attributable to 'religious' motivations. This assessment can only be completed by careful and empirically-grounded comparison. If a new explanation of terrorism is necessary, what are the puzzles that the 'old' paradigm cannot solve? My contention is that the departure from the past is not as pronounced as many accounts make it out to be. Today's terrorism is not a fundamentally or qualitatively 'new' phenomenon but grounded in an evolving historical context (for an example see Kalyvas 2001, 99–118).

The differences are of degree rather than kind. Contemporary terrorism shares many of the characteristics of past terrorism, dating back to the late nineteenth century. So far the accounts of a 'new' terrorism are based on insufficient knowledge of history and misinterpretation of contemporary terrorism. The 'new terrorism' literature so far has failed to do two things adequately. First, it does not precisely specify the concept and the distinction between 'new' and 'old'. What are the attributes of the 'new' terrorism? How are they different from those of the 'old'?

---

1 I have benefited from comments and questions following presentations of this argument at Irvine, Rutgers University, and at the Woodrow Wilson Center, in a lecture series co-sponsored by the Rand Corporation and the US Army's Eisenhower National Security Series.

Second, it needs to clarify which groups or practices belong in which category and explain how these cases satisfy the requirements of the definition. For example, accounts of the 'new' terrorism cite the common characteristic of religious doctrine as motivation. However, although the 'new' terrorists are all supposedly religious, not all religious groups are deemed to be 'new'. The groups that are typically cited as examples of the genre are radical or jihadi Islamists in general (al-Qaeda, al-Qaeda in Mesopotamia, Jamaah Islamiyah, the Abu Sayyaf Group, the Salafist Group for Preaching and Combat, and so on), the Christian Identity movement and its offshoots (including Timothy McVeigh, although it is not certain that he represented an organised group, and the attribution of a religious motivation to his violence seems problematic), Ramzi Youcef and his cohort (although some view him as a figure in the early years of al-Qaeda rather than an independent actor), Aum Shinrikyo, and the Jewish radical groups that plotted to blow up the Dome of the Rock and that assassinated Rabin. Hamas, however, is not included. The case of Hezbollah is problematic; it is included by some (see Hoffman 1998) but not others (see Simon and Benjamin 2003). In either case, the category of 'new' terrorists includes a diverse set of actors.

Clarification of the distinction between categories is hard to find. The MIPT Terrorism Knowledge Database, which is based on data collected by the Rand Corporation since 1968, lists 130 groups in the category of religious terrorism. Of these 130 cases, 124 are linked to group profiles, which indicate that only 54 of the cases are labelled as exclusively religious. Almost all the others are simultaneously classified as national separatist groups. If it is the case, as Simon argues, that 'the explicitly religious character of the "new terrorism" poses a profound security challenge for the United States', are we to understand the statement to mean those groups that are only religious or those groups that are both religious and nationalist?[2] Which orientation will determine their actions? (Simon 2003, Hoffman 1998).

If 'old' terrorism refers to secular groups or groups existing before 1990, we have over 400 examples, more if we go back to the nineteenth century. Accounts of the new terrorism are not specific or comprehensive on this score. For example, Steven Simon lists only the Irish Republican Army, the Red Brigades and the Palestine Liberation Organisation as examples of 'conventional' terrorist groups (Simon 2003).

There is a further problem. Even if a conceptual distinction between two types of terrorism can be established, it is not clear whether there is a chronological dimension. Should we assume that the 'new' is replacing the 'old'? When was the transition? If not, how do we explain the persistence of the 'old' as well as the emergence of the 'new'? David Rapoport has dealt with these questions in analysing the historical evolution of terrorism in terms of 'waves', which in his terms are 'cycles of activity in a given time period' characterised by a common international 'energy' or ideology (Cronin and Ludes 2004). All waves feature nationalist movements that take on different forms according to the nature of the 'wave', whether driven by anarchism,

---

2 It is important to look closely at the MIPT–Rand data, since it is the main source of the argument that religiously motivated terrorism is (1) increasing and (2) more lethal and indiscriminate than other forms.

anti-colonialism, 'New Left ideology' or now religion. He sees each wave ebbing as the new wave takes force. Although Rapoport does not espouse the idea that the religious wave is qualitatively different from preceding waves, he does see a process of replacement rather than coexistence. These issues need further empirical study to establish where there is continuity and where and why there is change.

The evolution of the concept of a 'new' terrorism is event-driven (as is much of the study of terrorism). The idea that the world confronted a 'new' threat took hold after the 1993 World Trade Center bombing, although Benjamin and Simon argue that the phenomenon itself began in 1990, with the assassination of Meir Kahane in New York (Simon and Benjamin 2003, 3–4; Morgenthau 1993, 18). The argument was well established, and had been criticised, by the time of the 9/11 attacks. The idea that there was a distinctively 'religious' terrorism began to develop with the growth of radical Islamic movements after the Iranian revolution (particularly as a reaction to the use of suicide bombings by Hezbollah in Lebanon) and was strengthened by the 1993 World Trade Center bombing and the discovery of subsequent ambitious plots directed by Ramzi Youcef (such as blowing up airliners over the Pacific). These suspicions were exacerbated by the fear that terrorist groups might acquire nuclear, chemical, biological or radiological weapons, especially considering the insecurity that followed the collapse of the Soviet Union. The new terrorism idea gained momentum with the 1995 Aum Shinrikyo sarin gas attacks on the Tokyo subway and the Oklahoma City bombing. Growing awareness of the extent of the al-Qaeda conspiracy caused more alarm (see Rose 1999).

The 1998 embassy bombings, the attack on the USS Cole in 2000, and the millennium plots strengthened the perception of a completely new threat. Not only the attacks of 9/11 but the following anthrax attacks also heightened concern. Although the risk of highly destructive terrorism was and is real, the 'new terrorism' school of thought is open to challenge. My critique of 'new terrorism' thinking analyses its propositions concerning the goals, methods and organisational structure and resources of groups practicing terrorism. I also question the historical application of the distinction between 'new' and 'old' terrorism. I challenge the soundness of the definition and its applicability to empirical data.

Goals

First, the *ends* of the 'new' terrorism are presumed to be both unlimited and non-negotiable. Fanaticism is the motivation, not political interest, according to Laqueur.[3] These aims are also considered largely incomprehensible and amorphous. In this view, the goals of 'new' terrorists are derived exclusively from religious doctrines

---

3 Laqueur's (1986) argument actually focuses more on the motivations or 'mind-sets' of the individual than the objectives of the group. He says, for example, that the new terrorists (who are characterised by rage, aggression, sadism, paranoia as well as fanaticism) can be found on the fringes of any extremist movement (p. 281). At other times he is contradictory; he seems to imply that the motive for terrorism, fanaticism, has not changed but that the availability of weapons has. At other times he suggests that religious fanaticism is different. The 'new breed' of terrorist enjoys killing (p. 231).

that emphasise transformational and apocalyptic beliefs, usually associated with Islam although present in all monotheistic religions. Millenarianism is key. The 'new' terrorists are presumed to hate Western and especially American values, culture, civilisation and existence. As Ambassador Bremer expressed it, it is not that they do not understand us: 'They hate America precisely because they *do* understand our society; they hate its freedoms, its commitment to equal rights and universal suffrage, its material successes and its appeals ...' (Bremer 2001, 24). President Bush described the enemy thus: 'we face an enemy which cannot stand freedom. It's an enemy which has an ideology that does not believe in free speech, free religion, free dissent, does not believe in women's rights, and they have a desire to impose their ideology on much of the world' (White House 2006). Further,

> we are not facing a set of grievances that can be soothed and addressed. We're facing a radical ideology with inalterable objectives: to enslave whole nations and intimidate the world. No act of ours invited the rage of the killers – and no concession, bribe, or act of appeasement would change or limit their plans for murder. (Bush 2002)

The new terrorism threat is compared to the existential threat of Communism during the Cold War, not past terrorism (Bush 2005a). It is considered a war on civilisation itself. The goals of terrorism are inextricably linked to the means, in this view. The new terrorists are fanatics unconstrained by any respect for human life. Violence is at the heart of their beliefs. There is some ambiguity about whether violence is 'strategic', since Simon and Benjamin argue that for the new actors terrorism is used strategically and not tactically, by which they mean killing is an end in itself (see for example Simon and Benjamin 2003, 419). If destruction is an end in itself rather than the means to an end, then it is not strategic but expressive. Rather than choosing among alternative ways of achieving political ends, the new terrorists seek primarily to kill. Lethality is their aim rather than their means. As Benjamin and Simon put it in an editorial in the *New York Times* in early 2000:

> The terrorists allied with Mr. bin Laden do not want a place at the table: they want to shatter the table. They are not constrained by secular political concerns. Their objective is not to influence, but to kill, and in large numbers—hence their declared interest in acquiring chemical and even nuclear weapons. It is just this combination—religious motivation and a desire to inflict catastrophic damage—that is new to terrorism. (Benjamin and Simon 2000)[4]

The goals of the 'old' terrorism, by contrast, are thought to have been negotiable and limited. Their ambitions were local, not global. The past aims of terrorism were understandable and tangible, typically related to issues of nationalism and territorial autonomy. Deals could be struck. The state could bargain with the 'old' terrorists. Conflicts could be resolved. In effect, these were presumably sensible terrorists whose objectives were realistic and pragmatic. Is this an accurate depiction of the old terrorism? Unobtainable ends and flamboyantly bloodthirsty rhetoric are not unique to religion or to the contemporary political environment. The European

---

4 This indicates perhaps that the new terrorists must be more than religious.

anarchist movement of the late nineteenth century (of which the proponents of terrorism were a fringe) sought to abolish all government as well as capitalist society (Coolsaet 2005). Sendero Luminoso wished to establish a Maoist regime in Peru. Its leader, Abimael Guzman, launched the war in 1980 with a speech titled 'We are the Initiators': 'we begin the strategic offensive for world revolution, the next 50 years will see imperialism's dominion swept away along with all exploiters ... The people's war will grow every day until the old order is pulled down, the world is entering a new era.' The speech continues on a lurid note,

> The people rear up, arm themselves, and rise in revolution to put the noose around the neck of imperialism and the reactionaries, seizing them by the throat and garrotting them. They are strangled, necessarily. The flesh of the reactionaries will rot away, converted into ragged threads, and this black filth will sink into the mud; that which remains will be burned and the ashes scattered by the earth's winds so that only the sinister memory will remain of that which will never return, because it neither can nor should return. (Gorriti 1999, 34–5)

In the 1970s, revolutionary organisations in Germany (the Red Army faction) and Italy (the Red Brigades), with little to no popular support, thought that they could overthrow well-established liberal democracies, bring down NATO, and deal a death blow to imperialism (see Alexander and Pluchinsky 1992). Separatist organisations are not immune from overreaching. ETA seeks to establish a Basque state that would include regions of both France and Spain. It was not particularly reasonable of Palestinian groups such as the Abu Nidal Organisation or the Popular Front for the Liberation of Palestine or Libya, to believe that they could destroy the state of Israel or bring about revolution in the Arab world. Patrick Seale, in a biography of Abu Nidal, describes his terrorism as 'fitful and purposeless', 'incoherent, incompetent, and invariably counterproductive to Palestinian interests'. There was no 'strategic vision':

> His claim that he wanted to prevent a compromise between the PLO and Israel so as to recover Palestine was not a credible objective. The vast imbalance of strength between Israel and its opponents made such pursuit suicidal. By degrading the Palestinian liberation struggle to mere criminal violence, Abu Nidal offered Israel the pretext for refusing to negotiate and to giving the Palestinians nothing but the sword. (Seale 1992, 231)

Do these assumptions about objectives describe the 'new' terrorism? Are such groups led by apocalyptic visionaries with no appreciation of reality? Groups claiming to act in the name of religious doctrine may be more extreme in their rhetoric than in their preferences (although analysis of their rhetoric is certainly worthwhile). They have often shown themselves to be astute political strategists, using terrorism successfully to compel the withdrawal of foreign military forces or to disrupt peace processes. Hezbollah is an excellent example, having transformed itself into a political party as well as a resistance organisation. Some regional experts have interpreted al-Qaeda's activities in pragmatic terms (see for example Doran 2002, 177–90; Wiktorowicz and Kaltner 2003, 76–92). Bin Laden's stated goal of expelling American military forces from Muslim territories is quite specific. He cites the encouraging historical precedents of Vietnam, Somalia and Lebanon, as well as the Soviet withdrawal from Afghanistan (Lawrence 2005). His interpretations may not be completely accurate, but they are not illogical. Just as secular nationalist groups such as ETA and even the IRA took on a Marxist–Leninist veneer when it was ideologically fashionable to do so, nationalistic groups today may take on an Islamic cast. Ideology and religion are useful recruiting and mobilising devices.

A finding that remains constant is that while some members of radical organisations are motivated by sincere beliefs in the cause, others are less committed to group values. Individual militants may be manipulated by their leaders. Undoubtedly all members of the groups designated as 'new terrorists' are not religious 'fanatics' (see Cullison, 2004, 55–70). As Stephen Holmes observed with regard to the 9/11 attacks:

> Many of the key actors in the 9/11 drama, admittedly, articulate their grievances using archaic religious language. But the very fact that the code involved is ancient while the behaviour we want to explain is recent suggests the inadequacy of causal theories that overemphasize the religious element. (Holmes, 2005; Simon and Stevenson 2005, 90–98)

Methods

Second, the *means* of the 'new' terrorism are also assumed to be radically different. The premise is that because the ends of the new terrorism are unlimited, so, too, are the means that groups espousing these goals are willing to use. The 'new' terrorists are supposed to be dedicated to causing the largest possible number of casualties among their enemies and also to be willing to sacrifice any number of their own in the process. What happens afterward is of no concern. Thus the 'new' terrorists are also thought to be significantly more inclined than secular groups to use 'weapons of mass destruction' because their purpose is simply to kill as many people as possible. Apocalyptic motivations are said to lead to a desire for unprecedented lethality. According to Steven Simon, 'Religiously motivated terrorism, as Bruce Hoffman of the Rand Corporation first noted in 1997, is inextricably linked to pursuit of mass casualties' (Simon 2003, 18). Presumably for the 'new' terrorists the means have become an end in themselves, not a way of reaching an audience other than a deity. They are not concerned with public support. The 'new' terrorists seek only to destroy, and their deaths will result only in the reaching of the millennium and a place in paradise, not political change in the here and now.

The 'old' terrorism is considered to be much more restrained and specific in targeting. The traditional terrorist wanted people watching, not people dead, according to Brian Jenkins' now famous aphorism. Hoffman describes the old terrorists as selective and discriminating (Hoffman 1998, 197). Benjamin and Simon say past terrorists used 'carefully calibrated violence' because 'they knew that excessive brutality would deny them the place they sought at the bargaining table' (Benjamin and Simon 2000). These terrorists imposed restraints on their actions because they aimed to change the attitudes of audiences who could help them achieve their goals. Although capable of being more destructive, they chose not to be. Their audiences and reference groups were tangible and present. They were limited by their dependence on constituencies and by their political interests. Their pursuit of legitimacy, in effect, restrained their behaviour.

However, the 'old' terrorists were not always discriminating in their choice of targets. Levels of selectivity and restraint vary across groups and across time, but not according to a religious–secular or past–present divide. A few examples show that killing large numbers is not restricted to groups espousing religious doctrines, although no single attacks were near as deadly as 9/11 (see also Quillen 2002, 279–302). The French anarchists of the 1880s bombed restaurants frequented by the bourgeoisie in order to show the working class who the true enemy was. 'No bourgeois is innocent' was their slogan. The history of anarchism in Spain was particularly violent. Martin Miller refers to a 'will to destroy' in the European anarchist movement (Miller 1995). The concept of 'propaganda of the deed', which is still at the heart of terrorism, was introduced by Peter Kropotkin in 1880. In 1946, the bombing of the King David Hotel in Jerusalem killed 91 and injured 45 (Bell 1977, 172). During the Algerian war, the FLN attacked Europeans indiscriminately, leaving bombs in cafes, on beaches, in soccer stadiums, and at bus stops in Algiers during the famous 'Battle of Algiers'. Their bombs often killed Algerians as well as Europeans. (The FLN also considered bombing the Eiffel Tower, in a campaign to bring the war home to France. They did bomb oil refineries near Marseille). The Japanese Red Army's attack on the Tel Aviv airport in 1972 killed 24 and wounded 80 people, most Puerto Rican pilgrims. A Sikh extremist group was probably responsible for the midair bombing of Air India Flight 182 in 1985 (killing 329 people), and the secular regime of Colonel Qaddafi (since rehabilitated) bombed Pan Am 103 in 1988, leaving 270 dead. Far right extremists with no religious connections whatsoever have also been willing and able to cause mass casualties; for instance, 85 people were killed in the bombing of the Bologna railroad station in 1980. As the Algerian war concluded, the OAS (Organisation de l'armée secrète) adopted a scorched earth policy of indiscriminate terrorism against Muslims. For example, on May 2, 1962, a car bomb on the Algiers docks killed 62 and wounded 110 among a crowd of Algerians waiting for day work (Droz and Lever 1982, 337; Harrison 1989).

Moreover, contrary to the expectations of new terrorism thinking, religious terrorists have not been quick to resort to weapons of mass destruction. Aum Shinrikyo's attack on the Tokyo subway is the only example of a deliberate use of chemical weapons against a civilian population.[5] Terrorists have not used nuclear or radiological weapons despite official concern over the prospect since at least 1976 (Central Intelligence Agency 1976).

Moreover, while the September 11 hijackings caused the highest number of casualties of any single terrorist attack in history, other al-Qaeda or al-Qaeda related

---

5 Another possible example is the LTTE's use of chlorine gas in an attack on a Sri Lankan army base, but their use appears to have been circumstantial and opportunistic, not planned. See in general Tucker (2000). According to this study, there have so far been only nine instances of what might be defined as chemical or biological terrorism, which included deliberate food poisonings. The anthrax mailings of 2001 could be added to the list. See also Falkenrath et al. (1998) and Stern (1999). There are also reports that al-Qaeda tried to acquire chemical weapons.

terrorism has (fortunately) caused fewer casualties (overall and per incident) and has not involved such innovative methods or sophisticated planning. The bombings in Bali in 2002 (202 killed), Madrid in 2004 (191 killed), and London in 2005 (52 killed) were tragically destructive, but not fundamentally dissimilar to past bombings by secular groups in crowded public venues.[6] The simultaneous explosions are a hallmark of al-Qaeda, but such a tactic was and is within the reach of many groups. More evidence of strategic discrimination in targeting is found in the July 2005 letter from Ayman al-Zawahiri to the late Abu Musab al-Zarqawi. The document is sharply critical of indiscriminate terrorism against ordinary Shia, especially attacks on mosques. Zawahiri warns that it will undermine the popular support that is essential to seizing power in the Sunni areas following an American withdrawal in order to establish a territorial base. Any action that the masses do not understand or approve must be avoided, and he notes numerous questions about the wisdom and rightness of anti-Shia terrorism that are circulating among even Zarqawi's supporters.[7]

The 20 most lethal of the groups classified as religious in the MIPT Terrorism Knowledge Database were each responsible for over 100 total fatalities through December of 2005.[8] However, only nine of the twenty are classified as exclusively religious. They include al-Qaeda and al-Qaeda affiliates in Europe, the Armed Islamic Group in Algeria, the Lord's Resistance Army, Jamaah Islamiyah in Indonesia, al-Gama'a al-Islamiya in Egypt, the Taliban in Afghanistan, and, curiously, Ansar Allah, which is regarded as an offshoot of Hezbollah, an organisation with mixed motives. (Ansar Allah is thought to have bombed Jewish and Israeli targets in Argentina in the 1990s.) Ansar al-Sunnah in Iraq is considered purely religious, while other Iraqi groups are defined as national separatist as well. The other hybrid groups are (1) Palestinian (Hamas and Palestinian Islamic Jihad), (2) three associated with the struggle in Chechnya, (3) three originating in the war in Iraq, (4) Lashkar-e-Taiba in Kashmir and Pakistan, (5) the Abu Sayyaf Group, (6) Hezbollah, and (7) the Moro Islamic Liberation Front. Thus pure religious groups killed a total of 6,120 people, and the hybrid groups killed 4,657. Rank orderings from the database are below. (Note that the combined Caucasus conflict-related groups caused 924 fatalities,

---

6 Figures are from BBC Online.

7 Text accessed on the Office of the Director of National Intelligence website, where it was posted on 11 October 2005: <http://www.dni.gov/letter_in_english.pdf>. I am assuming that it is authentic.

8 The database did not include domestic incidents until after 1998. Thus older groups that used extensive violence at home against local targets will be underweighted in the comparisons. For example, in 2003 the Peruvian Truth and Reconciliation Commission reported that between 1980 and 2000 Sendero Luminoso was responsible for 54 per cent of the 69,280 total deaths in the conflict, thus over 37,000 people – admittedly we might not define all of their violence as terrorism, even though the victims included in the tally were not from the security forces, but this is an extraordinary figure (<http://www.cverdad.org. pe/ingles/ifinal/conclusiones.php>). By contrast, the Terrorism Knowledge Database credits SL with 133 fatalities and 267 injuries from 1968 to the present. Furthermore, over time small-group or individual access to destructive technologies as well as their knowledge of target vulnerabilities has increased; if most new groups are also categorised as religious, the results will be biased.

which would place them third. The combined Iraqi groups caused 2,141 fatalities.) (See Table 3.1.)

Table 3.1 Religious Groups Responsible for over 100 Fatalities, 1968–2005

Group	Incidents	Injuries	Fatalities
Al-Qaeda	28	8,859	3,533
Al-Qaeda Organization in the Land of the Two Rivers*	179	2,719	1,463
Hezbollah*	180	1,538	838
Hamas*	545	2,904	595
Riyad us-Saliheyn Martyrs' Brigade* (Chechnya)	11	1,136	514
Armed Islamic Group	64	259	506
Lord's Resistance Army (LRA)	27	291	503
Ansar al-Sunnah Army	49	894	478
Taliban	168	239	339
Jemaah Islamiyah (JI)	4	699	261
Abu Hafs al-Masri Brigade (Al Qaeda in Europe)	9	826	249
Dagestan Liberation Army*	4	453	248
Tawhid and Jihad* (Iraq)	30	219	200
Abu Sayyaf Group (ASG)*	55	515	197
Palestinian Islamic Jihad (PIJ)*	119	971	186
Movsar Baryayev Gang* (Chechnya)	2	657	162
Lashkar-e-Taiba (LeT)*	17	276	150
Al-Gama'a al-Islamiyya (GAI)	36	229	134
Ansar Allah	3	236	117
Moro Islamic Liberation Front (MILF) *	29	311	104

*Classified as hybrid religious and national-separatist groups; note also that Hamas is not typically listed as a 'new terrorist' group even though it is religious and causes mass casualties.

Organisation

The organisation of the new terrorism is also thought to be fundamentally different from earlier structures of terrorism. The 'new' terrorists are said to be decentralised, with a 'flat' networked apparatus rather than a hierarchical or cellular structure.[9] Sub-units are supposed to have substantial autonomy, if not complete independence, and the scope is transnational (global reach). Much of the new terrorism is thought to be inspirational rather than directed from the top; it is diffuse rather than concentrated. The US Government now says that the war on terrorism is against an ideology rather than an entity. Laqueur says that the new terrorism uses smaller groups (which, in his view, makes them more radical) (Laqueur 1999, 5). Hoffman adds that the new groups are likely to be composed of amateurs rather than professional terrorists who devote their lives and careers to the cause; they are likely also to be less well trained and to rely on information they collect themselves, primarily from the internet (Hoffman 1998, 197 and 203).

By contrast, the 'old' terrorist structure was considered to be centralised and top-down. Orders were given, received, and followed by subordinates. There was a strict chain of command. Hierarchies operated. The classic cellular structure was paramount. Although al-Qaeda is a transnational actor, it is problematic to assume that it is entirely different from the past, that it is necessarily a model for the future, or that secular groups might not organise themselves similarly. First, among 'religious' groups, al-Qaeda is the only example of such a network or franchise/venture capital operation. Other 'religious' terrorist groups are more traditional in form (Hezbollah, Hamas or Egyptian Islamic Jihad). Aum Shinrikyo was extremely hierarchical; like Sendero Luminoso, it was dominated by a charismatic leader. Second, even the intelligence agencies do not completely understand how al-Qaeda is or was organised. There may be or have been much more centralisation than appears to the public eye. Certainly, extensive face-to-face communication occurred within the group, at least prior to 9/11. The importance of the shared experience and socialisation in Afghanistan and subsequent access to recruits from diasporas and from other conflict zones cannot be underestimated in the organisational development of al-Qaeda. The war in Iraq has also provided a training ground and magnet for terrorists. Without these specific historical circumstances and access to territorial bases, the 'new terrorism' might not have evolved.

Furthermore, the organisation of the 'old' terrorism was not always as centralised as it might have appeared. Peter Merkl, for example, has argued that the apparently monolithic quality of the Red Army Faction in West Germany was a myth (Merkl, 1995). The nineteenth-century anarchists formed a transnational conspiracy, linking activists in Russia, Germany, Switzerland, France, Spain, Italy and the United States. The essence of anarchism was antipathy to central direction, and much terrorism was locally generated or inspirational. The secular Palestinian groups of the 1970s and 1980s split, merged, resplit and remerged. The relationship of Black September to Arafat and Fatah was one of indirection and deniability. West German and Japanese groups cooperated with Palestinians; in fact, the Japanese Red Army relocated to Lebanon after being driven from Japan. In addition, some of the more hierarchical groups in the past actually allowed significant local autonomy. The Active Service

---

9 According to Ian Lesser, 'This new terrorism is increasingly networked … As a result, much existing counterterrorism experience may be losing its relevance as network forms of organisation replace the canonical terrorist hierarchies …' (Lesser et al. 1999, 87).

Units of the IRA, for example, sometimes acted autonomously, without the approval of the Army Council. The Italian Red Brigades were organised in independent 'columns' in different cities. The French *Action Directe* was actually two groups, one limited to France and the other operating internationally and linked to groups in Belgium.

The Appeal of the 'New Terrorism' Idea

Why is the idea of a fundamentally new terrorism attractive, if indeed it is as flawed as I claim? One reason may be that the conception of a 'new' terrorism supports the case for major policy change – a justification for a war on terrorism, a strategy of military preemption, and homeland security measures that restrict civil liberties. It is a way of defining the threat so as to mobilise both public and elite support for costly responses with long-term and uncertain pay-offs. Moreover, the shock of the surprise attacks of September 11 was a turning point, especially for officials such as Richard Clarke (and including Simon and Benjamin as former officials from the Clinton Administration National Security Council) who had long warned that terrorism could be a major danger and who felt that they had been ignored (Clarke 2004). The effect of 9/11 resembles the impact of the North Korean invasion of the South in cementing the ideas behind interpretations of the threat of Communism and the militarisation of containment.[10] It seemed and may still seem impossible to consider terrorism a 'first order threat' unless it is defined as unprecedented. If 9/11 had precedents, then we should have taken terrorism seriously and anticipated escalation.

Furthermore the new terrorism model permits top-down processing of information. If policy-makers can rely on a set of simple assumptions about terrorism, they need not worry about a contradictory and confusing reality. In the presence of incomplete and ambiguous information, policy-makers are prone to rely on prior cognitive assumptions. Doing so saves them time, energy and stress. They rely on metaphors, narratives, and analogies that make sense of what might otherwise be difficult to understand, if not incomprehensible. In the same vein, terrorism 'experts', especially newcomers to the field, might find it convenient not to have to take the time to study the complicated history of the phenomenon.[11] If the past is dismissed as irrelevant and only al-Qaeda matters, then the task of analysis becomes much easier. If religion is the cause of the sort of terrorism that poses a threat to national security, then we

---

10 Indeed Simon calls for a policy of containment, as the US contained the Soviet Union during the Cold War. A comparison of presidential speeches in the early Cold War years and the post-9/11 period would be instructive. (This is not to say that we should neglect the rhetoric of the second Clinton term) (Simon 2003).

11 Burnett and Whyte go further to say that 'It is certain that some elite groups will make a great deal of political and social capital out of this war on terror. It is equally certain that state interventions against the terrorists will continue to be supported by a manufactured conception of 'new terrorism' that is founded upon a highly questionable knowledge base' (Burnett and Whyte 2005, 15). They are particularly critical of the role of the Rand Corporation.

need to look no further for an explanation. Nor need we worry about other 'types' of terrorism.

Preliminary Conclusions

Rejecting our accumulated knowledge of terrorism by dismissing it as 'obsolete' is dangerous. A misdiagnosis of what the 'new' actually entails could lead to mistakes as grave as those attributed to lack of recognition. For example, the assumption that the sort of catastrophic terrorism that many defined as 'new' would necessarily involve the use of weapons of mass destruction turned out to be mistaken. The expectation was one factor in making surprise possible. Hijackings were thought to be a tactic of the past. Differences among groups and over time do exist, but they may be attributable to a changing environment (processes associated with what is termed globalisation, in particular, such as advances in communications and mobility), specific opportunity structures, and evolutionary progression, even learning. Observations about a 'new' terrorism lack a basis in sustained and systematic empirical research and they neglect history. This school of thought overestimates the effect of religious beliefs on terrorism. The distinction between religious and nationalist motivations is not clear or empirically substantiated, and the argument undervalues the power of nationalism.[12] The data on which the association between religion and mass casualties is based are incomplete, excluding as they do domestic terrorism prior to the late 1990s. Secular ideologies can also be fundamentalist, exclusive and totalitarian, as the Peruvian Truth and Reconciliation Commission concluded in the case of Sendero Luminoso.

---

12 Note Robert A. Pape's argument that suicide terrorism occurs when a resistance movement confronts a foreign military occupier of a different religious faith. I am not in complete agreement with his argument but it is worth considering in relation to this issue. See Pape (2005).

PART 2
Jihadi Terrorism Around the World

Chapter 4

Logics of Jihadi Violence in North Africa

Hugh Roberts

Movements pursuing strategies of violence for political purposes in the name of Islam have been a feature of the North African landscape since the mid-1970s. These groups have exhibited a considerable diversity, in scale and duration, in strategic vision, in method and tactical repertoire and even in motivation. But the effort to seize the logics underlying their emergence and activity has been consistently impeded by a number of important misconceptions and fallacies that have been regularly recycled in the discourse of Western and North African governments alike.

The Question of Ideology

A striking feature of current Western commentary on the various movements and organisations pursuing violent strategies in the Muslim world and, now, in Europe and North America is the insistent emphasis on ideology as the key explanatory variable. In part, this may be understood as a reaction against the earlier tendency to explain them in terms of economic and social deprivation, or at least relative deprivation, for it is now widely recognised that this does not work. It may help to explain why some young men from the towns of the Nile Valley and their counterparts from the run-down housing estates on the periphery of Algiers and the bidonvilles of Casablanca have joined armed movements or become suicide bombers. But it does not begin to explain the outlook of the founders and leaders of these movements, who have generally been from middle-class backgrounds, let alone why these movements – which have not made an issue of economic and social conditions, but something else altogether – have existed in the first place. But the turn to ideology as explanation owes a lot to the outlook and policies of Western governments. For the suggestion that the struggle against terrorism is, or should be, above all a 'battle of ideas' – a notion that certainly appears to have merit when weighed against the consequences of the 'war against terrorism' as taken literally and put into effect since 2001 – has been from the outset associated with the thesis that terrorism, at any rate when Muslims engage in it, is essentially the product of 'an evil ideology' and that it is this ideology which must be vanquished if terrorism itself is to be defeated. That this outlook contains the seeds, at least, of a dangerous drift towards the kind of authoritarian and strictly policed ideological conformism foreshadowed by George Orwell's *Nineteen Eighty-Four*, with subversive ideas assuming the explicit status of 'thought-crime', is by no means the only drawback in this view of things. An equally cogent objection to it is that it prevents us from understanding what we are looking at.

In its original version, developed in the 1980s and 1990s, this thesis suggested that Islamist ideology as such could explain the recourse to violent strategies. The Islamism that attracted attention was classified as 'radical' (see Sivan 1985) and represented as jihadist in tendency by definition.[1] The crystallisation of explicitly and consistently non-violent forms of Islamic activism over the last 15–20 years[2] has made such a sweeping claim no longer tenable, but a more discriminating variant of the same view now enjoys widespread currency, namely the thesis that the 'evil ideology' in question is a specific current within contemporary Islamism: 'jihadi salafism'. There are three objections to this thesis.

The first is that it amounts to a tautology. The Arabic term *al-Salafiyaa al-jihadiyya* refers to those Muslims professing their adherence to the salafi interpretation of Sunni Islam who engage in armed struggle. As such, it is a misuse of language to describe 'jihadi salafism' as an ideology; as far as ideas are concerned, it is merely an activist fashion. But the point is that to elevate it to the status of ideology and endow it with causal significance is to argue that jihadi salafis are jihadis because they are jihadi salafis. The circular character of this reasoning should be self-evident: it posits jihadi salafism as the cause of itself. It may well be because of the threadbare nature of this thesis that some Western observers have been increasingly disposed to identify salafism as such as the problem. There is an irony in this, in view of the generally positive evaluation which a previous generation of North Africanists made of the salafiyya movement (See also Gellner 1974, 277–310; Gellner 1981, 149–73; Hourani 1962; Kerr 1966; Abun-Nasr 1987; Etienne 1977). While its fundamentalist dimension was recognised, the fact that its emphasis on scripture inclined it to promote literacy and Arabic-language education – and so facilitate individual and egalitarian access to knowledge of God (as well as other kinds of knowledge) while tending to emancipate individual Muslims from tribal and other traditional parochial ties – meant that it had a very definite modernising impact and contributed in large measure to the development of national consciousness across the region in the 1920–50 period (Abun-Nasr 1987, 325). In addition, its doctrinal rigour and austere morality authorised comparisons with the Puritan movement in Protestant Christianity and were widely seen as offering a Muslim version of the Protestant ethic, with all that this could imply for economic and social development.

That there is an irony in contemporary commentators now excoriating this movement as the vector of the 'evil ideology' does not mean they are wrong to do so. But it should be noted that, if they are right, the truth they may claim to be stating is an extremely inconvenient and ominous one. The remarkable dynamism which the salafiyya has exhibited over the last thirty years, in expanding all around the

---

1　Thus a leading French author on this subject, Bruno Etienne, argued that the characteristic feature of mainstream Islamist religious activism, the mission of preaching and (re-)conversion, *al-dawa*, implied the jihad (Etienne, B., *L'Islamisme Radical* (Paris: Hachette, 1987), p. 142).

2　For a detailed discussion of the diversity within Sunni Islamic activism as different currents and tendencies have crystallised over the last two decades, see ICG (2005).

periphery of the Muslim world and in Europe in particular, owes a great deal to the fact that it thrives in the conditions created by globalisation (see also Roy 2002; ICG 2004a; Lubeck 1999; Lubeck and Britts 2001). In focusing on Muslim identity and individual conduct while simultaneously positing and invoking a global Ummah, salafism offers a definition of what it is to be a good Muslim that is extremely relevant to Muslims on the move, rural migrants arriving and trying to find a place in the anonymous and anomic environments of the cities and, above all, the millions of 'de-territorialised' Muslims living in or trying to join the Muslim diaspora in the West. If the processes of globalisation are not reined in, they will ensure that salafism will continue to grow for the foreseeable future. So, if salafism is indeed the 'evil ideology' that generates terrorism, there is a lot more trouble ahead.

In fact, however, these commentators are largely mistaken in suggesting that salafism as such produces jihadis. There is no necessary connection between resort to violent strategies and adherence to salafism. Not all the armed movements engaged in rebellion or terrorism in North Africa have been salafi and few salafis become jihadis. The mainstream salafiyya, often referred to nowadays as *al-Salafiyya al-'ilmiyya* ('the salafiyya of the scholars') to distinguish it from the minority jihadi trend, is above all a non-violent movement of ideas and missionary preaching and its leading lights have regularly condemned the recourse to jihadi violence except where jihad is mandated by classical – that is, not exclusively salafi – doctrine. In short, the ideology of salafism does not explain the phenomenon of jihadism. To pretend that it does is to engage in scapegoating if not witch hunts.

This leaves us with the problem of explaining why jihadi salafis are jihadi and, more generally, why any Muslims become jihadis. The alternative I wish to propose in respect of the North African experience at least is that recourse to armed struggle has been not so much the expression of an ideology as the response to a situation, or rather a set of responses to a number of situations which, while having certain things in common, are also quite specific and differ from one another in significant ways. In other words, it is the context, rather than the ideology, which explains what people actually do. In order to appreciate North Africa's various contexts, however, we still have some deck-clearing to do.

Islamism, Nationalism and Jihad in North Africa

The advent of movements committed to and engaging in armed struggle in the name of Islam in North Africa has conventionally been discussed in terms of two clichés which are in fact misconceptions rather than truisms. The first cliché conceives of these armed movements as the extreme end of a single spectrum of Islamist doctrine and practice. The second cliché posits an absolute opposition of Islamism to nationalism in the North African context. In this way Western observers have disabled themselves from grasping a large part of the reason why these movements have arisen when they have and why they have behaved as they have.

It is not the case that the variety of Islamist organisations and movements can be accurately or usefully ranged on a single spectrum of Islamist activism. Leaving aside the important differences between Sunni and Shiite Islamic activism,[3] the diversity within contemporary Sunni Islamic activism is not a matter of locations on a single spectrum but is of a completely different nature (see also ICG 2005). Three main currents can be distinguished:

- Political: the Islamic political movements (*al-harakât al-Islamiyya al-siyassiyya*) which seek power, or at least an influential role in the political sphere, operate (or seek permission to operate) as political parties within the constitutional and legal frameworks of the state, accept these frameworks even while criticising them on specific points, pursue non-violent and essentially reformist strategies, and abstain from counter-posing utopian conceptions of the 'Islamic state' to the states that actually exist;
- Missionary: the Islamic missions of preaching and conversion (*al-dawa*), exemplified by the highly diffuse salafiyya movement on the one hand and the highly structured tablighi movement on the other, neither of which seeks political power but rather the preservation of the Muslim identity and the Islamic faith and moral order against the forces of unbelief;
- Jihadi: the Islamic armed struggle (*al-jihad*) which exists in three main variants: defensive or irredentist (fighting to resist conquest by non-Muslim powers or to redeem land occupied and ruled by them); internal (combating nominally Muslim regimes considered impious); and global (combating the West).

The differences between the three main types of Sunni Islamic activism are not differences of degree. It is not a matter of the relative strength of people's convictions and the varying lengths to which they are prepared to go in bearing witness to them, as the 'moderate' vs. 'radical' dichotomy tends relentlessly to suggest and, arguably, presupposes. On the contrary, these different types of activism are premised on quite distinct diagnoses of the Muslim predicament and correspondingly distinct prescriptions of what can and should be done about it. As ICG has pointed out,

> political Islamists make an issue of Muslim misgovernment and social injustice and give priority to political reform to be achieved by political action (advocating new policies, contesting elections, etc.). Missionary Islamists make an issue of the corruption of Islamic values (*al-qiyam al-islamiyya*) and the weakening of faith (*al-iman*) and give priority to a form of moral and spiritual rearmament that champions individual virtue as the condition of good government as well as of collective salvation. Jihadi Islamists make an issue of the oppressive weight of non-Muslim political and military power in the Islamic world and give priority to armed resistance. (ICG 2005, ii)

Equally, the lumping together of all varieties of armed struggle, the indiscriminate labelling of them all as equally 'terrorist', and the claim that they all represent 'perversions' of Islam disable observers from grasping the dynamics and logics of these movements. Jihad as such, in the sense of armed struggle on behalf of the Ummah (the community of believers), is not at all a perversion of Islam. In both Sunni

---

3 These differences, of great importance in the Middle East and South Asia, are substantially irrelevant to contemporary North Africa, where almost all Muslims are Sunnis.

and Shia doctrine, recourse to armed struggle is certainly considered to be legitimate under certain conditions, and the Islamist thesis that jihad is, under these conditions, an obligation is not in itself a novel, let alone a perverted, view. Indeed, there is a strong case for the view that, in classical Islamic doctrine, the ruler of the Muslim state has the duty to lead jihad whenever defence of the Muslim state requires this, and that this doctrine has survived into the modern era and, in fact, to the present day. Western blindness to this rather fundamental fact has owed a lot to the mystificatory thesis that the states of North Africa have been ruled by secular nationalist regimes and that the Islamist movement in general, and the jihadi movements in particular, have arisen in absolute opposition to these. In fact, however, not one of these states has been a secular state in the sense in which France or the United States can be so described. Discussion of these matters has been relentlessly bedevilled by the tendency to resort to reductionist analyses, such as the thesis that the independent North African states are 'essentially' secular (that is, the patently non-secular aspects of these states are arbitrarily judged to be not 'essential' to them). The reality, to which only resolutely non-reductionist analytical approaches can do justice, is that each of these states is complex and accordingly *ambiguous*, combining elements of modernism in its constitution, form of government and policies with the potent Islamic heritage of the country as well as elements of the latter's pre-modern political tradition. The notion that at least some of them were 'essentially' secular and so un-Islamic was actively canvassed by the pan-Islamic axis of pro-Western states headed by Saudi Arabia during the 'Arab cold war' which pitted them against the Arab-nationalist republics in the 1950s and 1960s and was, of course, a major element of Sayyid Qutb's radical critique of the Free Officer's regime in Egypt. But it was never more than a half-truth at best and, in relentlessly recycling this half-truth, Western discourse has continually misrepresented key elements of what has been happening while simultaneously providing endorsement of Islamist challenges to the legitimacy of the state in North Africa.[4]

Islamic ideas and the Muslim identity were crucial ingredients of anti-colonial nationalism in Algeria, Morocco and Tunisia, both have been central to the strategies of legitimation of the Libyan state since 1951 – whether under the Sanussi monarchy or under Colonel Qadhafi's regime – and the Free Officers who seized power in Egypt in 1952 were in close contact with the Muslim Brothers at the time, included people who sympathised with them (notably Anwar Al-Sadat), and initially courted and enjoyed their support. Above all, in every case, from Morocco to Egypt, Islam has had, throughout, the constitutional status of the state religion, and as head of state a Muslim. The state has made a point of supervising the religious field through a specialist government ministry and state bodies grouping the senior religious authorities (the *ulama*) and has continuously sought religious legitimation for its policies. Even Tunisia, widely perceived, with some reason, as the most 'Western' and 'secular' of all, made a point of describing itself as an 'Islamic Republic' in its 1959 constitution.

---

4 Thus Western insistence that, for example, Egyptian nationalism was secular provided external endorsement of Sayyid Qutb's critique of it as un-Islamic.

The thesis that Islamist opposition to the state in North Africa has been grounded in an ideological rejection of secular nationalism is accordingly unsatisfactory and misleading. The thesis that the armed challenges to or rebellions against these states have, in invoking the idea of jihad, been invoking a spurious perversion of Islam is also groundless. On the contrary, these movements have been invoking an element of the Islamic tradition on which these states have themselves partly rested. The Algerian state is the product of a liberation war popularly conceived as a jihad. Within the National Liberation Front (Front de Libération Nationale, FLN) which conducted the war, this conception was not universally shared; it was rejected by modernist leftist elements in particular, notably the leaders of the FLN's organisation in France (see Haroun 1986).[5] But it was in fact officially consecrated by the FLN and the state it founded in various ways; for example, the title of the wartime FLN's main organ – and the state's principal daily newspaper throughout the first 27 years of independence – was *El Moudjahid* ('the warrior of jihad'), and one of the main national museums in Algiers devoted to the liberation war is called the Musée du Jihad. The Libyan state also consecrates its own jihadi tradition in the Libyan National Centre of Jihad.

It is not only the so-called 'radical' states of North Africa that have this tradition. Fulfilling the obligation to conduct jihad when necessary has been a condition of legitimation of the Moroccan sultanate since the sixteenth century CE. The Sharifian doctrine of the Moroccan sultanate as developed by the Sa'adian dynasty and further developed by the Alawi dynasty from the 1660s onwards explicitly included the duty of jihad among the obligations of the ruler (See Bennison 1999/2000). A corollary of this is the doctrine that the sultan (or, today, the king) has the title and authority of 'Commander of the Faithful' – *Amir al-Mu'minin*. This traditional condition of legitimation is arguably one which still applies to the contemporary monarchy. The legitimacy of independent Morocco's first king, Mohamed V, was unquestionably due in large part to his success in placing himself, qua Commander of the Faithful, at the head of the Moroccan national struggle for independence from France. His heir, Hassan II, whose position was extremely precarious in the early 1970s, when two attempted military coups occurred in rapid succession, recovered general legitimacy and authority through his effective leadership of Morocco's campaign to recover (or annex, as the Polisario Front sees it) the Western Sahara.[6] Even in Tunisia, that most 'moderate' and apparently 'secular' of North African states, official discourse throughout the first three decades of the post-colonial era routinely referred to President Bourguiba, who led the country to independence in 1956, as *le Combattant Suprême* ('the Greatest Fighter'), *al-mujahid al-akbar*.

It follows that what Islamist opposition currents in general, but also armed groups in particular, have been doing is to remobilise essential elements of the state's

---

5 That is, the Fédération de France du FLN (FFFLN).

6 This campaign began with the 'Green March' (green for Islam, march for jihad, albeit non-violent at that juncture) into the territory from the starting point of Qsar al-Suq (now renamed Al-Rashidiyya), the administrative capital of the Tafilalt region of south-eastern Morocco where the Alawi dynasty originated. The symbolism of all this was extremely potent and not lost on the Moroccan public.

own complex ideological tradition against the state or, at least, against the regime in power. The question is why they have done this, and what accounts for the variation that we can observe in forms of armed struggle that have been resorted to.

National Contexts I: The Propensity to Engage in Jihadi Activism

Jihadi activism is now a feature of all the states of North Africa with the notable exception of Libya. But, in the case of Morocco and Tunisia, the emergence of jihadi groups has occurred only since 2001 and in the context of al-Qaeda's global jihad and the West's response to this in the 'global war on terrorism'. The same is true of the development since 2004 of terrorism in Egypt's Sinai region, previously entirely unaffected by jihadi violence. Before 2001, armed movements engaged in violent strategies in the name of Islam were confined to the central regions of Egypt – that is, the Nile valley and delta – and Algeria. This calls for explanation.

The first Islamic armed movements emerged in Egypt in the middle and late 1970s and in Algeria in the early 1980s. They did so at a time when, under the regimes of President Sadat and President Chadli Bendjedid respectively, the Egyptian and Algerian states were engaged in dramatic changes of direction in both foreign and domestic policy. These changes were closely linked in their political implications. They amounted to the supersession of the state's previous nationalist project by a post-nationalist outlook and agenda (see also Roberts 2003, 358–65) and entailed a major reconfiguration of the regime's alliances at home and abroad. On the external front, a key feature was the abandonment of nationalist militancy (and its extension in the ambition to lead supra-national – pan-Arab, Third-Worldist – causes), while loosening ties with the Communist bloc and seeking rapprochement with the West and especially with the traditional external adversary (Israel, France). On the internal front, the regimes retreated from socialist economic policies, began to open up the economy to foreign capital and encourage the private sector. In order to change course in this way, they purged themselves of their nationalist and populist-socialist wings (Nasserists, Boumedienists) and suppressed the Left, while stressing their Muslim credentials and allowing unprecedented room for manoeuvre to Islamist tendencies (notably the Muslim Brothers in Egypt and their counterparts in Algeria). Thus, by simultaneously loosening their hold over nationalist sources of legitimacy while courting – and thereby empowering – Islamist sources of legitimation, the Egyptian and Algerian states encouraged the emergence, among other things, of opposition movements that retrieved and recycled elements of the nationalist project while articulating them in an Islamic idiom.

In Egypt, the first movements to plan violent actions against the Sadat regime in the mid-1970s were founded on the initiative of Palestinian activists resident in the country. When Egyptian jihadism cohered under Egyptian leadership in the Jihad Organization (Tanzim al-Jihad) in 1979–80, the state's separate peace with Israel was the main charge levelled against it, and a preoccupation with Palestine has continued to mark the Egyptian jihadi current to this day. In Algeria, a group of vaguely Islamic outlook, the Armed Islamic Movement (Mouvement Islamique Armé, MIA) was formed in 1982, at the very moment when, following François

Mitterrand's election to the French presidency the previous year, the Chadli regime was busy developing its rapprochement with Paris on the external front while courting Islamist support at home to cover its retreat from nationalism in both foreign policy (the tacit abandonment of militant, Third Worldist, non-alignment) and domestic policy (the abandonment of socialism and economic nationalism). The MIA's leader, Mustapha Bouyali, was a veteran both of the 1954–62 liberation struggle, as a member of the wartime FLN's guerrilla forces, the Armée de Libération Nationale (ALN), and of the brief armed rebellion of the so-called Socialist Forces Front (Front des Forces Socialistes, FFS) against the independent state in 1963–65. His motivation in launching his guerrilla movement in 1982 was a complex mixture of Islamic, nationalist and populist impulses combined with the prejudices of a former guerrilla fighter against civilian politicians, especially those with foreign connections. Viscerally anti-communist on religious grounds (and so both hostile to the late President Boumedienne's more radical socialistic policies and sympathetic to the Afghan jihad) (see Merah 1998), he was also bitterly critical of the corruption that he considered characterised the regime, especially hostile to those elements of the power elite who personified this or who had come to power on the backs of Boumedienne's 'army of the frontiers' in 1962,[7] but also suspicious and resentful of certain Islamist politicians, notably those linked to the Egyptian Muslim Brothers,[8] whose support for the regime was courting and who were clearly willing to be co-opted by it. Thus Bouyali's recourse to armed struggle in 1982 owed little or nothing to a specifically Islamist ideology.[9] As ICG has noted,

> It would be more accurate to classify Bouyali's MIA as a rebellious offshoot of the FLN-ALN tradition, which expressed itself in Islamist terms in deference to the ideological fashion of the 1980s much as the FFS's earlier rebellion had expressed itself in socialist terms in deference to the ideological fashion of the 1960s. (ICG 2004b, 2)

While Bouyali's guerrilla campaign in 1982–87 was a very limited affair, its significance is that it established the template of subsequent jihadi activism in

---

7 As a member of the ALN's guerrilla forces inside Algeria, Bouyali had strongly shared the resentment of these forces at the way Colonel Houari Boumedienne's 'army of the frontiers', which had been based in Tunisia and Morocco, seized power at their expense in 1962. This resentment, combined with hostility towards Algeria's first president, Ben Bella (perceived as a stooge of Gamal Abdel Nasser), had motivated the ALN veterans (Bouyali among them) who joined the FFS rebellion in 1963. Thereafter it strongly inclined them to regard the regime as lacking legitimacy, and to invoke the phenomenon of corruption as evidence of this.

8 Notably Sheikh Mahfoud Nahnah, whose Movement for an Islamic Society, founded in 1990 and later renamed Movement of Society for Peace, is regarded by the Egyptian Muslim Brothers as their Algerian sister party and has figured in Algeria's coalition governments since 1996.

9 An Algerian specialist on Islamism, Hmida Layachi, observed, 'When one analyses his discourse and references, one cannot speak of the Salafiyya jihadiyya. The MIA was not motivated by a strong and homogenous ideology. Bouyali's discourse included certain borrowings from the Salafiyya, but it was very simplistic, more populist than anything else' (quoted in ICG 2004b).

Algeria. It was veterans of the MIA – and *not* (as the Western media have relentlessly but erroneously suggested) radicalised members of the banned Islamist party, the Islamic Salvation Front (Front Islamique du Salut, FIS) – who launched the much more serious armed rebellion in 1992. Their reasons for doing so appear to have been a continuation of Bouyali's original motivations in the specific context of 1990–91, given that the regime's behaviour, notably its brutal repression of FIS demonstrations in June 1991 (see Roberts 1994, 428–89; Roberts 2003, chapter 3) and the army's coup in January 1992, suggested that the non-violent, constitutional, road to an Islamic state was an illusion. Thus in Algeria it is the nationalist guerrilla tradition (which dates back only to 1954), rather than the older tradition of Salafi Islamic activism (dating back to the 1920s if not earlier), which has been the main source of the jihadi tendency. And elements of the old nationalist discourse, in particular hostility to the traditional French enemy and the tendency to condemn the state in part because of its clientelist relationship with France and other Western states (notably, since 2001, the USA), has been an emphatic feature of the propaganda of the various armed movements in Algeria since then, including the Armed Islamic Group (Groupe Islamique Armé, GIA) in 1993–98 and, since 1998, the Salafi Group for Preaching and Combat (Groupe Salafiste pour la Prédication et le Combat, GSPC).

There can be little doubt that the end of the state's confrontation with its traditional external enemy was the most important change triggering, among other things, the development of a jihadi current of opposition in both Egypt and Algeria. That this is so is confirmed by the Moroccan and Tunisian cases. Neither the Moroccan nor the Tunisian state was constituted by a military revolution or has ever exhibited a missionary zeal in international affairs, both have always been conspicuously 'moderate' (notably on the Arab–Israeli conflict), and neither of them has engaged in abrupt and disorienting changes of direction and international outlook at any point. As a result, they have not been faced with home-grown jihadi movements at all. The substantial domestic Islamist movements that have posed real challenges to their regimes – Abdesselam Yassine's Justice and Charity Association (Jam'iyyat al-'Adl wa 'l-Ihsan) in Morocco and Rachid Ghannouchi's Al-Nahda movement in Tunisia – have been eminently political and have eschewed violent strategies, while the advent of jihadi terrorism in both countries has occurred only since the onset of the global war on terror and has been primarily an emanation of the Muslim diaspora in Europe and consequently oriented by exotic jihadi fashions.

Outlook and Focus: The Oscillation between External and Internal Enemies

The rise of a jihadi current of activism in Egypt and Algeria in the 1980s can thus be seen as involving the redeployment of jihadi energies from the external to the internal front, in which the original nationalist focus on 'the farther enemy' was replaced by the new, indeed novel, focus on 'the nearer enemy'. While this reorientation was a rather confused and doctrinally rudimentary affair in Algeria, it was explicitly proclaimed and rationalised in Egypt by the theoretician of Tanzim al-Jihad, Abd al-Salam Faraj, in his pamphlet *Al-Farida al-Gha'iba* (The Forgotten Obligation).

Not all such energies were redeployed to the internal front, however. Throughout the 1980s, many young Algerian and Egyptian men with activist impulses preferred to engage in the classic jihad against an unequivocally infidel enemy – the Soviet-backed Communist regime – that was under way in Afghanistan. During the 1990s, it was above all the cause of the Muslims in Bosnia which attracted these activists. With the clear defeat of the internal jihad in Egypt by 1997, those Egyptian jihadis still inclined to activism redeployed once more to the external front, where Osama bin Laden's al-Qaeda offered an outlet and framework for their impulses. A similar pattern is observable in the Algerian case, where the internal jihad against 'the impious state' has very clearly been defeated. Algerian activists have accordingly been redeploying to the external front, where they have been a prominent element of the foreign fighters drawn to Iraq since 2003. And, faced with the impossibility of realising its notional aim of overthrowing the regime, the last major Algerian jihadi movement, the GSPC, has at least nominally identified itself with the global jihad against the West by re-branding itself as 'al-Qaeda in the Lands of the Islamic Maghrib'. This development highlights an important change, however. In the original vision of the Egyptian jihadis, the nearer and farther enemies were distinct. The strategy of waging jihad against the nearer enemy was rationalised on the grounds that the revolutionary replacement of the impious state by a properly Islamic state was the necessary precondition of successfully resuming jihad against the farther enemy. With the rise to prominence of al-Qaeda since 1998 (and especially since 2001), strategic conceptions that were previously distinct have been combined and have accordingly become confused. While Iraq and Palestine may be conceived as terrains of classic jihad against infidel powers,[10] the global jihad is in practice an extremely ambiguous affair. Its least ambiguous aspect resides in jihadi activities undertaken in the West itself, in Europe and North America. Recent jihadi activities undertaken in Muslim countries, such as the terrorist attacks in Algeria, Morocco and Tunisia, are no longer oriented by a seriously revolutionary perspective of establishing properly Islamic states as the precondition of resuming the jihad against the farther enemy, but are now explicitly rationalised as engagements in the global jihad itself. As such, these developments express the logic of globalisation in two ways at once: the perception and stigmatisation of Muslim states as mere satellites and clients of the Western powers, and the supersession of specifically national strategies of armed struggle by a new, global fashion in violent activism.

National Contexts II: Strategies, Tactics and … Deviations

The distinctions between (1) defensive or irredentist, (2) internal and (3) global varieties of jihad established by ICG provided a base-line typology for analysing contemporary jihadi activism, but did not pretend to account for the full range of variations in this that can been observed. In so far as al-Qaeda's global jihad has, in practice, been parasitic on local jihads of both the irredentist-defensive and internal

---

10 Although the onset of vicious sectarian conflict pitting Sunnis against Shiites has certainly qualified perceptions of Iraq in this manner, the armed conflict between Al-Fatah and Hamas has similarly begun to qualify perceptions of the Palestinian case.

varieties (ICG 2005, 17), and to the extent that failing internal jihads are tending (as in Algeria today) to morph into local fronts of the global jihad, it may seem that these distinctions are already losing their relevance. But they remain extremely relevant at least for the purpose of understanding the history of modern jihadi activism. By far the most important type of jihad in the years prior to 11 September 2001 (if not up to the fatal invasion of Iraq in 2003) has been the internal jihad, and it is this which has been the field of the greatest diversity in jihadi behaviour. The global jihad is, in contrast, the field of fashion-following and emulation. But precisely because internal jihads have been conducted in particular national contexts, they have varied very considerably in ways which have reflected the specificities of these contexts.

In the Egyptian case, the most coherent and determined jihadi group, Tanzim al-Jihad, can be seen to be a characteristic product of the Egyptian revolutionary tradition as well as of the specific context of regime policy changes in the late 1970s and early 1980s. That tradition was, of course, established by the Free Officers who overthrew the monarchy in 1952. The 1952 revolution was a purely military, extremely elitist and conspiratorial affair. So was Tanzim al-Jihad. Just as the Free Officers had seen the overthrow of the monarchy and the seizure of the commanding heights of state power as the precondition of everything else they wanted to achieve, so Tanzim al-Jihad saw the assault on the apex of the regime as the crucial first stage of its strategy for establishing an Islamic state (Kepel 1993, chapter 7). Indeed, it would be fair to say that it never really thought out its strategy beyond this first stage. Concentrating almost exclusively on its conspiracies to assassinate senior power holders and mount occasional bomb attacks, it never seriously addressed the question of mobilising popular energies and harnessing them to the revolutionary purpose (Kepel 1993, chapter 7). It would seem that it could not do this because the example of the Free Officers was of no assistance to it in this respect and no other relevant example from Egyptian history was available. There was no element of the Islamic *dawa* (the religious mission of preaching and conversion) in its strategic vision or tactical repertoire, any more than there had been any element of political agitation in the vision and repertoire of Nasser and his associates. The 1952 Revolution was, of course, in reality a coup, not a revolution. It made possible what one might call a revolution from above thereafter, but it mobilised no social constituency or popular energies for the purpose of taking power. And so Tanzim al-Jihad had no example before it that could guide it. Lacking what the Free Officers possessed – an army – it could never come remotely near achieving its initial objective, let alone its ultimate aim. While it contrived to produce a statement of its doctrine (Farag's pamphlet), as Nasser produced his *Philosophy of the Revolution*, this amounted to little more than a justification of the recourse to jihad. Its function was to legitimate the group's activities, not guide them.

The contrast between Tanzim al-Jihad and the jihadi movements in Algeria – both the MIA of 1982–87 and the various groups active since 1992 – serves only to underline the critical importance of national traditions. We have already seen how the original MIA was an offshoot of the guerrilla tradition of the ALN and that it was veterans of the MIA, and thus products of this tradition at one remove, who launched the armed struggle against the regime in 1992. The tradition of the ALN was the tradition of the revolutionary *maquis*, and thus both a tradition of mobilising popular support for a protracted guerrilla war and a tradition that actually constituted the state. As such, this tradition did, in principle, provide guidance to the Algerian jihadis as to how they might achieve their purpose of overthrowing 'the impious state' and establishing an Islamic state in its place. If they failed to achieve this purpose, this was in large part because they were prevented from following the guidance of the national revolutionary tradition effectively.

Crucial to the failure of the armed rebellion of 1992 onwards was its inability to emulate the historic FLN–ALN in establishing a single, unified movement with a clear and intelligible objective and an agreed strategy for achieving this objective. Several attempts to unify the armed movements were made but they were all unsuccessful. There is no doubt that the Algerian army's intelligence services, which were able to infiltrate most if not all the various armed organisations, were instrumental in thwarting these attempts. But, if the intelligence services were able to play to great effect on the divisions within and between the armed organisations, this is because these divisions already existed. For the national tradition of the revolutionary, *maquis* was not the only source of orientation for the armed rebellion. Three other traditions were also available to them, and exercised a relentlessly disturbing effect.

The most obvious was the far newer tradition (so recent that it was not so much a tradition as a model and a fashion) of the Afghan jihad. Algerian veterans of the Afghan jihad played a major role in organising what soon became the most prominent movement, the GIA. Between 1993 and 1996 the GIA eclipsed all the other armed organisations and during this period it was led by a succession of veterans of the Afghan war. Three features of the GIA's behaviour quickly distinguished it from the other groups:

- The ferocity of its violence, including its assassination of prominent secularist intellectuals, its murderous attacks on foreigners resident in Algeria, its regular resort to beheadings (a practice which the FLN–ALN had rarely if ever engaged in) and its resort to indiscriminate terrorism, in the form of car bombings, in public places;
- Its coercive Islamisation, by means of terror, of the local communities in which it was present, a practice that tended to be at cross-purposes with the objective of winning and retaining popular support;
- Its explicit condemnation of the FIS in particular and Islamist political parties in general and its corresponding refusal of all and any political negotiation.

All three of these features of the GIA's behaviour represented what might be described as the pedantic acting out of the Afghan jihadi model – with an admixture of Tanzim al-Jihad's tactical repertoire (notably car bombings and assassinations) – in the very different Algerian context, a context in which these tactics were largely inappropriate and counter-productive, in that they unquestionably made it easier for the regime to rally public opinion to its side. They soon led the GIA into explicit conflict with other armed organisations, thereby producing a fourth feature of its behaviour, the extent to which it devoted its energies to combating rival movements, a feature which, of course, worked to the benefit of the regime and was very probably encouraged by the regime's intelligence agents. The resulting disagreements and tensions within the

GIA itself in turn resulted in a series of bloody purges, which precipitated the GIA's loss of external support from foreign sympathisers and eventually climaxed in its frenzied resort to indiscriminate massacres of civilians on the bizarre and entirely eccentric pretext that Algerian society as a whole had 'left Islam', that is, become apostate, such that ordinary Algerians were all licit objects of jihad (ICG 2004b, 13–14). While the impulse to put into practice the exotic Afghan and Egyptian jihadi model was a major obstacle to unity with those other groups which took their bearings from Algeria's own revolutionary tradition, it was not the only one. For Algeria's own traditions of recourse to violence against the state are in fact multiple. In addition to the revolutionary tradition of the FLN–ALN, two other traditions have been quietly in play. The first of these is the tradition of armed rebellion as a form of political strike or dissidence, a tradition which dates from the time of the Ottoman Regency, when tribes or local power-holders provisionally incorporated into the Regency's political system would periodically seek to renegotiate the terms of their allegiance by demonstrating their nuisance value. The second is the tradition of banditry, whether that of outlaws motivated by the traditional code of honour (what French sociologists call 'les bandits d'honneur' and English ones call 'social bandits') or the form of banditry that is mere predatory brigandage.

The difficulty which the various armed Islamic organisations found in emulating the truly revolutionary *maquis* of the FLN–ALN gave rise to the tendency for these organisations to revert to one or other of these less than revolutionary traditions. Thus, when most of the groups which had stayed outside the GIA cohered into a new movement calling itself the Islamic Salvation Army (Armée Islamique du Salut, AIS) and the AIS explicitly proclaimed its allegiance to the FIS and called for negotiations and a political solution, it was clear that the armed struggle in question was no longer a real jihad, in the sense of a war to overthrow the impious state, but had declined into a more modest rebellion, expressing a grievance against and a dissidence from the regime rather than a more radical objection to it and the revolutionary ambition to overthrow it. It was for this reason that the regime was willing to negotiate a cease-fire with the AIS leaders and eventually secured the dissolution of the AIS in exchange for a kind of amnesty. Equally, following the eventual disintegration of the GIA in 1997–98, there has been a clear tendency for many of the armed groups still active to decline into mere banditry.

Both of these tendencies can be seen to have been at work in the case of the main armed movement still active in Algeria in recent years, the GSPC. This originated in Zone 2 of the GIA (the eastern Mitidja and Kabylia), whose commander, Hassan Hattab, had increasingly distanced himself from the central GIA leadership on the ground that this had clearly deviated from the true path of jihad. Hattab entirely rejected the GIA's strategy of massacring civilians and the extremist doctrine that underpinned this, the doctrine of *takfir al-mujtama'* (condemnation of the whole society as infidel) and in September 1998 he explicitly broke with the GIA by renaming his organisation the GSPC. Under his leadership, the GSPC reverted to the orthodox jihadi doctrine of limiting *takfir* to the 'impious state' alone and concentrated its attacks on the state's security forces while sparing civilians. It was accordingly able to renew links with foreign sympathisers, notably bin Laden's al-Qaeda, while also gaining a measure of local popular support. As such, it situated itself within the same jihadi current as the GIA of 1993–95 before the deviations began, that of the *Salafiyya jihadiyya*. In practice, however, the GSPC increasingly behaved just like the MIA and the AIS, as if it was in reality, rhetoric notwithstanding, an offshoot of the national jihadi tradition. It success in preserving local popular support, especially in western Kabylia, was very probably connected to this fact.

While militarily effective, however, the GSPC was unable to make serious headway towards its notional revolutionary objective of overthrowing the state, and by 2001 if not earlier Hattab seems to have been seeking a negotiated end to his campaign along lines similar to that of the AIS. In the meantime, however, elements of the GSPC in other parts of Algeria, especially the Tebessa area near the Tunisian frontier, had become deeply involved in smuggling activities, and it was these elements which expanded into the Sahara in 2003 by sensationally abducting 32 Western tourists and holding them for ransom. This was an astonishing development, given the unsuitability of the desert terrain for guerrilla activity and the ease with which the security forces had insulated the Sahara from terrorist violence throughout the 1992–2002 period.[11] Moreover, it clearly signified the decline into brigandage rather than adherence to a revolutionary jihadi purpose. It was nonetheless interpreted by the Western media as proof of a serious jihadi threat in the Sahara and the Sahel, and thus justification of the US Government's 'Pan-Sahel Initiative' (subsequently renamed the Trans-Saharan Counter-Terrorism Initiative and now the Trans-Saharan Counter-Terrorism Partnership). At the same time, the Saharan tourists affair also signalled Hattab's loss of control over the group, and by the autumn of 2003 he had been deposed, an event that simultaneously signified the scotching of any prospect of a negotiated end to the GSPC's campaign. Since then, under Hattab's successors, the GSPC has increasingly reverted to the tactical repertoire of the old GIA, notably in its massive resort to car bombings, a tactic Hattab had little or no use for. At the same time, it has appeared to link its own survival to increasing emphasis on its connection with al-Qaeda, a development which reached its conclusion with its announcement that it had changed its name to 'al-Qaeda in the Lands of the Islamic Maghreb'. In other words, it appears that the mutation of the GSPC into a local affiliate of al-Qaeda is, among other things, a function of the fact that it has exhausted its other strategic options and so a sign of weakness rather than strength. At the same time, it is by no means clear that this mutation is much more than skin deep. The use of suicide bombers in the attacks on the *Palais du Gouvernement* in central Algiers and a police station in the Bab Ezzouar district on 11 April 2007 was almost certainly intended to underline the new connection with bin Laden's global jihad by adopting its characteristic operational style. But it remains the case that

---

11 It should be noted that virtually no guerrilla activity occurred in the Sahara throughout the Algerian war of liberation. For this and other reasons, enormous question marks hang over the GSPC's supposed expansion into the Saharan theatre. Many seasoned observers of Algeria have expressed the suspicion that the entire episode has owed a great deal to manipulations by Algerian military intelligence. See Keenan, J., 'Conspiracy Theories and Terrorists: How the war on terror is placing new responsibilities on anthropology', *Anthropology Today*, 22(6) (2006): 4–9. See also Mellah, S. and Rivoire, J-B, 'Petites manipulations algéro-américaines. Enquête sur l'Étrange Ben Laden du Sahara', *Le Monde Diplomatique*, February 2005.

the movement's targets, whatever it calls itself, are essentially internal ones. The rebranding of the group can thus perhaps be best understood as responding to the need for fresh and primarily external legitimation of a jihadi agenda which remains essentially confined in its purposes to Algeria.

Conclusion

This essay has sought to broach the question of the diversity to be found within the single category of Sunni jihadism and the scale and character of the differences – of doctrine, of source of inspiration, of purpose, strategy and tactics – that can be observed between the various jihadi organisations in North Africa. As such, it has had the character of a preliminary and somewhat rapid reconnoitre of this difficult terrain and much of the argument should be understood to be provisional and tentative. I have not at all pretended to offer a definitive analysis, let alone a complete theorisation, of this diversity. My object has been to draw attention to it and make the case that it matters and requires further investigation.

To the extent that I have taken the argument beyond this case, I have suggested that the observable diversity cannot be adequately appreciated or comprehended within the conceptual framework that has been central to the discourse on jihadism or 'Islamic terrorism' (a very problematic as well as controversial term) of Western governments and the Western media. It follows that a new and more appropriate conceptual framework is badly needed and must be developed. This is a question which I intend to address in future work.

Chapter 5

Kinship and Radicalisation Process in Jamaah Islamiyah's Transnational Terrorist Organisation[1]

Noor Huda Ismail

Jamaah Islamiyah (JI) is a transnational terrorist organisation. The phenomenon of transnational terrorism emerged as a main focal point during the 1970s (see Swanstorm and Bjornehed 2004, 328–49). The term was used to describe the engagement in violent struggle by sub-state groups on an international level. The word 'transnational' indicates activity that crosses state boundaries but does not involve the state as an institution. It has commonly been used to denote economic and industrial activities, such as transnational corporations (TNCs) (Guelke 1995, 145).

The combination of development of means of travel and light, hard-to-detect, effective weapons and materials facilitates the movement of human agents as instruments of violence. One defining characteristic of transnational terrorist organisations is their presence in more that one country and their attacks directed against civilians in other states rather than their own, or targets within their host state that are associated with another state. It also includes directing an attack against internationally positioned targets such as aircrafts.[2] In the case of JI, the organisation has established a presence ranging from southern Thailand through Malaysia, Mindanao, Singapore and Indonesia. Although the JI was founded in the mid-1990s, the organisation did not initiate a terror act until 2000. The organisation spent a lot of time laying the groundwork for a long-term sustainable environment (Abuza 2003, 10). Many of the cells are 'sleeper' cells and/or agents. This means that the individuals within the cell are waiting to be activated. Meanwhile they lead normal lives, far from any connection with terrorist activities. This is what makes individuals of a cell so hard to detect, and one may say they live undercover (White Paper 2003, 129). Use of such a cell structure, as is found in contemporary terrorism, has a discouraging impact on the conventional methods utilised in counterterrorism. The utilisation of numerous autonomous cells makes it extremely hard, if not impossible,

---

1 This chapter is an expansion of an article that was published in *Terrorism Monitor*, 4(11) (2 June 2006). It can be accessed at <http://jamestown.org/terrorism/news/article.php?articleid=2370016>.

2 <http://db.mipt.org/rand.tc.cfm>.

for authorities to foresee and thus prevent future terrorist attacks since there are few messages to intercept or communications to wiretap.

The formal induction into JI often took place in conflict places such as Afghanistan when the novice pledged *baya*, a formal oath of loyalty, to JI leader, Abdullah Sungkar (White Paper 2003, 91). 'Joining the jihad' is understood here as the decision to go somewhere for training, whether Afghanistan (the most common destination), Bosnia, the Philippines, Malaysia or Indonesia. Embedded in the above discussion is the notion of a pathway to terrorism. The assumption that being involved in a jihadi movement is something to be understood absent of its social context and which furthermore can be characterised as a physiological state of some kind, disconnected from its context and history, leads necessarily to a focused attempt to identify unique and/or personal qualities (Taylor and Horgan 2006, 9).

Table 5.1 Education of Embassy Bombers

Name	Education
Son Hadi	Ngruki 1988–91
Syaifuddin Umar alias Abu Fida	Lecturer, Universitas an-Nur 2000–2002
Gempur Budi Angkoro alias Jabir	Ngruki 1993–96; Darussyahada 1996–98, taught 1999–2004
Suranto alias Muhammad Faiz alias Deni	Ngruki 1992–95; al Husein (Indramayu, also JI School) 1995–97; an Nur 2002–2003
Bagus Budi Pranoto alias Urwah	Al Muttaqien (Jepara, also JI School) 1990–96; an Nur 2000–2003
Lutfi Haidaroh alias Ubeid	Ngruki 1992–95; Darusysyahada 1995–98; an Nur 2000–2003
Heri alias Umar (Ubeid's brother)	An Nur
Heri Sigu Samboja alias al- Anshori	Ngruki 2002–2003

Since the 2002 Bali bombings that killed more than 200 people, mostly foreigners, with several hundred more injured, JI has been weakened by arrests and other counter-terrorism measures. However, terrorists have carried out murderous attacks twice in Jakarta and once more in Bali since the first major bombings. Most of JI's targets are 'highly symbolic Western interests'. According to the group, there was no need to go to Iraq or Afghanistan; the jihad could be waged at home.[3] The repudiation of the West constitutes a common thread running through various

---

3 It may not be coincidence that around this time a pamphlet was circulating in jihadi groups that was a translation from Arabic into Indonesian of an article that first appeared in the al-Qaeda on-line magazine *Sawt al-Jihad*. Entitled 'You Don't Need to Go to Iraq for Jihad', it was written in 2003 by a Saudi jihadi, Muhammad bin Ahmad as-Salim (ICG 2006b).

Islamist movements that have emerged in the contemporary Muslim world. Those attacks by JI members show that all parts of the terrorist network have not ceased jihadi operations. The 'grass-roots enlistment' in JI seems to exist along a 'bottom up' rather than a 'top down' perspective in that individuals in jihadi networks bring in other family members (about 20 per cent), friends, co-worshippers or co-workers (about 70 per cent). The rest are recruited mostly through school.[4] Certainly, people are driven to join religious movements by personal needs and these needs are rooted in identified social conditions (see Beckford 1988; Bruce 1996). These two tables summarise the school ties of the operatives in the Hotel Marriot bombing and the Australian bombing (ICG 2006b, 4 and 7) (see Tables 5.1 and 5.2).

Table 5.2 Education of Marriot Bombers

Name	Education
Noordin Moh Top	Lukmanul Hakiem, 1998–2002
Azhari Husin	Lukmanul Hakiem, 1998–2002
Indrawan alias Toni Togar	Ngruki, 1987–90
Mohammad Rais	Ngruki, 1991–95; Lukmanul Hakiem, 1996–99, 2001–2002
Asmar Latin Sani	Ngruki, 1991–95
Ismail alias Mohammad Ikhwan	Lukmanul Hakiem, 1991–98
Sardona Siliwangi	Ngruki, 1993–97
Masrizal bin Ali Umar alias Tohir	Ngruki, 1990–94; Lukmanul Hakiem, 1998, 2000
Mohammad Ihsan alias Jhoni Indrawan alias Idris	Ngruki, 1989–93

Indonesia's president, Yudhoyono also acknowledged that the police forces have made progress in cracking the network, killing Jamaah Islamiyah's alleged explosives expert Azahari bin Husin in 2005, but noted that alleged mastermind Noordin M. Top remains on the run. Noordin, seen as the group's real strategist and one of its main recruiters, 'is continuing his activities', said Yudhoyono in his annual address to Indonesia's parliament, calling on security forces to keep up their guard (AP 2005). In our society there is a wide consensus that eliminating poverty from society also alleviates crime. Therefore, it is not surprising that in the aftermath of the tragic events of September 11, 2001, several prominent observers – ranging from former Vice President Al Gore to President George W. Bush, as well as academics, including Joseph Nye, former Dean of the Kennedy School of Government, Laura Tyson, Dean

---

4 This is the hypothesis of the Global Network Terrorism project that was presented in an NSC briefing (White House, Washington DC, 28 April 2006). The author has been working in this project as a graduate researcher. The project is supported by the National Science Foundations and AFOSR-MURI.

of the London Business School, and Richard D. Sokolsky and Joseph McMillan of the National Defence University, just to name a few – have called for increased aid and educational assistance to end terrorism.[5] Also, at a gathering of Nobel Peace Prize laureates, South Africa's Archbishop Desmond Tutu and South Korea's Kim Dae-jong opined: 'At the bottom of terrorism is poverty'. Elie Wiesel and the Dalai Lama, for their part, concluded, 'Education is the way to eliminate terrorism' (Ismail 2005). Indonesian Defence Minister Juwono Sudarsono also said Southeast Asian nations must fight terrorism on their 'own terms' or risk being seeing as lackeys of nations such as the United States and Australia. And he warned in an interview with AFP that it would take at least a decade for Indonesia to address the root causes of terrorism – poverty, unequal wealth distribution and corruption (Yeo 2006).

But poverty and lack of education are clearly not the main root causes of terrorism. Osama bin Laden is both highly educated and very wealthy, and JI mastermind Azahari bin Husin – who was killed in a shootout with Indonesian police on October 2005 – earned a PhD in Britain. In May 2005, on the outskirts of Jakarta, the author interviewed Tajul Arifin, a jihadi who robbed Bank Central Asia in 1999 and was alleged to have taken part in an attempt to assassinate Indonesian politician Matori Abdul Jalil, a one-time leader of the Awakening and Justice Party. He is not poor and is the son of an Indonesian military man. Another former jihadi the author interviewed was Fauzi Isman. He was arrested in 1989 for subversion and released ten years later. Isman comes from a military family and graduated from the Jakarta State Academy of Statistics in 1989. In his house in Curug, East Jakarta, he said that he wanted to overthrow the Indonesian government and replace it with an Islamic state.

While these individual cases may not suggest a larger trend, a Singapore parliamentary report substantiates the claim after conducting a thorough review of detained terrorist operatives. The report noted that of the 31 captured operatives from JI and other al-Qaeda allies in Southeast Asia:

> These men were not ignorant, destitute or disenfranchised. All thirty-one had received secular education ... Like many of their counterparts in militant Islamic organisations in the region, they held normal, respectable jobs. As a group, most of the detainees regarded religion as their most important personal value ... secrecy over the true knowledge of jihad helped create a sense of sharing and empowerment vis-à-vis others. (Yeo 2006)

Terrorism may in some cases offer greater benefits for those with more education (Kruger and Maleckova 2003). For example, well-educated individuals may participate disproportionately in terrorist groups if they think that they will assume leadership positions if they succeed; or if they identify more strongly with the goals of the terrorist organisation than less educated individuals; or if they live in a society where the relative pay advantage of well-educated individuals is greater for participation in terrorist organisations than in the legal sector. Furthermore, terrorist organisations may prefer to select those who have better education. Between 1996

---

5 President George W. Bush refrained from drawing a connection between poverty and terrorism for a time, but on 22 March 2002 he announced in Monterrey, Mexico: 'We fight against poverty because hope is an answer to terror'. (<http://www.whitehouse.gov/news/2002/03/20020322-1.html>).

and 1999, Nasra Hassan (2001), a relief worker for the United Nations, interviewed nearly 250 militants and associates of militants, including failed suicide bombers. One Hamas leader interviewed, claimed: 'Our biggest problem is the hordes of young men who knock on our doors, clamouring to be sent (on a suicide mission). It is difficult to select only a few.' A planner for Islamic Jihad explained to Ms Hassan that his group scrutinises the motives of a potential bomber to be sure that the individual is committed to carrying out the task. Apparently, most groups generally deny suicide bombing missions to 'those who are under eighteen, who are the sole wage earners in their family, or who are married and have family responsibility'. Higher levels of educational achievement are probably a sign of one's commitment to a cause and determination, as well as of one's ability to prepare for an assignment and carry it out. This demand for educated operatives is an often-neglected element of terrorism (Kruger and Maleckova 2003). Discussions that attempt to root terrorism in poverty and civil strife alone miss the fundamental attributes of terrorism as noted early in this chapter. Terrorism is defined primarily as a strategy and a tactic open to any group regardless of their background.

However, if one looks at organisations like JI, it seems that JI utilises marriage to a large extend to ensure loyalty, to collect information about members, and to facilitate further recruitment. Therefore, it is critical to understand 'kinship ties' in the jihadi network in Indonesia and beyond. Without such ties, many alienated young Muslim men would not have become or remained jihadis. Kinship is particularly important in a clandestine organisation like JI, where maintaining relations of trust and confidence is crucial for survival. Additionally, jihadi organisations have the unusual advantage of having their own religiously qualified members available to officiate at the creation of new marital bonds.

Pattern of Kinship in Jamaah Islamiyah

What role, if any, does kinship play in the ability of JI to rejuvenate itself? The author hopes to show how the conceptions of kinship have important ramifications in the way these jihadis conceive political authority among their recruits. And how they capitalise the perceived grievances suffered by Muslims worldwide to galvanise the anger among marginalised young Muslims in the region. Although kinship is the most arcane aspect of anthropological study, it nonetheless must be studied if we want to understand the ties of affinity. The crucial point of kinship for this research is the blood relations and parenthood, not the more general rituals of kinship (such as the spiritual kinship in respect to Christian societies) (Parkin 1997, 124).

Utilising JI as a case study offers several examples that highlight the complexity of kinship links in terrorism, such as relationships between two or more male siblings, between in-laws, between fathers and sons, as well as more distant kinship relations. The following section considers the different roles of kinship in a possible contribution to terrorist activities and the important role kinship maintains in helping to keep the network secure from infiltration.

Sibling Relationships

The use of sibling relationships in jihadi recruitment is meant to provide further ideological support for the recruits that extend beyond the group itself. Sometimes two or more brothers are recruited for jihad, helping each other during an operation and providing each other inspiration and reassurance. This particular type of recruitment is an effective use of kinship to ensure deeper engagement with the cause and group. One example of such sibling kinship and terrorism is the family of Achmad Kandai. In the 1950s he belonged to the hard-core movement Darul Islam, which tried to assassinate the first Indonesian President Sukarno in 1957. Nasir, a brother of Kandai's, worked with Abdullah Sungkar and Abubakar Ba'asyir, two successive spiritual heads of JI in Malaysia in the 1980s and 1990s. Kandai's sons Farihin bin Ahmad, Abdul Jabar, Mohammed Islam and Solahudin all became jihadists. In August 2000 Ahmad and Jabar participated in the attack on the Philippine ambassador's Jakarta residence that killed two people and injured 22 others, including Ambassador Leonides Caday.[6] Mohammed Islam, the third brother, became involved in several bombings during the religious conflict in Poso in Central Sulawesi where violence between Muslims and Christians led to hundreds of deaths on both sides between late 1998 and 2002 (and where intermittent violence continues to this day).[7] The fourth brother, Solahudin, was among those arrested in the 29 April 2006 raid in Wonosobo, Central Java. He is now under police custody for his involvement in a series of terrorist attacks including the bombing of the Atrium shopping mall in August 2001, where the designated bomber lost his leg and was arrested after the bomb he was carrying blew up prematurely.[8] The complex kinship relations found in terrorism, illustrated by the Kandai family, is not an anomaly in the JI terrorist faction. The al-Ghozi family is another jihadi family. Faturrahman al-Ghozi, who was shot and killed by the Philippine police in 2003, was one of JI's main bomb-makers. Among other actions, he was the perpetrator of the devastating Rizal Day bombing in Manila in 2000 that killed 12 people and wounded 19 others. Al-Ghozi's father was a Darul Islam member who was jailed during the Suharto era. A younger brother, Ahmad Rofiq Ridho, is now standing trial on several charges including sheltering the Malaysian JI member Noordin Mohammed Top. Last year, Ridho set a precedent for JI by marrying his brother's widow in a ceremony in a Jakarta police detention facility.[9] Gempur Angkoro, whose alias is Jabir, is al-Ghozi's cousin and was one of Top's most trusted men; he too was killed in the raid of 29 April 2006. Jabir assembled the bombs used in the deadly attacks in Jakarta at the JW Marriott hotel in 2003 and at the Australian Embassy in 2004. The first Bali

---

6 *Washington Diplomat*, 1 August 2000.

7 In interviews in 2005, Nasir Abas, head of Mantiqi 3, one of JI's strategic area divisions, which covered the geographical region of the Philippines and Sulawesi and was responsible for military training and arms supplies, said that Poso had the potential to develop into a *qoidah aminah*, a secure area where residents can live by Islamic principles and law. In their view, such a base could then serve as the building block of an Islamic state; Maluku and Poso, therefore, remain a focus for religious outreach and recruitment efforts.

8 An interview with Farihin bin Ahmad in Jakarta in 2005.

9 An interview with Ahmad Rofiq Ridho in Jakarta prison in 2005.

bombing introduced three brothers to the outside world: Ali Ghufron (Mukhlas), Amrozi and Ali Imron. The first two are now on death row. Ali Ghufron was in charge of overall supervision of the bombing. Amrozi procured the chemicals and vehicles needed for the attack, while the third brother coordinated transport of the bomb.[10] Another set of brothers, Herlambang and Hernianto, were also involved. Hernianto later died in jail, allegedly of a kidney complaint. Hambali and Rusman Gunawan, whose alias is Gun Gun, are another set of JI brothers. Hambali, now in US detention, was JI's liaison with al-Qaeda. Gun Gun was involved in the Marriott hotel bombing in 2003. He attended university in Pakistan and in late 2002 he became the intermediary for e-mail messages between al-Qaeda and Hambali, who was then hiding in Cambodia.[11] There was also a set of JI brothers in Singapore, Faiz and Fatihi bin Abu Bakar Bafana. Faiz was treasurer of the first JI region or Mantiqi 1 (JI's regional division that provides the economic wherewithal for JI operations), and has admitted receiving funds from Osama bin Laden via Hambali. Fatihi carried out reconnaissance against Western targets in Singapore.[12] Mantiqi 1 was initially led by Hambali who was subsequently replaced by Ali Ghufron (Mukhlas) in 2001.[13]

In-Law Relationships

Kinship ties also include in-laws. Ali Ghufron married Farida, younger sister of Nasir bin Abas, a Malaysian who once served as Mantiqi 3 chairman. Nasir, who abandoned the JI cause and wrote a book entitled *Exposing Jamaah Islamiyah*, was sufficiently loyal to his brother-in-law to write that he had been the best possible husband for his sister. Another JI member, Syamsul Bahri, is another of Nasir's brothers-in-laws (ICG, 2003). Taufiq Abdul Halim, the Malaysian who lost part of his leg in the Atrium bombing, is the brother-in-law of Zulkifli Hir, a leader of a Malaysian jihadi group which was responsible for a series of crimes including the assassination of a state assemblyman (White Paper 2003). Another example is Datuk Rajo Ameh, who participated in the Christmas Eve bombing in 2000 among other attacks. He is the father-in-law of JI member Joni Hendrawan, who was involved in the first Bali bombing and the 2003 Marriott attack.[14] Mohammad Rais, another Marriott figure, is the brother-in-law of Top. Rais recruited a suicide bomber for the Marriott bombing.[15]

Fathers and Sons

Anxious for their offspring's safety and with an eye to regenerating JI, senior members sent their children to study in Karachi, where they formed the so-called *al-Ghuraba* (the foreigners) cell. During university break, some members of the group

---

10 An interview with Ali Imron in Jakarta Prison in 2005.

11 *Ibid.*

12 An interview with Ali Imron in Jakarta Prison in 2005.

13 An interview with Rusman Gunawan in Jakarta Prison in 2005.

14 An interview with Joni Hendrawan in Jakarta Prison in 2005.

15 An interview with Muhammad Rais in Jakarta Prison in 2005.

went to Afghanistan for a course in urban warfare. Six of them travelled to Pakistan-controlled parts of Kashmir where Lashkar-e-Toiba, a guerrilla movement affiliated with al-Qaeda, gave them a month of physical and military training. Pakistan's Inter-Services Intelligence (ISI) agency discovered the group in September 2003. Abdul Rohim, Abubakar Ba'asyir's son, was the cell leader.[16] One of its members was Abu Dzar, whose father is a long-time associate of Hambali and two of his uncles are JI members. Abu Dzar's uncle, Muhamad Ismail Anwarul, who drove a taxi in Singapore, would later attend an al-Qaeda training camp in Kandahar during 2001. His sister had recently married Masran bin Arshad, the leader of Khalid Sheikh Mohammad's alleged suicide cell. Another cell member was the Malaysian Muhammad Ikhwan, whose father, Abdullah Daud, attended an al-Qaeda surveillance course in Kabul in 2000. Ikhwan's older sister married another JI member. Likewise, the father of Singaporean student Mohammad Riza was sent by JI's Mantiqi 1 for military training in Mindanao.

Arranged Marriages

Establishing arranged marriages between members of JI families was the ideal way of forging permanent alliances for the organisation. These marriages were meant to keep the JI organisation a close-knit one. JI spiritual leaders could play the role of matchmaker and marriage celebrant. It is suggested to those who feel ready to marry to go to their *ustadz* (religious teacher) and to tell him of their intentions. Usually an *ustadz* will give his wife(s) the task of finding a girl ready for marriage. Through the mediation of the *ustadz* and his wife(s), a meeting between the future bride and bridegroom is arranged. At that meeting the would-be-bride is allowed to see the face of the would-be-bridegroom in the presence of their mediators.[17] Abdullah Sungkar married two of his stepdaughters to senior jihadis – Ferial Muchlis bin Abdul Halim, a head of the Selangor JI cell, and Syawal Yassin, a prominent South Sulawesi figure and former military trainer in Afghanistan. Sungkar had been the celebrant at the 1984 marriage of future Mantiqi 4 leader Abdul Rohim Ayub and the Australian Rabiyah (ICG 2003).

Haris Fadillah is a hard-core Darul Islam militia leader who fought and died in communal religious conflict in Ambon, Maluku, where thousands of Muslims and Christians lost their lives; many villages and places of worship were destroyed. He arranged the marriage of his daughter, Mira Augustina, to Indonesia-based al-Qaeda operative Omar al-Faruq. Following her husband's arrest in June 2002, Mira acknowledged that she had married al-Faruq the first day she met him.[18]

In the same vein, Jack Thomas, an Australian jihadi, married an Indonesian, Maryati, in South Africa on the recommendation of his JI friends. Thomas, who even adopted the name 'Jihad', likewise married his wife the day he met her. A Singapore jihadi called Jauhari testified in court that the Indonesian preacher, Abu Jibril, had helped to choose his wife for him and that Abdullah Sungkar had married

---

16 An interview with Abdur Rahim in Solo, Central Java in 2004.

17 An interview with Farihin in 2005.

18 An interview with Mira Agustina in Bogor, West Java in 2004.

them at Abu Jibril's house (ICG 2003). As for Hambali, he married a part-Chinese woman, Noralwizah Lee, who converted to Islam. Like male JI members, Lee used several aliases and was active in recruiting women to the cause. The couple first met at a gathering held by one of the women's groups under Abdullah Sungkar's auspices. The author established in interviews with one of the participating lecturers that one topic offered was 'Women and Jihad'.[19] Lee shared Hambali's fate by being arrested in Thailand with him in August 2003. Noordin Mohammed Top found time to take a second wife; he was still married to Mohammad Rais's sister from Riau. Noordin heard about Munfiatun al-Fitri, a young woman who had expressed interest in marrying a mujahedeen warrior for Islam. The marriage was arranged by Surabaya JI member Abu Fida in 2004. Like Ali Ghufron's wife, Munfiatun is well educated and graduated in agriculture at East Java's Brawijaya University. In search of security, women do not hesitate to be the second or third or even the fourth wife of a jihadi man. This seems to be a rational choice for them because finding a good man who understands their 'position' is not an easy task.

Kinship and the Individual's Engagement to Terrorism

In a series of interviews conducted by this author with terrorists identified above, diverse examples provide evidence to conclude that terrorists are ordinary people who make choices in the contexts in which they find themselves (discussed at length by Taylor 1993). There seem to be no discernible pathological qualities in terrorists that can identify them in any clinical sense as different from others in the community from which they originate (Taylor and Quayle 1993). Nonetheless, the world was outraged by Amrozi's reaction upon hearing his sentence. Amrozi is one of several jihadis convicted of the October 2002 Bali bombing. In court, Amrozi smiled broadly and raised his two thumbs in approval over the judge's decision to sentence him to the death penalty. The image from the Bali courtroom of a smiling Amrozi will remain etched in many people's mind.[20]

Interviews also demonstrate that the commitment of these people to a religious clandestine movement, like JI, had been preceded by their association with the Darul Islam movement. This movement has the characteristics of a strict religious organisation, demanding complete loyalty, unwavering belief and rigid adherence similar to a sect. Laurance R. Iannaccone defines it as 'a religious organisation with a high commitment, voluntary and converted membership, a separatist orientation, an exclusive social structure, a spirit of orientation, and attitude of ethical austerity and demanding asceticism' (Iannaccone 1994; see also Stark and Bainbridge 1985; Robbins 1988).

Iannaccone underscores the significance of social ties in determining one's engagement in a strict religious movement. He argues that people who lack extensive social ties to friends and family outside the sect are more likely to join (or remain active) and are still more likely to join if they have friends or family in the sect. On the contrary, those who have extensive social ties are less likely to join the sect.

---

19 An interview with Muyazin in Solo in 2004.
20 The author was present to cover the event for the *Washington Post*.

He emphasises that a potential member's social ties predict conversion far more accurately than his or her psychological profile (Iannaccone 1994, 1200–201).

The choice to become a terrorist or engage in terrorist activities is a gradual process with many routes toward this mien of political violence. Triggering-events such as police brutality, massacres or some other significantly provocative incidents, increase the likelihood that people will become involved in terrorism activities. Thinking about terrorism as a process of course reflects its complexity, but thinking in this way can also help us to draw better policy recommendations. This can be seen in the case of Ahmad Rofiq Ridho, a JI member based in Solo, Central Java and the younger brother of Fathurrahman al-Ghozi. In an interview with the author in December 2005, he described in great detail (not all of which is presented below) how his involvement in jihadi activities affected him and his family:

> 'Honestly, I do not have any personal inclination to jihadi activities. I used to keep my hair long. I just loved to hang out with friends and sometimes to race with a motorcycle. [Laughs …] I gained my first jihadi experiences in 2000 in Ambon [there was a communal conflict between Muslims and Christians in this area]. My brother recruited me to help my Muslim brothers in Ambon confronting attacks from a Christian group of Red RMS for nine months. I went there as a humanitarian of KOMPAK [JI financial section]. When I was arrested last year [2005], my mother told me not to worry about my arrest. She said that it was not new in our family. "I was in jail when your sister was a baby" my mother told to me. I am very proud of my late brother and I want to be like him: to die as a martyr. He is my hero. He is not a terrorist. He is an Islamic guardian. America and Israel are terrorists! To respect him, I married his wife last month. I am very lucky to be born in a jihadi family.'[21]

His late father was arrested during the Suharto regime for his involvement in the Jihad Command movement. After his release, Ridho's father became a member of a local legislative council in East Java. Ridho belonged to an Islamic charity called KOMPAK, which made videos documenting alleged atrocities against Muslims in Poso, Central Sulawesi and in Ambon, Maluku. A number of features of this account suggest the following tentative qualities. The encouragement from Ridho's brother to participate in jihadi activities in a conflict area can be perceived as a catalyst for his involvement with JI. As previously noted, two or more brothers were often recruited for jihad in order to help each other during operations and provide each other with inspiration and reassurance. This particular type of recruitment is an effective use of kinship to ensure deeper engagement with a terrorist cause or group.

There appears to be a deep sense of personal identification with his brother's role as a *mujahedeen* and those victimised in the conflict in Ambon. He was easily able to justify involvement and engagement in terrorism as part of a defensive reaction. He sees it is his duty to take up arms in defence of his 'brothers' as part of a collective identity as a good Muslim. Being *syaheed* (martyr) is one of the lures that can increase engagement in terrorist activities. The sense that initial involvement in terrorism may develop from a series of incremental steps is powerful. As Horgan contends, the tendency to think about involvement in terrorism being determined

---

21 An interview with Ahmad Rofiq Rido in Jakarta police detention in December 2005.

by the drama of particular terrorist events obscures the incremental process (Horgan 2005, 95).

Hundaine, for example, describes the incremental process through which youngsters become committed insiders of counter-culture youth groups (Hundaine 2003, 107–27). She suggests the idea of a 'community of practice' as an informal social learning environment. This environment allows the individual to exchange views with other members. Essentially, she asserts: 'over time, this collective learning results in practices that reflect both the pursuit of our enterprises and the attendant social relations'.

Conclusion and Recommendations

In mid-August 2006 President Bush stated the country's war on terrorism will last 'for years to come' (Murphy 2006). The open-ended nature of this war and feelings of public vulnerability, generated by reports of plans like the air-bombing plot uncovered in London in August 2006, create great scepticism among US allies about the effectiveness of its tactics. Therefore, it is not surprising that many in Indonesia still view the whole war against terrorism as a plan to weaken Islam. Some even ask: 'is the terrorist threat real or hocus-pocus?' (Zulaika and Douglas 1996, 8).

Indeed, Indonesia is still in the process of transition and Islam, as a moral force in support of reform, has played a strong and positive role. Although it must also be acknowledged that there have been times when the actions of Muslim militants and extremists have generated many of the problems Indonesia continues to grapple with today.

In the last three years, Southeast Asia witnessed considerable success in dismantling JI networks. However, the JI networks are far from eradicated and due to their ability to recruit, indoctrinate and reconstitute themselves, they are still an organisation that poses a threat to all nations of the region. The terrorist threat has mutated and continues to create new challenges. These people have been using 'jihad' as a way to gain support from Southeast Asian Muslims who feel alienated in the process of democratisation. As Jason Burke writes, 'they represent the lunatic thought in the Islamic world; more certainly not connected to the big Islamic movements which have meanwhile opted for democratic rules or at least reject violence as a mode of operation.'

Like any other organisation, JI has had to respond to external developments and internal disruptions. It has a capacity to regenerate, made possible by deep roots in Indonesia that go far back, before JI officially even came into being. JI has survived partly because it is held together by an intricate pattern of kinship. Generally, people do not join JI due to some individual pathology. Indeed, most recruits look, dress and behave like normal individuals, at least until they are given a deadly mission or are deeply engaged with the JI ideology and group. The choice to become a terrorist or engage in terrorist activities is a gradual process with many routes toward this type of political violence. As this research has demonstrated, once inside the group, JI members tend to cement ideological and other bonds by marrying the sisters and daughters of their comrades-in-arms. This is a unique tool utilised for recruitment and for further engagement in the JI cause, thus limiting disengagement options for JI members and blocking effective counterterrorism tactics. Evidence throughout this study shows that kinship bonds make defection from JI difficult by imposing a belief that defection is tantamount to betraying ones own family. Furthermore, these close ties of kinship maintain a system that is nearly impenetrable to outsiders such as security services aiming to disrupt terrorist organisations.

Therefore, relatives of identified terrorists need to be closely monitored and investigated wherever they reside. Especially important are those who went to the same mosque and school or who participated in the same military training either in local areas or abroad, such as in Afghanistan or in Moro Islamic Liberation Front camps. It implies that we need to prevent the emergence of the kind of international training centre that Afghanistan provided in the past. The personal bonds established there are almost certainly more important than ideology or money in facilitating partnerships among jihads groups. It is essential not to underestimate previous informal membership in action-oriented groups, such as soccer or cricket clubs, that may facilitate the passage from radicalisation to jihad and on to joining suicide attack teams. Profiling of jihadi families by looking at their social backgrounds is useful. It is also crucial to look at the ways in which a person gets drawn into terrorism and from that to develop counterterrorism strategies. Democratic reforms, especially an impartial, credible legal system, a neutral and competent law enforcement agency, and better access to justice, remain absolutely essential in preventing the kind of vigilantism that radical groups can manipulate.

The challenge of the JI phenomenon is an ideological one. Like other governments, the Indonesian government can take security and law enforcement measures to contain the perceived threat. However, if the challenge posed by the ideological radicalism underlying the belief systems of these individuals is not countered with an effective response, there will be no guarantee of preventing the possibility of another generation of JI recruits. JI's singular concept of jihad as a violent struggle and an obligation for all good Muslims to pursue, their rejection of the secular state, their personal allegiances to al-Qaeda and their belief that terrorism is a legitimate means in pursuit of the larger cause of defending Muslims and Islam are some of the key issues which need to be addressed by the Indonesian government and Muslim leaders. Failure to do so will simply guarantee that Indonesia will remain a target for terrorists. Only through a combination of effective public policy, education and dialogue can the spread of al-Qaeda's brand of radical ideology be neutralised.

To prevent the spread of ideas, such as Samudra's, it is critical to de-legitimise leaders – not simply arrest or kill them. The ideas of these leaders are often very significant and are inextricably connected to the organisation's very existence. Therefore, the public diplomacy campaign to discredit these ideas is as, or even more important than the actual arrest or killing of terrorists. Understanding the dynamic of the ideas of the group together with its arrangement of psychological and cultural relationships is crucial. To do that, the Indonesian government may be able to copy the concept of Yemen's Committee for Dialogue (Taarnby 2005). The committee was established in August 2002, when Yemeni President Ali Abdullah Salih summoned five senior clerics who subsequently formed the nucleus of this pioneering enterprise. The clerics who approached the jihadi detainees insisted that the dialogue would centre on the interpretation of the Holy Scriptures. If the detainee could persuade the clerics of the legitimacy of their jihad they would join them. If not, the detainees would have to give up the idea of armed struggle. This effort demands more patience and there is no magic bullet to solve the terrorist problem.

For the international community the real challenge is, therefore, not to counter specific terrorist groups but to conceive effective measures of prevention against those individuals who could engage in a terror campaign because of an imagined connection with other people's struggle and suffering (Volpi 2002, 17).

These 'emotional' connections constitute one elusive and enduring legacy of events such as the Algerian civil conflict, the Palestinian struggle, the Gulf War, the Afghan tragedy, the Southern Thailand insurgency, the Moro liberation movement, and so on. Indeed, that terrorism is a marginal symptom tells us a lot, as does any symptom, and obliges everybody (above all Muslims) to transcend wishful thinking, misgivings and passivity (Roy 2004, 340).

Chapter 6

Jihadi Terrorists in Europe and Global Salafi Jihadis

Edwin Bakker[1]

Of the different types of terrorism[2] in Europe, jihadi terrorism[3] is relatively new. This threat started to emerge in the 1990s. Until 9/11 the threat posed by jihadi terrorism was, however, often underestimated, overlooked and misunderstood. The Madrid bombings in 2004 came more or less as a surprise and had a deep impact on threat perceptions of the general public. Although at that time jihadi terrorism had taken root in Europe already for more than a decade – in France in particular – it was still perceived by many as a foreign, external threat that had not 'reached' the continent. Even after 'Madrid', the threat continued to be regarded as an external one. Politicians, intelligence and security forces primarily focused on international jihadi networks operating from outside Europe that were comparable to those responsible for 9/11. Thus, the idea that the threat of jihadi terrorism could also come from radicalised members of Muslim communities within Europe came as a very unpleasant surprise. The subsequent killing of Dutch filmmaker Theo van Gogh and the attacks on the London Underground confirmed that jihadi terrorism also had a malicious home-grown dimension. Terrorist plots in Spain, Italy, France, Germany, Belgium and the Netherlands have added to growing awareness of this dimension and the seriousness of the threat of jihadi terrorism in Europe.

The increasing awareness of the threat has been followed by a growing number of professional and academic publications on jihadi terrorism. In particular the development, ideology and *modus operandi* of the al-Qaeda network have been studied in detail. Less attention has been given to the European context and the specific

---

1 The author would like to thank Michael Andrew Berger for reading the first draft and offering his valuable suggestions.

2 The term terrorism as used in this study is taken from that formulated by the Council of the European Union. It refers to intentional acts that were committed with the aim of seriously intimidating a population, or unduly compelling a government or international organisation to perform or abstain from performing any act, or seriously destabilising or destroying the fundamental political, constitutional, economic or social structures of a country or an international organisation.

3 In this study, the term jihad refers to a violent form of the 'lesser jihad'. A person who engages in it is called a jihadi or jihadi terrorist – the latter depending on the kind of activities in which they are involved. The violent acts of these jihadis are claimed to be in furtherance of the goals of Islam. These goals may include the establishment of a (pan-)Islamic theocracy and the restoration of the Caliphate.

characteristics of jihadi terrorism in Europe. There are, however, exceptions that need mentioning. These include biographies and studies by journalists of individuals and individual networks associated with jihadi terrorism. Such publications are of much value to learn about these networks and individuals and to understand why and how they turned into jihadis. In addition there are a growing number of studies by government agencies on individuals, networks and communities that have been involved in terrorist activities in Europe. Other valuable governmental documents on jihadi terrorists include transcripts of legal proceedings – charges and verdicts – and the reporting on terrorist issues to national parliaments. The relatively small body of scholarly research on jihadi terrorism and terrorist networks in Europe includes studies by Lorenzo Vidino, Robert Leiken, Fidel Sendagorta, Javier Jordan and Nicola Horsburgh, and Petter Nesser (see Vidino 2005; Leiken 2005; Sendagorta 2005; Nesser 2006). Also a number of valuable country studies need mentioning, among others a study on jihadi terrorism in Spain by Javier Jordan and Nicola Horsburgh, and one on jihadi activity in Denmark by Michael Taarnby Jensen (see Jordan and Horsburgh 2005; Taarnby 2006). Additionally, considerable research has been conducted on Islam and Islamism in Europe, including publications of leading French experts, Olivier Roy and Gilles Kepel (see Roy 2004; Kepel 2002; Kepel 2004).

Most valuable to a better understanding of individual jihadi terrorists, as well as their cells and networks is the research by Marc Sageman. In *Understanding Terror Networks* he focuses on the individuals and networks behind the global salafi network linked to al-Qaeda for the years up to 2003 (see Sageman 2004b). His study investigates 172 individual cases and four clusters of jihadi terrorists and provides important insight into the development of individual terrorists and terrorist networks. Unfortunately, the number of evidence-based studies like that of Sageman is rather limited.[4] This type of research is, however, of vital importance to be able to track trends and developments with regard to terrorism. This chapter aims to contribute to a better understanding of jihadi terrorism in Europe by investigating the characteristics of the individuals that have been behind jihadi terrorist activities in Europe and by comparing them with the characteristics of jihadi terrorists elsewhere. For this comparison the chapter focuses on the above-mentioned group of 172 individuals studied by Sageman. The outline of the chapter is as follows. First it gives an overview of the research of Sageman and its methodological framework. Next it identifies 31 cases of jihadi terrorism in Europe and describes the social, psychological and situational variables that make up the 'biographies' of the almost 250 persons that are behind these cases. Finally, the characteristics of these European jihadi terrorists are compared with those of the 172 global salafi jihadis.

---

4 Other valuable evidence-based studies of this kind include the earlier mentioned study by Robert Pape and Robert Leiken, 'Bearers of Global Jihad? Immigration and National Security after 9/11', Nixon Center, 2004.

Understanding Terror Networks

In his study *Understanding Terror Networks*, Marc Sageman searches for common features explaining why individuals become involved in jihadi terrorism. The author analyses a set of biographies of 172 global salafi jihadis that were involved in terrorist activities in the 1990s and the early 2000s. To this end, he identified seventeen key variables that are divided in three general categories: 'social background', 'psychological make-up' and 'circumstances of joining the jihad' (see Table 6.1).

Table 6.1 Variables used by Marc Sageman

'Social background'	'Circumstances of joining the Jihad'
Geographical origins	Age
Socio-economic status	Place of recruitment
Education	Faith
Faith as youth	Employment
Occupation	Relative deprivation
Family status	Friendship
	Kinship
'Psychological make-up'	
Mental illness	Discipleship
Terrorist personality	Worship

Source: Sageman, M. (2004), *Understanding Terror Networks* (Philadelphia, PA: University of Pennsylvania Press).

Based on his analyses of these variables, Sageman concludes that there is no typical jihadi terrorist. In fact he argues that there are many profiles, which he divided into four clusters of mujahedeen: the central core of al-Qaeda, North African Arabs, 'Core Arabs' and Southeast Asians. With regard to their individual characteristics, Sageman does observe a number of commonalities. At the time they joined the jihad they were not particularly young. The average age of joining the jihad was 26 years. Out of 165 mujahedeen on whom he found information, 115 (70 per cent) joined the jihad in a country where they had not grown up. They were expatriates – students, workers, refugees, fighters (in the jihad against the Soviets) – away from home and family. Another 14 (8 per cent) were second-generation citizens in France, the United Kingdom and the United States. With regard to the circumstances of joining the jihad, Sageman also observes a number of common patterns. 'Just before they joined the jihad, the prospective mujahedeen were socially and spiritually alienated and probably in some form of distress' (Sageman 2004b, 98).

Analysing the joining of the jihad by the 172 terrorists, he rejects the common notions of recruitment and brainwashing to account for this process. Instead, he argues for a three-prong process: social affiliation with the jihad accomplished through friendship, kinship and discipleship; progressive intensification of beliefs and faith leading to acceptance of the global salafi jihadi ideology; and formal acceptance to the jihad through the encounter of a link to the global salafi network. Without it, the potential jihadi groups will undergo a process of progressive isolation or they may try to participate in the jihad, but without know-how or resources (Sageman 2004b, 120). Sageman concludes that social bonds are the crucial element in this process (Sageman 2004b, 135).

The author shows that friendship bonds between persons often pre-existed before these individuals went on to join the jihad. Most of them joined the jihad in small clusters of friends. Kinship also played a role in the joining of the jihad. The combined figures for friendship and kinship, eliminating overlap, indicate that about 75 per cent of mujahedeen joined the jihad as a group with friends or relatives, or had pre-existing social bonds to members already involved in the global jihad. The third affiliation, discipleship, is unique to the group of Southeast Asians. These individuals are followers of the leaders of two Islamic boarding schools in Indonesia and Malaysia (Sageman 2004b, 72). With regard to worship, Sageman stresses that places of worship do figure prominently in the affiliation to the global salafi jihad. He argues that these mosques served many functions in the transformation of young alienated Muslims into global salafi mujahedeen.

According to Sageman, the above-described processes of social affiliation with potential members of the jihad and intensification of beliefs and faith are necessary, but not sufficient conditions for joining the jihad. He states that the critical and specific element to joining the jihad is the *accessibility* of a link to the organisation of the global jihad. Without someone able to make arrangements with the al-Qaeda leadership, prospective candidates would remain sympathisers rather than full-fledged mujahedeen (Sageman 2004b, 112).

New Developments

Understanding terrorist networks is based on data gathered up to 2003. Since then, the shape and size of jihadi terrorism has changed. Especially in Europe, new questions have risen following the attacks and thwarted plots in Europe. Investigations into the Madrid, Amsterdam and London attacks do not show a clear link with al-Qaeda or any other global salafi network. In the case of Amsterdam and London, the jihadi terrorists were home-grown and operated more or less autonomously.[5] The same holds for the some thirty foiled and failed attacks in Europe.

This situation indicates that the need for and necessity of formal recognition of al-Qaeda and its support has diminished. Today, many jihadis appear to be 'self-organised' and 'self-recognised' groups or networks. They do not need the consent or the financial or operational support of what Sageman calls the 'Central Staff' (see Coolsaet 2005; Coolsaet and van de Voorde 2006; Gorka 2004). These developments call for specific questions regarding present-day jihadi terrorists in Europe: are

---

5 'Report of the Official Account of the Bombings in London on 7th July 2005', The Stationery Office, 11 May 2006; General Intelligence and Security Service, *Violent Jihad in the Netherlands: Current trends in the Islamist terrorist threat* (AIVD, 2006).

these individuals very different from Sageman's global salafi terrorists? And are the circumstances in which the latter joined the jihad fundamentally different from those in Europe? Before answering these questions, the chapter focuses on the various cases of jihadi terrorism in Europe and the characteristics of those behind it.

Cases of Jihadi Terrorism in Europe

Since 9/11 Europe has been confronted with several dozen jihadi terrorist incidents. To make a complete and reliable list of these acts and the persons behind them is complicated for a number of reasons. Since the attacks on the United States in September 2001, hundreds of persons have been arrested in Europe on suspicion of jihadi terrorist activities. The overwhelming majority of these arrests, however, have not been followed by formal charges and convictions. In fact, most detainees were released within a few days or a few weeks. In addition, there is the limitation of the use of open sources, such as the reliability and the apparent bias of different journalistic and other publications, including official documents and reports. Moreover, open source information on terrorist cases is often incomplete. Undeniably, these obstacles and limitations had an influence on both the quantity and quality of information used for this study.

In spite of these difficulties, individuals, networks and incidents are identified using the following procedure. First, information was gathered on terrorist incidents in Europe, including (failed) terrorist attacks and thwarted plots that have been reported in the media in the period September 2001 to October 2006. In addition, official reports and statements were collected from websites of ministries, courts and other governmental agencies. The dataset of the Terrorism Knowledge Base and other corroborated overviews of terrorist incidents were also explored. Based on this inventory of reports and data on possible jihadi terrorist incidents, those cases were selected in which terrorists (were or) claimed to be jihadi fighters and adhered to Islamist political ideologies. The next step involved the selection of those cases in which people had been formally charged and taken into custody for an extended period of time; in which they were convicted for terrorist activities, or; in which they committed suicide during the attack (the first London bombings) or after the attack (the Madrid bombings).

Following the above-mentioned steps, the following 31 jihadi terrorist incidents were identified:

1. Foiled attack on the US embassy in Paris: France, Belgium, The Netherlands – September 2001
2. Foiled attack on Belgian air base Kleine Brogel: Belgium – September 2001
3. Foiled attack on the Stade de France: France – October 2001
4. Failed 'shoe bomber attack': UK, France, The Netherlands, United States – December 2001
5. Plot to attack Jewish targets in Germany: Germany – April 2002
6. Plot to attack British and US warships in the Strait of Gibraltar: UK (Gibraltar), Morocco – June 2002

7. Plot by 'the Chechen Network': France – December 2002
8. The 'cyanide and ricin plot': UK – January 2003
9. Plot to make bombs: UK – April 2003
10. Plot to attack unknown target in the UK: UK – October 2003
11. Plot to attack targets in northern Italy and to recruit terrorists: Italy – October 2003
12. The Madrid bombings: Spain – March 2004
13. Plot to attack with home made napalm: Spain – March 2004
14. 'London Fertilizer plot': UK, Canada – March 2004
15. Plot to incite hatred and possession of a terrorist manual: UK – May 2004
16. 'The Asparagus Case': Belgium – June 2004
17. Plot to attack financial institutions in the US and targets in the UK: US, UK – August 2004
18. Plot to threaten Dutch politicians and to make an explosive device: The Netherlands – September 2004
19. Plot to establish a terrorist network called 'Martyrs of Morocco': Spain – October 2004
20. The killing of the Dutch film maker Theo van Gogh: The Netherlands – November 2004
21. Plot to attack existing structures and terrorising Dutch society: The Netherlands – November 2004
22. Plot to prepare a terrorist attack and attempt to recruit a fellow-prisoner: The Netherlands – March 2005
23. The first London bombings: UK – July 2005
24. Failed attack on the London Underground: UK – July 2005
25. Inciting local Muslims to carry out acts of terrorism: Denmark – September 2005
26. Foiled attack on public transport in France: France – September 2005
27. Plot to attack politicians and a government building: The Netherlands – October 2005
28. Plot to commit terrorist acts in Europe: UK, Denmark, Bosnia-Herzegovina – October 2005
29. Plot to attack targets in Italy: Italy – November 2005
30. Failed attack on German trains: Germany – July 2006
31. Foiled transatlantic aircraft attack: UK – August 2006

Besides the above-mentioned 31 cases, there were a number of possible jihadi terrorist incidents that have not been included in the sample. A number of recently discovered plots and foiled attacks could not be included. Some cases had not been brought to court yet or there was too little open source information to include them in this research.

Characteristics of Individual Jihadi Terrorists in Europe

The 31 cases of jihadi terrorism in Europe involved at least 242 persons. This section explores their characteristics. It follows Sageman's methodological framework and looks at their 'social background', 'psychological make-up' and 'circumstances of joining the jihad'. In addition it focuses on gender as the group of European terrorists includes both men and women.

Geographical, Social Background and Psychological Make-up

The geographical background of the 242 individuals is determined in four different ways: by family origin, by country in which people were raised, by place of residence and by nationality. If one looks at family origin, most persons in the European sample are of non-European origin and are first, second or third generation immigrants. In fact, very few terrorists' families originate from Europe (17 persons). If they do, the person often is a convert, child of a mixed marriage or from Bosnia-Herzegovina. The region from which most persons in the European sample originate is North Africa (Morocco, Algeria and Tunisia). Other typical regions and countries of origin include Pakistan and the Horn of Africa (see Table 6.2). A significant part of these persons of non-European origin were born and raised in Europe: for example the group of second and third generation immigrants. This was the case of 56 out of the 146 cases in which the country in which the jihadi terrorists grew up could be determined.[6] Looking at places of residence, the overwhelming majority of the jihadi terrorists in the European sample are residents of a European country (211 out of 219 persons). In fact, very few of the jihadi terrorists resided in other parts of the world before being involved in terrorist activities in Europe (eight persons in total). Focusing on nationalities, a few are very prominent. Out of the 227 individuals on whom information on nationality could be found, 59 are Moroccans, 55 Algerians and 46 Britons. Other prominent nationalities include 15 Pakistani, 15 French, 10 Dutch, 8 Belgians and 8 Spanish. About 20 per cent of them have dual citizenship (56 persons).

With regard to the socio-economic background of the jihadi terrorists the study follows Sageman's distinction between 'lower'-, 'middle'- and 'upper'-class background.[7] Of the 72 persons on whom socio-economic data could be gathered, only three can be regarded as upper class, 30 as middle class and 39 as lower class. From this data it appears that very few jihadi terrorists in Europe come from higher socio-economic classes. More than half of the individuals are from the lower classes within society. Given the immigrant background of the families of origin, however,

---

6 Some jihadi terrorists migrated with their parents to Europe at a young age. Those who migrated after the age of ten are considered to have been raised in the country of origin.

7 As a measurement the dominant occupational background of a person and his or her family was selected: for example unskilled worker is lower class; semi-skilled worker is middle class, and; high-skilled worker is upper class. Depending on the type of business, entrepreneurs are classified as middle or upper class: for example a shopkeeper versus someone managing a large company.

this situation may, above all, simply be a reflection of the general socio-economic character of Europe's immigrant communities originating from Muslim countries.

Despite the many media reports and the detailed description of persons in transcripts of legal proceedings, surprisingly little is to be found on the educational background of the 242 persons in the European sample.[8] From the 48 persons on whom information on education could be gathered, a majority finished secondary education (42 persons). Fifteen of them finished college or university. It should be stressed that of those persons on whom no information could be found, some were arrested at a young age (18 persons were 20 years old or younger). These individuals were still students at the time and simply could not have finished university, college or even secondary education.

Table 6.2 Top Ten Geographical Backgrounds in Terms of Place of Residence, Nationality and Family of Origin

Country of residence (N = 219)	Nationality (N = 277*)	Country of the family of origin (N = 215**)
UK (62)	Morocco (59)	Algeria (64)
Spain (58)	Algeria (55)	Morocco (64)
France (36)	UK (46)	Pakistan (24)
Netherlands (15)	France (15)	Lebanon (7)
Belgium (13)	Pakistan (15)	Ethiopia (5)
Germany (8)	Netherlands (10)	France (5)
Italy (8)	Belgium (8)	'Palestine' (6)
Denmark (6)	Spain (8)	Tunisia (5)
Afghanistan (3)	Lebanon (6)	Syria (4)
Lebanon (3)	Denmark (5)	UK (4)

*Includes 'double counts' as some persons have more than one nationality (56)
**Includes 'double counts' as some persons are of mixed marriage (4)

Information on the childhood faith was found for 50 persons. Fourteen of them were converts: 13 persons with a Christian and one with a Hindu background. Of the rest, 11 were raised in a religious family and 25 did not have a particularly religious childhood. The latter were raised in families not actively practicing their religion and 'rediscovered' their faith at a later age. Of the 103 persons on whom information could be collected on their occupation, 34 were unskilled workers, 19 persons

---

8 As a measurement of educational background the highest level of education the person had completed was selected. This means, for instance, that (former) students at university that did not finish their studies fall within the category 'secondary education'.

had semi-skilled occupations and 12 had a job that can be described as skilled.[9] In addition there were 12 entrepreneurs, mostly shopkeepers. About 15 per cent of the persons in this sample were unemployed at the time of their arrest. Seventeen persons were students. The relative number of unskilled workers and unemployed in the sample is very high compared to national averages. However, these figures reflect the occupational situation of many persons belonging to the aforementioned immigrant communities in Europe. Consequently, the data of the European sample do not uphold the general notion that jihadi terrorists are typically unemployed or have much lower-skilled jobs than other persons within their communities. Moreover, the figures are generally reflective of European averages. For instance, the average unemployment rate of the persons in the sample is about 15 per cent. This is higher than that of the European Union, which is 8.2 per cent, but it is lower than the unemployment rate for this age group. The EU figure for those under 25 is 17.7 per cent.[10] This is an important point to consider, as a clear majority of the unemployed in the European sample is also under 25.

Information on family status was collected for more than 100 persons. However, in only 66 cases could these data could be labelled as very reliable. Among them, 39 individuals were married or engaged at the time of their arrest and 8 had been divorced. Twenty-five of them had children. Twenty-two persons were single. Of the persons in the European sample, at least 58 had a criminal record while involved in jihadi terrorist activities. This means that almost a quarter of the jihadi terrorists in Europe had previously been convicted by court before their arrest for terrorist offences. A few of these criminal records can be linked to the terrorist activities for which they had been arrested or convicted at an earlier stage. This is the case for half a dozen persons. Most of them have been sentenced for the illegal possession of arms.

The biographies of the persons within the European sample indicate that 11 of them suffer from mental illness. This figure represents almost 5 per cent of the total sample. This percentage is significantly higher than the world base rate, which, according to Sageman, is about 1 per cent (Sageman 2004b). Two of the mentally ill suffer from paranoia. It should be mentioned that four of the terrorists have become ill after their arrest.

Circumstances of Joining the Jihad

In the European sample of 242, the date of birth or the age at the time of their arrest was found for 224 persons. Their average age while participating in the jihad (measured at the time of their arrest) is 27.3. The statistical distribution of age is very spread out. The standard deviation is more than seven. The youngest jihadi terrorists were 16 and 17. The oldest person in the European sample was 59 when he was arrested. It should be noted that since March 2004, jihadi terrorist incidents

---

9 Unskilled workers include cleaners and factory workers. Examples of semi-skilled workers are electricians and administrators. Highly skilled workers are medical doctors, army officers, scientists, etc.

10 Eurostat, Euro indicators, Newsletter, July 2006, p. 6.

in Europe involved relatively more persons under 25, including several teenagers. For instance, the average age of those behind the Madrid bombings was over 30, whereas those behind the 'successful' and the failed London bombings were on average just over 20.

Conventional wisdom has it that terrorists are male. The sample of jihadi terrorists in Europe confirms this general notion: it includes 237 males and only five females. Most of the 70 persons on whom information could be found on their place of recruitment were recruited in Europe: most of them in the countries in which they were resident. Among these countries, the United Kingdom ranks first (26 persons), followed by Spain (15), The Netherlands (13), France (7) and Germany and Denmark (6). Outside the European Union, persons have been radicalised and recruited in Arab countries (5), Afghanistan (3) and Bosnia (2). With regard to the faith of persons at the time of joining the jihad, it is not surprising to see that in many cases (58 of the 61 in which reliable information could be found) faith increased in the months before recruitment. The would-be jihadi terrorists participated in courses on the Quran (at home or abroad) or were vigorously debating Islam on the Internet. Others tried to convert acquaintances or colleagues, or changed liberal mosques for more orthodox or extremist ones.

Concrete information about full-time or part-time employment of persons in the European sample is rare. This variable was extrapolated from data on the occupational situation of persons at the time of their arrest. Over 50 per cent of the terrorists appeared to have had full-time jobs (47 out of 76 cases for which information could be gathered). Fifteen persons held part-time jobs and 14 persons were unemployed. With regard to the idea of relative deprivation, not enough information was found to indicate whether or not this concept was relevant to jihadi terrorists in Europe. In 23 cases there was evidence of a situation of relative deprivation. In the European sample 43 situations were observed in which persons were friends at the time of their joining of the jihad. A slightly stronger indicator for social affiliation between jihadi terrorists is kinship. Of the 242 persons, 50 were related through kinship. In other words, in more than 35 per cent of the sample social affiliation may have played a role in recruitment. In one extreme case, that of the Benchellali family, six family members were arrested for terrorist activities of which four have been convicted. Moreover, there are half a dozen (half) brothers who joined the same jihadi terrorist network.

Studying the characteristics of the 242 jihadi terrorists in the European sample leads to one obvious disclaimer and one evident conclusion. Starting with the first; it is impossible to gather complete information from open sources for all variables for the more than 200 persons in Europe. This means that generalisations sometimes required some crude judgement. The evident conclusion of this chapter is that there is no standard jihadi terrorist in Europe. Our sample includes very young ones and persons in their forties and fifties. Some have no education, others finished university, and so on.

Nonetheless, there are a number of, more or less, common traits. A clear majority of them are from Arab countries and have roots especially in North Africa (on the European continent) and Pakistan (in the case of the UK). Many of these first, second or third generation immigrants also have in common that they come from the lower strata of society. A strikingly high number of persons had a criminal record; at least a quarter of the sample. Finally it should be noted that almost all jihadi terrorists in Europe are male, and that many of them relate to each other through kinship or friendship.

Comparing Samples

As mentioned earlier, recent developments in Europe indicate that the characteristics of jihadi terrorists in Europe and the circumstances of joining the jihad may differ from those of Sageman's global mujahedeen. This paragraph compares the 'biographies' of the 242 jihadi terrorists in the European sample and those of the 172 global salafi jihadis that were studied by Sageman.[11]

Geographical, Social Background and Psychological Make-up

There is a striking difference between the nationality of the global salafi jihadis and that of the jihadi terrorists in Europe. The former mainly come from Saudi Arabia (31), Egypt (24) and France (18). In the European sample, the dominating nationalities are that of Morocco (59), Algeria (55) and the United Kingdom (46). Most of these Moroccans and Algerians live in Europe and many of them were born and raised in a European country. Compared to the sample of Sageman, the number of 'Core Arabs' and Southeast Asians is very small. Moreover, in the European sample there are no persons that can be regarded as belonging to the 'Central Staff' of the global salafi network.

Apart from the above-mentioned countries, the two samples show a wide range of geographical backgrounds in terms of nationality and country of family origins. With regard to place of residence, the geographical background of Sageman's 172 terrorists is a truly global one, whereas the network of jihadi terrorists operating in Europe is both global – 29 different nationalities and 26 countries of origin – and very 'European' – only 8 jihadi terrorists resided in other parts of the world before becoming involved in terrorist activities in Europe.

There is a difference in socio-economic background between jihadi terrorists in Europe and those in Sageman's sample. Sageman states that 18 individuals in his group are upper class, 56 middle class and 28 lower class. In short, a clear majority is middle class. However, Sageman notes that this is different for the 'excluded' North African Arabs in France and a large part of the Western converts to Islam. They are predominantly lower class. Nonetheless, Sageman refutes the theory that terrorists are mainly from the lower strata of society.

---

11 It should be noted that there is some overlap between the samples. We collected information on individuals involved in terrorist activities since September 2001 and Sageman's sample covers the period 1990s – 2003. As a consequence, nine persons are in both samples.

Our sample, however, shows relatively many persons from the lower class. Among the individuals of whom information could be found, 40 belong to this socio-economic part of society, followed by middle class (30) and upper class (3). These figures are similar to those of the 'North African Arab' cluster in Sageman's sample. This is partly explained by the fact that the European sample is dominated by persons from North Africa.

The educational levels of terrorists in the European sample and that in Sageman's are difficult to compare. In the latter case, no less than 42 per cent finished university. In the European sample there are too few data on the educational background to be able to compare it with the 137 persons on whom Sageman could gather information. The educational background could be determined of only 47 persons, of which 14 finished university.

In Sageman's sample, about half of the persons he could find information on were secular during their youth (53 out of 108 persons). He notes that in the case of the North African Arabs this percentage is higher. Many of them lived in France, a very secular country. In the European sample, more than a third of the jihadi terrorists were (born and) raised in France, the UK and other secular European countries. It shows that the number of persons (not including converts) that were secular during their youth is twice as large as the number of persons that were faithful during this phase of life (24 compared to 11). Similar to the groups studied by Sageman, the European sample has a significant number of converts (14 persons).

Among jihadi terrorists in Europe the predominant occupational category is that of unskilled occupations. Also the group of semi-skilled occupations is relatively large. Together they account for more than 70 per cent of those on which information could be found. The categories dominating the sample of Sageman are skilled occupations and professionals (57 out of 134 persons). This is not the case within the cluster of North African Arabs in which unskilled and semi-skilled occupations are the dominant ones (90 per cent). Again, this particular cluster shows many similarities with jihadi terrorists in Europe. In both samples, a significant percentage of the terrorists were unemployed at the time they joined the violent jihad or were involved in terrorist activities: about 10 per cent in the case of Sageman, some 15 per cent in the case of jihadi terrorists in Europe.

Information on the marital status of the jihadists was collected for only a quarter of the persons studied. This figure is lower than in Sageman's sample. Contrary to Sageman, in Europe there were a number of divorced men and women. In his sample most of the men were married and most of them had children. In the European sample there were only 38 persons being married, of whom 24 had children. Despite limited information, it is safe to say that Sageman's image of 'married mujahedeen' does not apply to the case of jihadi terrorists in Europe. Moreover, the situation in Europe does not contradict the typical image of single males.

Of the global mujahedeen, about one quarter had been involved in criminal activities (forgery, document trafficking and petty crime) by the time they joined the jihad. In the European sample the number of persons with a criminal record appeared to be similarly high. Also about a quarter of the jihadi terrorists in Europe had a criminal record. Of those without a criminal record, many had been involved in criminal activities without having been in prison or sentenced in a different way.

Among jihadi terrorists in Europe 11 individuals were suffering from mental illness or a psychological disorder. This is a much higher percentage of the population than in the sample of Sageman (5 per cent compared to 1 per cent). It should be stressed, however, that the absolute numbers are very low for both samples.

Circumstances of Joining the Jihad

In Sageman's sample the average age is 25.7 years. The average in the European sample is somewhat higher at 27.3 years. In both cases, most persons joined the jihad well past adolescence, often in their mid- or late-twenties. It should be noted that there are a significant number of exceptions to this general picture as the range of ages within both samples is quite wide. Moreover, the average age of those involved in jihadi terrorism in Europe after 2004 is considerably lower than that of those behind plots and attacks in the first three years after 9/11.

In Sageman's sample, all 172 individuals are male. In the European sample only five out of 242 people are female. Based on this data, it is safe to say that terrorism is attempted mainly by males, both in Europe and within global salafi networks. Sageman noted that recruitment for the jihad was high amongst men that were 'cut off' from their original roots, far from their families and friends. Seventy per cent joined the jihad in a foreign country. In Europe the situation seems to be rather different. The overwhelming majority (more than 80 per cent) of the persons on whom information could be gathered were recruited in their country of residence. Most of them were second- or third-generation immigrants who were born and raised in these countries. If one wants to regard this situation as one in which a person is being cut off from cultural and social origins, it supports Sageman's assumption that being away from 'home' is a very important factor in the process of joining the jihad. However, most of the 242 jihadi terrorists in Europe were not far from their families and friends, and in many ways were at home in the countries of recruitment. Therefore, the term 'home-grown' is regarded as very appropriate to the European group of jihadis. Hence the two samples differ significantly on this issue. Both in the sample of Sageman and ours, almost all persons on which information could be found became more devout before joining the jihad and being involved in terrorist activities. Thus, these findings support Sageman's conclusion that before joining the jihad and getting involved in terrorist activities most people become more religious.

In the European sample there were few examples of full-time terrorists. Most people had a 'normal life' and most of the persons on whom information could be gathered had full-time jobs. This general picture is quite different from that of the global mujahedeen in Sageman's sample. He found many examples of full-time jihadis as well as many students that can be considered as such. In Europe, in contrast, participating in terrorist activities seemed to be a 'part-time activity'.

Given the fact that not enough information could be collected to indicate whether or not the concept of relative deprivation was relevant to jihadi terrorists in Europe, the two samples can not be compared on this variable. In the European sample there are 92 cases of social affiliation at the time people started to get involved in jihadi terrorist activities. Kinship was the dominant one (49 cases), followed by friendship bonds (43 cases). No evidence was found of discipleship. The figures for kinship and friendship represent about 35 per cent of the total sample. This is a much lower percentage than that of Sageman. Among his global mujahedeen a clear majority of persons had social bonds with network members at the time of their joining the jihad (150 out of 172 persons). In his sample friendship bonds were far more important than kinship bonds.

In his study, Sageman stressed the importance of formal acceptance of potential candidates to the jihadi through discovering a link to the global salafi network as the final part of the process of joining the jihad. Within the group of 242 jihadi terrorists in Europe, there were only a few cases of (possible) foreign connections and links with global salafi networks. There was no concrete information that supports the existence of formal acceptance by a global network in Europe. But there were situations in which individuals seemed to join the jihad more or less entirely on their own. Hence, in Europe this process seems to be fundamentally different from that of the global jihadis.

Overall Characterisation

Comparing the sample of the European group with that of Sageman's members of global salafi networks, the main conclusion must be that there are more dissimilarities than similarities between the two. First, there is the difference in average age between Sageman's jihadis (25.7 years) and those in Europe (27.3). Moreover, whereas the former mainly consists of married man, the jihadi terrorists in Europe were predominantly single. The two groups also differ very much with regard to socio-economic status and occupational background. The subgroup within Sageman's sample that comes closest to the group of Islamist terrorist in Europe is that of the North African Arabs. Both groups share a socio-economic background, faith as youth, type of occupation and the fact that many of them have a criminal record. As stated earlier, these similarities are partly explained by the fact that persons from North Africa dominate the European sample.

Differences between the two samples are less explicit with regard to circumstances in which individuals in both groups joined the jihad. Whereas most members of global salafi networks were recruited far from their families and friends, European terrorists joined the jihad under opposite circumstances. Thus, the situation in Europe goes against Sageman's assumption that people were recruited while away from home. It should also be noted that instead of the term 'recruitment', the term 'self-recruitment' seems more appropriate in the European setting. Most of the jihadi terrorists in Europe joined the jihad by a process of radicalisation and recruitment with very limited or no outside interference.

Other circumstances that are rather different include employment and social affiliation. Most jihadi terrorists in Europe have work or study, some are married with children and others live with their parents or friends. Basically, they seem to live 'normal' lives that look similar to those of most of the people within their communities. Sageman's global mujahedeen, however, were often full-time jihadis. In both cases social affiliation played a role in joining the jihad. In the case of Europe though, kinship was more important than friendship; while in the case of global jihadi terrorists it was the other way around. That being said, in general the above-mentioned differences in the circumstances for joining the jihad cannot be regarded as fundamental. Social affiliation, the most crucial factor in this process, played a role in both samples.

Finally, the final phase of the process of joining the jihad as described by Sageman, that of formal acceptance of potential jihadi fighters by global salafi networks, such as al-Qaeda, does not seem to be a vital phase in the case of jihadi terrorists in Europe. As mentioned above, most of the jihadi terrorists in Europe joined the jihad with very limited or no outside intrusion.

Final Remarks

Comparing the sample of the European group with that of Sageman's 172 members of global salafi networks leads to the conclusion that European jihadi terrorists are rather different from Sageman's global salafi terrorists, with the exception of the important role of social affiliation in joining the jihad. What both group of jihadis very much have in common is that they are very heterogeneous. The conclusion that follows is that there is no standard jihadi terrorist.

For policy makers, the latter conclusion has implications for the idea of profiling certain groups of people that are considered likely to commit a terrorist crime. Based on the analysis of Sageman and this study, such a policy does not promise to be very fruitful. Not only at the individual level, but also at group level there is no general picture of jihadi terrorists. Even the conclusion that many would-be terrorists join the jihad as groups of friends or relatives does not provide clear indicators that would make it easier for the intelligence community to spot jihadi networks at an early stage. There are uncountable groups of friends and family members and the European sample also includes groups of persons that lack pre-existing social ties. Moreover, there are also examples of persons that seem to have operated almost entirely on their own, the so-called 'lone wolves'.

A second recommendation that can be derived from studying both samples relates to the search to address root causes of jihadi terrorism. With regard to the circumstances in which persons join the violent jihad, there seems to be some room to address the different factors that may be of influence. Some of these factors can not be changed at all, such as age, family status, psychological make-up, and friendship and kinship. Other factors such as education, occupation and employment, however, may be influenced by social policies. This requires large socio-economic projects, in particular aimed at immigrant communities. Even more so, it requires far more research into the links between such factors on the one hand, and radicalisation and recruitment on the other. Unless we know more about these links and processes, socio-economic policies may seem to make sense, but might just as well make no difference at all. Moreover, such policies may even make things worse, for instance by stereotyping immigrant and Muslim communities as possible jihadi terrorists.

Basically, we need to know more about these persons and the circumstances and processes that lead to jihadi terrorist activities. Given the current limited number of evidence-based studies, it should be stressed that the picture of the puzzle of jihadi terrorists, whether in Europe or elsewhere, is still very much incomplete. Given the heterogeneity of this category of terrorists and the fact that terrorism is a constantly changing social phenomenon, it remains to be seen if we will ever have clear insight into their characteristics. The same holds for circumstances and processes of joining the jihad.

This is not to say that further research is futile. Comparative studies can be helpful in identifying new developments in different parts of the world and in testing various hypotheses or common wisdom. In addition, it should be stressed that further research is much needed. Gathering data on individuals as well as updating knowledge on the process of joining the jihad are essential to keep track of trends and to prevent unpleasant 'surprises', such as the 'discovery' of suicide terrorists in July 2005 in Britain or the recent arrests of very young home-grown jihadi terrorists in Europe.

Chapter 7

The Islamist Networks in Belgium: Between Nationalism and Globalisation

Alain Grignard

Radical Islamism remains a subject where subjectivity and approximation are omnipresent. Receptacle of all our fears, this has also become a very lucrative market, but where scientific and objective analysis is all too often lacking. We still lack the necessary historical hindsight to apprehend correctly such a complex phenomenon, particularly in the light of its latest developments. This chapter consequently has an ambition to fill some gaps, by presenting a number of general observations, based on more than twenty years of police work in this field.

The law enforcement approach, although not a scientific discipline *stricto sensu*, proceeds nevertheless knowingly in utilising sources duly compiled and compared in order to constitute elements for convicting (or discharging) suspects by tribunals in a democratic state. Thus, in a certain sense such an approach closely resembles the science of historical critique … It is in this approach that we will assess the evolution of the jihadi movement that Belgium has been confronted with since the end of the 1980s. Belgium has succeeded in dismantling eight major networks and sentencing more than 60 suspected terrorists (see Table 7.1).[1]

Table 7.1. Main Dismantled Networks in Belgium, 1995–2007

	Network	Nature
1995	Zaoui	Nationalist, focused on Algeria
1998	Mellouk	Moving towards internationalisation, linked to what was to become al-Qaeda
2001	Trabelsi and Massoud	Internationalist, linked to al-Qaeda
2003	GICM (Asparagus)	Post-Afghan, globalised re-deployment after loss of Afghan sanctuary
2005–2007	Post-Iraq	Transnational networks issued from mobilisation in favour of Iraq, influenced by jihadi ideology

---

1 One has to bear in mind that up to 2003 terrorism was not included as such as a misdemeanour in the Belgian penal code. Sentences were obtained based upon peripheral offences of common law.

First and foremost, it is important to acknowledge that Belgium has never been directly involved in Arab-Muslim states or their conflicts. Its modest size makes it relatively unnoticed by the rest of the world and it has never played an important role either politically or economically in this area. That said, the importance of the immigrant community of Muslim origin makes it a receptacle of all the ideological currents of the Ummah, the community of 1.3 billion Muslims worldwide. The immigrant community of Muslim origin in Belgium is estimated at some 400,000 people, all nationalities, illegal immigrants and converts included. More important, it is a young community: in major cities such as Brussels and Antwerp, individuals of Muslim origin, native born or not, constitute a majority within the 18–25 age group. Mostly due to economic and financial reasons, this community also tends to be concentrated in ghetto-like districts and has traditionally been subjected to discrimination. The history and the reasons of this inequity will not be addressed in this chapter.

Belgian police started to investigate the field of political Islam in the 1980s, in particular after the terrorist attacks that rattled Paris in 1986. Here lies the origin of the so-called 'Fouad Ali Saleh' network. This network, related to the Iranian regime, provoked a grave crisis between France and Iran.[2] The emergence of this brand of terrorism, linked to religion, led to the establishment of a specific entity entirely dedicated to radical Islamism within the existing antiterrorist unit that was part of the Special Investigation Sections[3] of the Brussels division of the Gendarmerie. At that time, the investigators only had a very rough and superficial understanding of the new phenomenon, since it had been more focused on the extreme-left terrorist threat that had been present in Belgium since the early 1980s. As a result, the period between 1986 and 1992 constituted a real learning process for the Belgian police forces.

In the early 1990s terrorism was dominated by the events in Algeria. Indeed, the attempts by the Islamist party Front Islamique du Salut to gain power through political action were denied by the cancellation of the elections in 1991. As a result almost the entire party tipped into violence. They joined forces with the first members of the resistance, the Bouyalistes,[4] and formed the Groupe Islamiste Armée (GIA) (see Labat 1995; Grignard 2001). Despite the small size of the Algerian community in Belgium, numerous FIS-directed propaganda and fundraising activities were in evidence. At that time, violent actions were not yet part of the picture.

Studying the seized documents that circulated within Muslim communities permitted the Belgian police to establish the foundation of its expertise on the

---

2 Following a bombing campaign in Paris, the dismantled network of which Fouad Ali Saleh was a member, led inspectors to an official within the Iranian Embassy in Paris, Walid Gordji. He fled into the embassy compound to avoid being apprehended.

3 BSR, Brigade de surveillance et de recherche.

4 In 1986 'Sheykh' Mustafa Bouyali had already organised the first clandestine cells, composed of veterans from the Afghan war against the Soviet Union. He was killed by police forces in 1987.

Islamist phenomenon. The internal decision within the police to enable some of its members to start studying the Arab language subsequently proved timely.[5]

March 1995: The 'Zaoui' Network, an Islamo-Nationalist Structure

In March 1995, tipped off by intelligence from the French intelligence services and from its Belgian counterpart, the Sûreté de l'Etat, our counter-terrorism unit was able to dismantle the so-called 'Zaoui network'. This network was primarily focused on the Algerian problem and was composed mostly of Algerians.[6] Its membership, however, reflected the diversity of the Algerian movement. It is important to remember that at that time already the cleavage between the 'Algerianists' (limiting their action to Algeria and aiming at establishing a theocracy-based state) and the 'Internationalists' or Afghan veterans (who considered the events in Algeria just a prelude to the more imperative global Islamist jihad) was already present. Some protagonists positioned themselves in the lineage of the political FIS. Others wanted to transform the party into a military force, called the Armée Islamique du Salut. Others still were already subscribing to the ideas of the GIA. As a group, they gave the impression of being a 'national' entity since they acted as a logistical network that assisted rebels in their country of origin, who wanted to overthrow the Algerian regime.

But nevertheless, some aspects caught our attention. On the one hand, some members of the network appeared to be involved in something beyond mere logistical support. Indeed, we seized materials linking members of the Belgian network to key players of the terror campaign that was going to hit France soon after.[7] On the other hand, an international dimension seemed to emerge. Not only did we discover leaflets related to the Libyan Groupe islamique combattant libyen, we also noticed materials linked to the Afghan theatre that foreshadowed what was going to take place in the following years.

Besides a number of visits by different protagonists of the Belgian network to the tribal Pakistani–Afghan zone, one particular document drew the attention of the investigators. It was a 'training manual for the jihad' on a computer disk comprising some 8,000 pages. The document assessed every aspect of the armed struggle, from the principles of guerrilla warfare to the research of intelligence and counter-intelligence, as well as the fabrication of explosives and the most diverse engines. The document signed by the Mekhtab Al-Khidemat

---

5 The analysis of these publications enabled the identifying of more than 60 publications related to different movements operating in Algeria as well as in different other regions of the world (see Grignard 1997).

6 Even though some marginal Moroccans played a role of executants (for example, the El-Majda family).

7 Notably concerning Ali Touchent, alias Tarek, Boualem Ben Said and Ait Belkacem, incriminated later in the attacks in France that started with the assassination in July 1995 of sheykh Sahraoui in his Mosque in Myrrha street.

Al-Mujahideen ('The Office of Services for the Mujahedeen')[8] was dedicated to 'the Dear Brother Abou Abdullah Osama bin Laden ... and the martyr Abdallah Azzam'. It proved to be an essential element, because it was according to the model of that 'Service Office' that the al-Qaeda was going to function later on, expanding its struggle against the Soviets to the entire non-Muslim world under the leadership of Osama bin Laden. In summary, this first 'Islamo-nationalist' network already carried the seeds of a movement intending to act at the scale of the Ummah.

March 1998: The 'Mellouk' Network

The three years that followed the break-up of the 'Zaoui' network were dedicated to the instruction of the dossier and the dismantlement of the network and its spin-offs. Its first objective was nevertheless the support of the Algerian struggle, but new hotbeds were appearing (for instance in Bosnia). It is also during those years that the Taliban took over most of Afghanistan and established their 'Islamic emirate'. During that time, numerous investigations converged pointing at frequent links with Great Britain, more precisely with a jihadi 'ideological core' established in London.[9] This resulted in an operation against a second network, the so-called 'Mellouk' network. The intelligence that led to the operation was provided by the Belgian intelligence services converging with similar indications from investigations headed by foreign services (Great Britain and Italy). Immediately, the operation was going to be spectacular since shots were fired during the police raid on an apartment building. The original seven persons that were arrested pointed at a new type of structure. Indeed, many nationalities were now involved. Among the suspects were Algerians, Moroccans, Tunisians, Syrians and others. Furthermore, we clearly were in presence of something that went beyond a mere logistical structure, since explosives and detonators were discovered. Moreover, the analysis of the rich stock of printed material found on the spot established links with almost all armed groups active at that time in Morocco, Tunisia, Libya and elsewhere (GSPC, GICT, GICL[10]). Links with the majority of the important European Islamist figures also came to light. Connections with Afghanistan and the Taliban were also abundant and obvious via jihad manuals and through diverse protagonists connected to the dossier and having completed journeys to Afghan camps or being very close to the al-Qaeda core and its leader bin Laden.[11] During the house searches an important document

---

8 Structure created in 1982 by Osama bin Laden and Abdullah Azzam to assist and train jihadis and to conduct them to Afghanistan to fight the Soviets.

9 The principal propaganda centre for the GIA was in London, constituted around ideologues such as Abu Qatada al-Falestiny, Abu Mussab al-Sury, Abu Hamza al-Misri and so on (see, for more details, Thomas, D., *Londonistan, la voix du Jihâd* (Paris: Michalon, 2003).

10 Groupe salafite pour la prédication et le combat, groupe islamique combattant tunisien, groupe islamique combattant lybien.

11 Notably Abou Zoubeyda, Abou Doha aka Rachid Boukhalfa aka Dr Haydar.

was also discovered: a pamphlet of about 60 pages representing the 'birth certificate' of the Moroccan *Groupe islamique combattant marocain* (GICM). It amounted to a declaration of intent by a group that was later to become famous.[12] This 'Mellouk' network was particularly noteworthy because it represented a major step in a process of globalisation of the networks. Indeed, the structure, in close contact with the Pakistani–Afghan region, had at its disposal a panoply of sophisticated fake identity papers and stamps. It was a kind of small-scale replica of the previous 'Office of Services' that could operate without bias for all the Islamist organisations, present and operational in Europe. Finally, the Mellouk cell also seemed to be on the eve of committing a terrorist attack on an unknown target that has still not been identified.

From 1998 to 2001: Internationalisation

From 1999 on the Belgian intelligence services were confronted increasingly with networks organising the transport of volunteers to Afghanistan. Simultaneously, the ideological and logistical role played by London became more explicit by the day. Two major dossiers were initiated in this period, one concerning the Tunisian jihadi Nizar Trabelsi ('dossier WAWA'), and another linked to a Tunisian network ('dossier MEZZE').

Investigating petty crime related to radical Islamism was going to allow the identification of Nizar Trabelsi. He was connected to a core of petty criminals with contacts in France and Holland.[13] In June 2001 wiretaps by foreign intelligence services indicated that Trabelsi, in contact with the Belgian group, had prepared a suicide attack. The attack also appeared to be part of a wider plot that involved Jamel Beghal, a French jihadi arrested in the Emirate upon his return from Afghanistan. The investigations intended at locating Trabelsi and circumscribing his environment, received a boost from the 9/11 attacks. He was arrested together with his accomplices within days of the attacks, on 13 September 2001. During the house-search an important quantity of components for building explosives was discovered. Later on, Trabelsi confessed that he was indeed on the eve of committing a suicide attack against a US military base. He explained that the operation was planned in Afghanistan with the active support of Osama bin Laden. Trabelsi himself was convicted to a ten-year jail sentence and his accomplices to lesser sentences. However, some grey areas continue to persist in this dossier. Simultaneously, the entire Tunisian network was dismantled. Via London, where the masterminds of the

---

12 Announced in a periodical *al-Ansâr* and then in *L'écho du Maroc–Sâ'ada al-Maghrib*, the phantasmagoria of the creation of a Moroccan resistance group, based on the GIA model, had become reality. The manifest called for the elimination of King Hassan II and of his impious regime.

13 This splinter group functioned according to *takfiri principle*, arguing that petty crime was permissible when done for jihadi purposes.

network lived in the entourage of Abû Qatâda,[14] this network had helped to escort jihadis to foreign countries.

The second investigation ('dossier MEZZE') led the Belgian intelligence service to identify the two suicide bombers that killed the Afghan guerrilla leader Massoud on 9 September 2001. These two men had stayed for several years in Belgium and had been infiltrated in Afghanistan by the network a few months earlier. The break-up of the complete cell was a major anti-terrorist success for the Belgian police forces.

These two investigations resulted in, thanks to multiple interrogations and the examination of a wealth of documents, the discovery of the *modus operandi* of these transnational networks and how these groups organised themselves in the Afghan camps, under the umbrella of al-Qaeda and its relays in London. Although each group had their own camps in Afghanistan, they established links among themselves. Some of their members were chosen by bin Laden himself and his associates to commit terrorist acts all around the world, being able, once back in the West, to benefit from the logistical support of the relationships they had forged. These camps were, however, totally disrupted with the US-led intervention in Afghanistan after 9/11.

The 'Dossier Asparagus': The GICM, Prototype of Post-Afghan Networks

As mentioned above, the first indications pointing at the GICM go back to 1998, at the time of the break-up of the Mellouk cell. In the following years several individuals linked to this Moroccan Islamist movement were signalled on many occasions. They were notably in contact with the Afghan groups that were exposed during the Trabelsi and the Massoud cases. It thus became clear that the hub of these Moroccans cells was situated in the Turk–Syrian region and in the North of Iraq. The last of the Moroccan mujahedeen to have joined Afghanistan before Enduring Freedom started took principally the route Syria–Turkey–Iran–Afghanistan.

The American intervention at the end of 2001 forced a substantial exodus of jihadis, who had to leave their Afghan safe haven. After a massive and improvised departure through Pakistan and Iran, the networks that had contributed to infiltrate the jihadis into Afghanistan put in place ex-filtration routes. This was notably the case for the Moroccan networks. It is in this context that the 'dossier Asparagus' started in Belgium. After a few months of observations, police was able to identify a group structured around Afghan veterans directing a network of re-infiltration (leaving Afghanistan and introducing them into other theatres). Right from the start, the international links with France, Spain and Morocco gave the structure an international dimension. The surveillance of the network was, however, interrupted by the Madrid attacks on 11 March 2004. Indeed, the media repeatedly hinted at GICM-linked networks that had found refuge in Belgium. As a consequence, police

---

14 Notably Sayfallah Ben Hassine, who joined Afghanistan in 2001 to take over leadership of the network. In London he was replaced by his aide Kamel Ben Moussa.

operations were initiated. They proceeded in two phases and led, after months of investigations, to the sentencing of a number of individuals for membership of a terrorist organisation.

The GICM network had a polymorphous character. After having, in a first stage, helped the repatriation of Afghan veterans, they provided them with a temporary shelter in Belgium and other European countries (France, Spain and others). They also facilitated the return of some individuals to Morocco, so as to be able to return to the original objectives of the movement: the jihad in Morocco, supported by the worldwide *Al-Salafiyya al-Jihadiyya* or jihadi movement. The different cells established over the entire European continent could also function as sleeping cells, assisting if and when needed by other cells (as was the case for the cell in Brussels that sheltered some of the perpetrators of the Madrid bombing). Finally, these structures were also able to transfer some volunteers to new jihadi theatres.[15] Investigations enabled the establishment of links with networks in Iraq and Saudi Arabia.[16]

This type of network represented a kind of completion: in terms of ideology and national aspirations (the desire to establish an armed force able to challenge the tyrants in their country) blended with the global vision (participating in the global struggle between the world of Islam – Dar al-Islam – and the world of the disbelievers – Dar al-Kufr). Logistically, the relationships established in Afghanistan and inside the ideological platform in London, allowed the constitution of a global network in which every jihadi, of whatever origin, is likely to collaborate, obeying the slogans provided by the residual core of al-Qaeda and others. After the dismantlement of the GICM, investigations highlighted additional links with Spain and the Madrid bombings, the Dutch Hofstad group, some armed groups in Saudi Arabia and networks under construction in Morocco.

Conclusions and Perspectives

If the years between 1986 and 2003 saw the appearance – and dismantlement – of new types of networks, the 2003 Gulf War and the ensuing occupation of Iraq has brought us at present into a new dimension, far more complex than before. The war has changed the equation by fostering a new frustration amongst the Muslim communities worldwide and in Belgium. It has spawned many networks conveying mujahedeen to and from the Iraqi battlefield.

Recent investigations point at a new generation of structures where converts mix with those who were born Muslims, independent of their country of origin (Morocco, Tunisia …). The Iraq situation has boosted these new networks. The feelings of frustration have never been so strong within the Muslim world. New vectors of frustration have merged with older ones, the Palestinian tragedy in particular: the war in Afghanistan, the simmering war in Chechnya and, especially, the third Gulf

---

15 As revealed, for example, by the discovery of the tracks of the passage in Brussels of Mohamed Afallah on the run after Leganès. He died afterwards in Iraq.

16 For example, the links with Saudi Arabia of Abdelkader Hakimi and the links of Karim el-Mejati who afterwards died in a police operation in Saudi Arabia.

War and the ensuing occupation of Iraq. The 2006 Lebanon war has made this development even worse.

The problem is two-sided here: on the one hand, this frustration and the corollary resentment are shared by the near totality of Muslims and, on the other hand, the gap continues to grow between our two worlds, particularly within the immigrant communities. Each act of violence[17] indeed tends to increase the degree of suspicion with respect to Muslims or those perceived as such, and the glance charged with mistrust which is thus carried towards the other will often be the catalyst driving the other to become precisely what one would not like him to be ... (Grignard 2005).

In another register, the absence of perspectives and the marginalisation also push many youngsters towards a world of the 'righteous', characterised by an attractive fraternity. The failure of the affirmation of their individual identity in our post-modern societies will naturally lead them towards a community which embraces them wholeheartedly. Paroxysm is reached here on the level of recruitment in prisons: the misdemeanours themselves will be seen as part of a defence against an unfair society. Put at the service of the cause, these misdemeanours become legitimate – and even redeeming.[18]

Converts hold a particular place. Often emanating from marginalised segments of society, they hope to find in their 'new world' a solidarity and ideals which are missing to them in their world of origin. Their zeal to prove the depth of their engagement with respect to the Muslims of origin will unsurprisingly push them to burn through the stages of the radicalisation.

These heteroclite networks have international ramifications right from the start. They are also intimately blended with criminality, since many among the members of these networks have a serious judicial history. The dismantlement in Belgium of the first network of this type caused a great deal media hype due to the character of a native Belgian involved in the network: Muriel Degauque. She was a convert and died in a suicide attack in Iraq that activated 'operation KARI' in November 2005. The police action of dismantlement was the result of several months of surveillance and research that enabled the detection of a recruitment network for Iraq on Belgian soil. The instruction of this file will soon be closed and the protagonists will probably be brought to justice before the end of 2007.

Concluding, we have thus seen that since the late 1980s the networks turned from an Islamo-nationalist project to an internationalist one, having taken *mutatis mutandis* the relay of the radical leftwing extremists, or *internationales communistes combattantes* as they called themselves. Not only did the ideology go global (from the struggle against the local dictator to the confrontation against the world of unbelievers), but the methodology also evolved through the fusion of all the original entities. This fusion has taken place in Afghanistan and 'Londonistan'. Belgium, contrary to some clichés, is neither a rear base nor a weak spot in the European fight against terrorism. Belgium forms only one piece of the puzzle in which we find all the other European countries without exception.

---

17 It can be labelled as ironic that most of the victims of acts of violence in the name of Islam are Muslims. See: Chapter 2 in this book, by Rik Coolsaet and Teun Van de Voorde.

18 This is one of the core aspects of Takfiri ideology.

In addition, despite its modest dimension and its limited resources, and thanks to its very early involvement in the fight against jihadism early in the 1980s, Belgium has obtained clear successes against these new forms of criminality.

PART 3
Radicalisation in Western Europe: The Root Causes

Chapter 8

Muslims in Europe and the Risk of Radicalism

Jocelyne Cesari

The appeal of jihadi movements to young European Muslims is not new and, contrary to popular opinion, did not begin with al-Qaeda. Rather, mujahedeen resistance to the Soviet occupation in Afghanistan attracted Muslim youth from Europe starting in the 1980s. A well-known example is the case of Redouane Hammadi and Stephane Ait Iddir – French citizens sentenced to death in Morocco for an attack on a Marrakech hotel in 1994 – who received their training in Afghanistan. Converts Joseph Jaime and David Vallat also met in a camp in Afghanistan and were subsequently imprisoned on charges related to the 1995 Paris metro bombings. Nine Britons have been detained in Guantanamo Bay for fighting for the Taliban. A French convert, David Courtailler, has been charged with links to the March 11 Madrid bombings and the Belgian group that aided the assassination of the leader of the Northern Alliance in Afghanistan.

Each new conflict between the West and the Muslim world fuels radical activities. Moreover, since the dismantling of its bases in Afghanistan, al-Qaeda seems to regard Europe as a promising recruitment area for foot soldiers. Since the war in Iraq, French anti-terrorist services have been concerned by the influence of al-Qaeda among Muslims in Europe, especially converts and women. British police are also focusing on radical converts, especially from the Afro-Caribbean community, and have called on Muslim leaders for assistance in identifying radical activists operating in mosques or Islamic organisations. Dominant explanations of this phenomenon are too often socio-psychological. It is tempting to attribute the attraction to movements like al-Qaeda and the violent rejection of the West to social and economic frustration. Social approaches insist on material deprivation and marginality as major causes for radicalisation. Thus, the mujahedeen is painted as a highly frustrated person who is full of hatred and this predicament, caused by socio-economic marginalisation, goes on to fuel a sense of humiliation. However, many Western mujahedeen are neither marginalised nor delinquents and most of the data on terrorists contradict such assessments. They show that terrorists are usually 'ordinary people in ordinary places'. Marc Sageman's research sheds light on the ordinary profile of most terrorists involved in al-Qaeda: they belong to the middle class, are educated, married and have jobs (see Sageman 2004b). Thus, the conventional image of the single, disenfranchised young man is not an accurate representation of reality. These social explanations are often combined with psychological causes: the terrorist has pathological features such as narcissism or paranoia that prompt his attraction to radical groups. The underlying assumption of most such interpretations is that participation in terrorist movements is the result of an individual rational choice. Ironically, such an approach converges with the testimonies of mujahedeen who describe their involvement as an act of self-consciousness motivated by the search for truth.

Using Marc Sageman's findings, an alternative approach to those mentioned above can be posited. First, the emphasis must be on the social context: in other words, joining the jihad is a social process and not simply an individual decision, despite the 'romanticised' narrative offered by the mujahedeen themselves. This process is made possible through the conjunction of four main factors: the preeminence of salafi[1] doctrine in the West, especially in Europe; the culturally-marginalised status of some segments of urban European youth; the growing discrimination in Europe against Muslims and Islam as a religion; and the lack of credible ideologies to counter the decline of nationalism and liberalism.

The Dominance of Salafi Interpretations in Europe: The Spread of a Theology of Intolerance

According to research, even though it does not incite terrorism directly, salafi doctrine does provide the same religious framework that is used by radical groups such as al-Qaeda. As such, it therefore contributes to the sense of familiarity or proximity that terrorists experience in joining radical groups. Although salafi doctrine is not the exclusive interpretation of Islam available in European societies, it has become central in the way that Muslims deal with their religious tradition in the West. Most of the materials provided to teach or learn about Islam in Europe follow this particular interpretation of the Islamic religion. Western countries have thus paradoxically proven to be fertile ground for the growth of puritanical and intolerant interpretations of Islam. This is only an apparent contradiction, however, as the globalisation of culture tends to promote fundamentalism or puritanism in almost all religions, not just Islam (see Rudolph and Piscatori 1997; Eickelman and Piscatori 1996).

What, then, is the salafi intellectual framework? It may be generally defined as a variant of 'pan-Islamism'. This term refers to those religious or political transnational movements that emphasise the unity of the Ummah (the community of believers) over specific cultural, national or ethnic loyalties. The idea of the Ummah has been an important element of Islamic thought, particularly during the decline of the Ottoman Empire before the First World War, and has been closely associated with the preservation of the Caliphate. Today, communication technology and the circulation of people and ideas make the Ummah all the more effective as a concept, especially considering that nationalist ideologies have been on the wane. The imagined Ummah takes a variety of forms. The most influential of these forms are fundamentalist in the sense that they emphasise the revealed Text and a Muslim unity which transcends national and cultural diversity. It is for these reasons that

---

1 In the Islamic tradition, salaf refers to the devout elders who served as companions to the Prophet Muhammed. In contemporary Islam, the term denotes groups or movements that refer back to the Quran.

these groups may be described as pan-Islamist (the restoration of the Caliphate is no longer a major element of such movements).[2] These pan-Islamist movements should not be constructed as monolithically reactionary or defensive. A distinction must be drawn between the wahhabi/salafi and tablighi movements on the one hand, and the Muslim Brotherhood on the other.

The wahhabi interpretation of Islamic tradition emerged in the eighteenth century in the Arabian peninsula in the teachings of Muhammad Ibn Abdel Wahab (1703–92). Wahab's literalist interpretations of the Quran became the official doctrine of the Saudi kingdom upon its creation in 1924. Wahhabism is characterised by an extreme hostility to any kind of intellectualised criticism of tradition. Mystical approaches and historical interpretations alike are held in contempt. Orthodox practice can be defined as a direct relation to the revealed Text, with no recourse to the historical contributions of the various juridical schools (*madhab*). In this literalist interpretation of Islam, nothing must come between the believer and the Quran. Such mediators as customs, culture and Sufism must all be done away with.

The contemporary heirs of this rigorist and puritanical line of thought are known as salafi. The chief difference between modern salafi Islam and the original wahhabi period, therefore, is that the decisions and interpretations of salafism are no longer limited to the Saudi kingdom, but spread throughout the entire Muslim world. 'Salaf' refers to the devout elders who served as companions to the Prophet Mohammed, but salafiyya was initially a reformist movement created in the nineteenth century. Though the early salafi leaders, including Mohammed Abduh, Jamal al-Din al-Afghani and Rashid Rida, promoted a return to the revealed Text and the Hadith, they were not by any means anti-intellectuals and were in their time considered progressive.[3] Nonetheless, by the end of the 1970s, the Saudi government had succeeded in transforming salafiyya into a conservative theology. The fatwas of Sheikh Abdul Aziz Ibn Baaz, Grand Mufti of the Saudi Kingdom, who died in 1999, and of Sheikh Al-Albani are the shared points of reference for their disciples in Europe and the United States. The movement has succeeded in imposing their beliefs not as one interpretation among many, but as the orthodox doctrine of Sunni Islam. The considerable financial resources of the Saudi government have certainly helped in creating this religious monopoly.

In the past two decades, the rivalry between Saudi Arabia, India, Pakistan and Iran over leadership of the Muslim world has rapidly intensified. Within this atmosphere of competition, Europe and the United States have become crucial battlegrounds, evidence of which can be seen in the massive rise in the sum of petrodollars distributed in these parts of the world. The proliferation of brochures, free Qurans and new

---

2 The Hizb ut-Tahrir party is one of the most important contemporary pan-Islamist movements arguing for the restoration of the Caliphate. Founded in Jerusalem in 1953, it claims branches in the Muslim world as well as in Europe and the United States. In Great Britain, the party is known under the name Muhajirrun, and has been active in the public sphere, particularly before 9/11 (see Taji-Farouki 1996).

3 For example, the position taken by Mohamed Abduh, Grand Mufti of Egypt, who toward the end of the nineteenth century came out against polygamy and for equality in divorce proceedings.

Islamic centres in Malaga, Madrid, Milan, Mantes-la-Jolie, Edinburgh, Brussels, Lisbon, Zagreb, Washington, Chicago and Toronto; the financing of Islamic Studies chairs in American universities; the growth of Internet sites: all of these elements have facilitated access to wahhabi teachings and the promotion of wahhabism as the sole legitimate guardian of Islamic thought.[4]

It is extremely difficult to gauge the precise influence exerted by wahhabism on Muslim religious practice. In the case of European and American Muslims, the influence cannot be measured by statistics alone. In a minority culture which lacks both institutions for religious education and the means to produce new forms of knowledge, the accessibility of salafism is a primary reason behind its popularity. The widespread diffusion of salafi teachings means that even non-salafi Muslims evaluate their Islamic practice by wahhabi standards. In other words, even if most Muslims do not follow wahhabi dress codes – a white tunic, a head covering, and a beard for men; *nikab*[5] for women – the salafi model has nonetheless come to define the behaviour of the 'good Muslim'.

Another group that takes a traditionalist and legalistic approach to Islam is the tabligh, sometimes referred to as the 'Jehovah's Witnesses of Islam'. The tabligh is usually described as a pietist and apolitical movement whose primary aim is to strengthen Muslim orthodoxy (Nadwi 1964). A sub-sect within the larger deobandi movement, the tabligh movement was founded in 1927 by Maulana Muhammad Ilyas, a devout Muslim scholar who lived in New Delhi and died in 1944. The essential principle of tabligh is that every Muslim can be a vehicle for the values and practices of Islam.[6] The most important aspect of Islamic practice is the mission, which consists of the missionary devoting one hour per day, one day per week, one week per month or one month per year to go and spread the word of Islam. The mission can take place in the city of the missionary, in his country or in more distant destinations outside of India and Pakistan. The annual gathering of tabligh in Lahore is the largest regular gathering of Muslims, excepting only the pilgrimage to Mecca. Today, competition rages in the West between tablighis and salafis, and anathemas rain down from both sides. One 1997 fatwa from Sheikh Ibn Baaz named the tabligh, as well as the Muslim Brotherhood, as one of the 72 heretical sects of Islam.[7] These movements indicate the emergence of fundamentalism as a global phenomenon. Global fundamentalism is defined, above all, by an exclusive and hierarchical vision of the world, as well as by a taxonomy of religions that places Islam at the top. The expanded use of the term *kafir* (infidel or heretic), for example, is very common among wahhabis (more than among tablighis). In the classical Islamic tradition,

---

4 See <http://www.saudinf.com>.

5 Cloth covering the face, according to wahhabi law.

6 The six principles of tabligh are: 1) *Kalima* (the attestation of faith), 2) *Namaz* (prayer), 3) *Ilm* and *Dhikr* (knowledge and remembrance of God), 4) *Ikram-e-Muslim* (respect for Muslims), 5) *Iklas-e-Niyat* (purity of intention and sincerity), 6) *Tafri-e-waqt* (taking time for tablighi duties, self-reformation and proselytising). (See Ali 2003).

7 For the complete English text of this fatwa, see <http://www.allaahuakbar.net/ tableegi_ jamaat/>. Sheikh Abdul Azeez Ibn Baaz, born in 1909 in Riyadh, began his religious education in the family of Ibn Abdul Wahab. He held numerous posts within the kingdom's religious hierarchy, and was Grand Mufti of Saudi Arabia from 1992 until his death in 1999.

kafir is used only for polytheists, not for members of competing monotheistic faiths. In globalised fundamentalist groups, however, it has been extended to include Jews, Christians and sometimes even non-practising Muslims (Cesari 2004). A representative example of this approach is the following fatwa on whether Jews and Christians can be considered infidels, published on the Belgian website Assabyle. com. After referencing several applicable Sura (chapters of the Quran), the sheikh concludes that, 'Jews and Christians who do not believe in Mohammed and deny his Prophecy, are infidels'. But his argument goes still further, eventually concluding that, 'He who does not consider to be a infidel one who follows a religion other than Islam, such as the Christians, or who doubts their vileness or approves of their ways, he himself is an infidel.'[8]

The salafi world is thus divided into Muslims and infidels, and the West, seen as the breeding ground for moral depravity, is always placed in a negative light. Such logic informs an essay entitled *The Choice Between the Burka and the Bikini*, by Abid Ullah Jan,[9] in which the author contrasts women's respectable status in Islam to their status in the West, bound to the dictates of fashion and the constant objects of Western sexual depravity. This dichotomy can also be seen in the writings of Sheikh Abdur Raman Abdum Khaliq. He opines on Assabyle.com that the role of every good Muslim is to declare that Muslims are members of the greatest nation that humanity has ever known, and to proclaim the superiority of Islam throughout the world: 'It suffices to note that the call to unify the religions, the effort to bring the various religions together, and their presentation as a homogenous and unified vision is a ploy on the part of the infidels that seeks to confuse truth and lies, and to eradicate Islam by torpedoing its foundations and leading Muslims into wholesale apostasy.'[10]

Another characteristic common to these movements is a worldview that sorts the different aspects of life – such as family, work and leisure – according to the opposition between *haram* (forbidden) and *halal* (permitted). Everything that did not already exist or happen during the time of the Prophet is an innovation and is thus *haram*. Khaled Abou El Fadl has called this mode of interpretation 'The Culture of Mamnu' ('It is forbidden') (Abou El Fadl 2002, 125). Islam as it existed during the time of the Prophet, especially during Muhammad's residency in Medina, is idealised and essentialised, functioning as an 'epic past' (Bakhtin 1981) and an ideal model for life in the present. The smallest aspect of this period serves as the basis for the present day, for 'in this era, everything is good, and all the good things have already come to pass' (Bakhtin 1981, 15). Another characteristic common to both tablighis and salafis is their extreme inflexibility regarding the status of women. The rules determining proper attire for women – namely a *hijab*, a long loose garment covering the entire body – are presented as absolute. Salafis are more extreme in their views on dress than the tablighis; for the former group, a woman must cover not only her hair but her face and hands as well. The *nikab*, gloves and the long tunic fashionable in Saudi Arabia distinguish the salafi woman from the tablighi.

---

8 See <http://assabyle.com/index.php?id=510>.
9 See <http://www.allaahuakbar.net/womens/choice_between_burqa_ and_bikini.htm>.
10 See <http://www.assabyle.com>.

The latter also wears a long tunic, but in a neutral colour (not necessarily black), and covers her hair with the *hijab*. Tablighi men, for their part, wear tunics that go down to their ankles, while salafi tunics come just below the knees. This puritanical interpretation of women's behaviour includes not only dress, but also women's roles as wives, mothers, daughters and participants (or non-participants) in the community. Mixed-gender interaction is forbidden in both public spaces and schools, and male superiority is constantly reaffirmed, along with the Quranic legitimacy of corporal punishment for women.[11] It is the question of women's status within the family and society that allows the various interpretations of Islam to be placed on a spectrum from reactionary to liberal.[12] Additional criteria are the respective opinions of the radical movements on political participation and citizenship, in both Western and non-Western societies. Fundamentalist movements, in particular the salafis, reject political participation, holding that the believer must maintain a separatist stance in relation to public institutions. An example of this position is the 1996 fatwa, issued by an American salafi group, approving the actions of Abdul Rauf, a black Muslim basketball player who refused to rise for the singing of the US national anthem (Abou El Fadl 2001).

Today, a fundamental question is whether these interpretations of Islam, based on anachronistic and ahistorical readings of scripture, have a necessary correlation with the violence and development of jihadi movements, particularly among young Muslims in the West. These radical interpretations do contain similarities with jihadi discourse, using the same vocabulary (especially when discussing the West) and often even the same religious terminology. This fact may explain the connection many young people perceive between wahhabism and jihadism. One must not therefore assume, however, that all wahhabis eventually become jihadis. Other factors, such as the level of political socialisation and the education of the youths in question, are also decisive in this respect (Cesari 2004). We should note that the majority of movements – such as Hamas in Palestine, GIA in Algeria or Jamaat Islamiyya in Egypt – are not pan-Islamists. The obvious exception here is al-Qaeda, which has brought jihad to the global level.

The Weakness of Social Networks, or Lack Thereof

If such essentialised approaches play a key role in recruiting youths into radical groups, so too does the social status of the young Muslims in question. A prerequisite for engagement in radical groups is 'disembeddedness' from society – that is, a

---

11 The Quran, 4:34.

12 A distinction must be introduced here regarding the status of women in the tabligh. Because married women are allowed to do missionary work, they receive an intense Islamic education and can be taken away from the family circle and their conjugal duties. A dissonance is thus created between the theoretical vision of the ideal woman and the reality of women within tabligh. In other words, one consequence of women's participation in tabligh is to modernise, in a certain fashion, the condition of women and to make women more autonomous – in spite of the extremely conservative discourse on the role of the Muslim woman which dominates tabligh (Sikand 2002).

circumstance in which an individual or group lacks strong social affiliations and networks. According to Sageman's findings, the absence of social networks and the atomisation of individuals seems a precondition for involvement in destructive mass movements. Taking up arms for transnational political causes is not a new phenomenon. Such men are in many ways reminiscent of the young people who flocked from all over Europe to fight in the Spanish Civil War, as well as those who fought for anti-colonialism movements in the post-1945 Third World. What is more surprising in the case of Islamic radicalism is that many of its demagogues and ideologues live not in the Muslim world, but in countries of the industrialised West.[13] That is, the most vocal and virulent proponents of jihad against the West reside in the West. We must therefore distinguish between the ideologues of jihad and the foot soldiers of jihad. The foot soldiers are those who take up arms in Afghanist. Bosnia or Iraq, who build bombs, who plant them, and so forth. The ideologue. deliver fatwas and preach inflammatory rhetoric against the West.

Some of the soldiers who take up arms in the name of jihad are the sons of Arab or South Asian and Inner Asian immigrants; others are recent converts to Islam. It is tempting to attribute the attraction to movements like al-Qaeda and the violent rejection of the West to social and economic frustration, a pattern that would mirror those that exist in the Muslim world. Many Western Talibanis, however, have been neither marginalised persons nor delinquents. John Walker Lindh, for example, is the only son of a well-off family in California. He was raised in a liberal environment – both in terms of his religious education and his schooling – in a prosperous town north of San Francisco. He attended an alternative school that provided him with a great deal of educational freedom. He developed an interest in Islam through Spike Lee's film *Malcolm X*, and converted at the age of sixteen. Lindh went to Yemen to learn Arabic, then from Yemen to a madrasa in the north of Pakistan, and finally, in May 2001, he went to Afghanistan (see Rousselot 2001). Zaccarias Moussaoui, the alleged 'twentieth hijacker' of the 9/11 attacks, is also well-grounded in Western culture. Born in 1968 at Saint Jean de Luz, the French-Moroccan Moussaoui was raised by his mother. He went to England to complete his university training and learn English, receiving his degree in international business from the South Bank University in London in 1995. It was during this time that he became an Islamic militant. Like Richard Reid, the so-called 'shoe bomber', Moussaoui frequented the Brixton mosque, which eventually expelled him for extremism. Richard Reid, born to an English mother and a Jamaican father in a poor suburb to the south of London, fits somewhat better the profile of the social and economic outsider. His father was in jail for the greater part of his childhood, and he himself spent time in prison for a variety of petty crimes. It was in prison that he converted to Islam. He, too, attended the Brixton mosque – known for being home to many converts – and eventually came into contact with members of the jihadi movement.

One reason for the disembeddedness of the above persons is related to the conditions of life in major globalised cities in the West. The 'global city' is the primary

---

13 It should be noted that many ideologues of national liberation movements in the first half of the century – e.g. Bourguiba and Gandhi – also began their struggles in the capitals of the Western world.

environment for the installation and adaptation of Muslim immigrants within their new national and social contexts. Paris, Berlin and London are now centres of the Muslim world by virtue of the large concentration of Muslim immigrants that live there. However, for many inhabitants of these multicultural cities, the permanent contact with other cultures does not necessarily make them cosmopolitan. This is especially the case with the European Talibanis, who, transnational though they may be, are diametrically opposed to cosmopolitanism. For them, taking up arms against the West expresses the rejection of what is close, familiar and at the same time inaccessible. Their immersion in Western culture only reinforces their need to preserve the purity of Islam and to limit interactions with the surrounding environment. The lack of cultural roots of these soldiers is also demonstrated by the fact that most are apprentices or novices in Islam. Whether because of their conversion to Islam or because their family's emigration disrupted a normal transmission of tradition, their education in Islam begins not in the family but in the fundamentalist groups of the tabligh or the salafis. Zaccarias Moussaoui, Richard Reid, Hervé Djamel Loiseau (the French Talibani discovered frozen to death in the Afghan mountains) – all have a common background of intense Islamisation through the tabligh. The tabligh is, of course, not directly responsible for anyone's involvement in jihadi movements. In most cases, tablighi who join a jihadi movement do so after having left the tabligh structure.

Thus, the temporary loss of embeddedness made these jihadis vulnerable to salafi mosques and their attendant networks. Salafi groups can facilitate social affiliation with jihad, and the decision to become an agent of jihadi movements involves familiarity with like-minded individuals. In other words, becoming a mujahedeen involves entering membership through cliques. According to Sageman, 'Cliques are often built on human similarities. Friendships reflect common background, education and beliefs, but the dense network that members of a clique form are local and based on face to face encounters, attraction and development of long-term bonds'. A clique is like an enclave of like-minded people, prone to polarisation of visions, views and interpretations of the world. In this regard, salafi doctrine provides an intellectual framework conducive to the clique by supplying a binary vision of the world that can then be implemented in violent jihadi action.

Reinforcement of the Clique via Post-9/11 Perceptions of Islam and Muslims in Europe

Muslims in post-9/11 Europe have become increasingly mistrustful, in response to what they consider to be discriminatory security policies. Fears that Muslims are suspected and despised have created an increased sense of community among European Muslims. Muslims do not feel accepted as full members of European society, due to widespread anti-Muslim sentiments, negative stereotypes in the media, discrimination in various areas of society (such as employment), prejudiced remarks by political leaders, and counter-terrorism legislation disproportionately affecting Muslims. Eurobarometer (an international European poll) indicates that about one in five Europeans do not want to have other cultures within their nation-states. Beyond that, growing majorities (approaching two thirds) believe that there are limits to the possibilities of multiculturalism. For over a decade, a stable 40 per cent of Europeans have held that legal immigrants should not have the same civil rights as native citizens, and a growing minority of about 20 per cent believes that legal immigrants should be repatriated to their countries of origin. These numbers were particularly high in Belgium and Greece. In general, about half of respondents in the European Union show resistance to immigrants and diversity. In Northern and Western Europe, there seems to be little sense of immigrants as a serious threat to the dominant ethnic group, but such negative attitudes are more prevalent in Mediterranean nations.[14]

Attitudes toward Muslims in particular are likewise mixed. In Germany, a survey in December 2003 found that 65 per cent of participants thought that Islam could not coexist within the West, while majorities opposed any new immigration and would feel uncomfortable living in a neighbourhood with Muslims (Schmitt 2003). Such sentiments are mirrored in the rising numbers of Turks in Germany who feel they are being discriminated.[15] A 2003 study showed substantial anti-Muslim attitudes in Italy. 56 per cent of Italians believe that Muslims have 'cruel and barbaric laws', 47 per cent consider them 'religious fundamentalists and fanatics', and 33 per cent are convinced that they are invading Italy (Palmieri-Billig 2003). Since 2001, the European Monitoring Centre on Racism has noted an increase of discrimination and perception of discrimination by Muslims across Europe.[16]

Research has shown that the more discrimination and social exclusion members of a minority confront, the more they tend to unite around the perceived cause of their discrimination, such as their religious affiliation. Such a situation can be a factor in strengthening a defensive identification with Islam among Muslims in Europe. However, this is not sufficient to explain involvement in radical groups, and thus has to be combined with the other conditions discussed in this chapter.

Islam as Anti-Imperialism: The Lack of an Alternative Ideology

All of the major post-Second World War ideologies – nationalism, communism, liberalism, and so forth – have failed and have not been replaced. The structures of the European Union lack political appeal to numerous segments of the European population, most especially youth. A case in point is the increase in right-wing extremist parties exploiting anti-European and anti-immigrant feelings, as shown

---

14 According to the European Monitoring Center on Racism and Xenophobia, 2003.

15 '80 percent of German Turks Feel Discriminated Against', *Turks.us*, 27 November 2004.

16 From 'Muslims in the European Union: Discrimination and Islamophobia: A Report from the EU Monitoring Centre for Racism and Xenophobia', 2006. However, results from the Pew Forum show a more nuanced Muslim perception of the Muslim situation in Europe. See <http://pewresearch.org/pubs/232/muslims-in-europe>. For a critique of Islamophobia in Europe, see Cesari, J., *Muslims in Western Europe: Why is the Term Islamophobia More a Predicament Than an Explanation?*, report to the European Commission, June 2006, available at <http://www.euro-islam.info/PDFs/ChallengeProjectReport.pdf%20-4.pdf>.

in the June 2004 European elections. For some young Europeans, adherence to radical Islam provides a viable alternative ideology, comparable to those of radical leftist groups in the 1970s (such as Rote Armee Fraktion, Brigata Rossa, and Action Directe) that attracted European youth on the grounds of anti-imperialist thought and action.

Today, the anti-imperialist narrative is provided by Islamist rhetoric, from its mild to its radical versions. Adherence to a radical and politicised Islam satisfies the need for collective meaning and at the same time provides spiritual fulfilment. The proponents of political violence dream of an idealised community in opposition to the dehumanisation of the post-modern world. The Ummah is synonymous with solidarity and friendship, in contrast to the cold inhumanity of post-modern society. The binary approach to the world advocated by radical groups encourages radicalisation against an enemy: in this case, the West. Cold is opposed to warmth, order to chaos, and individuals to the community. Islam appears as both a system of personal beliefs and as an ideology of resistance to Western oppression. The transition from this kind of ideology to an armed warfare that takes young people as far as Afghanistan is often due to a taste for adventure that urban life is not likely to satisfy. The figure of the hero and the idea of resistance are glamorised. Thus David Courtailler (the brother of Jerôme), charged in 1999 with 'associating with malefactors in relation to a terrorist enterprise', describes his involvement in Islam:

> I was suffocating; I wanted a change of scenery, to do something, no matter what. My friends told me that in Brighton, in England, I could do something. So I left. That was in 1990. Just like that, without a cent. I even hitchhiked … I went to a mosque for the first time with some Muslim friends. It was really something, all those people praying. There was just this serenity streaming from their faces. The people were nice. I made friends. I learned Arabic. Then one day I made the leap: I converted … Some friends had spoken to me about Afghanistan, Pakistan. I was curious, and besides, I had never really travelled anywhere. I thought it would be great to go over there. So I went. They totally took care of everything.

Thus, a dominant salafi interpretation of Islam – along with weak social networking, a sense of alienation, and a lack of ideologies – can explain the attraction of jihadi groups to some segments of European Muslim Youth.

Conclusion

As Muslims face difficult social and economic situations in the West, these types of activities are likely to provoke further sentiments of alienation. If Muslims begin to feel that they are not legitimate members of the nation, then this may well lead to negative reactions against the nation (Cesari 2004, 91–109). Three scenarios are possible: acceptance, avoidance or resistance (see Postiglione 1983). These three attitudes subtend the multiplicity of discourses and actions in the name of Islam, whether oriented towards Muslims or non-Muslims. Acceptance means that the dominant discourse is accepted by Muslims, and is accompanied by cultural amnesia and a definite will to assimilate. This trend is marginal amongst immigrant Muslims.

Avoidance refers to behaviours or discourses that attempt to separate Muslim societies from the non-Muslim environment by developing, for example, a sectarian usage of Islamic religious beliefs. Resistance means refusing the status given to Islam within dominant discourses and politics. Resistance need not be violent: it can involve, for example, taking a view opposite to that of dominant narratives, and producing a voluminous literature that functions as an apologetic for Islam. Regarding practices, certain forms of resistance involve what Erving Goffman calls 'contact terrorism', wherein certain Islamic symbols linked to clothing or behaviour are used in order to provoke the Other's fear and repulsion. Resistance can also take on more radical forms, such as involvement in violent Islamist movements. Although these latter forms of resistance are not dominant, they are highly visible and more and more influential on the ways Islam is perceived in Europe. However, there do exist positive forms of resistance through which Muslims re-appropriate elements of Islamic practice, acknowledging a personal commitment to their faith while simultaneously accepting European societies as their own.

What, then, are the options available to European governments? First, governments must put an end to the 'ghettoisation' of Islam in political discourse and policymaking. When politicians speak about Islam to their constituents, they should disconnect international issues (such as the 'war on terror') from domestic ones (such as the status of Muslims as a religious minority). Issues relating to the latter category – Islamic schools, the construction of mosques, and the training of imams – should be discussed apart from international concerns of terrorism. Second, European governments ought to open multilateral dialogues on all religions – not merely Islam – when questions of secularism and religious freedom are raised. Singling Islam out for separate discussion increases the sensation of alienation for many Muslims. Third, governments ought to provide opportunities for Islamic education in public schools in a non-religious manner, thus increasing familiarity with Islam in various historical and cultural contexts among the young. Fourth, and finally, governments ought to foster conditions favourable to critical Islamic studies, in a manner comparable to critical biblical studies. Simultaneously, they ought to focus on increasing the recruitment of Muslim scholars in the social sciences and the humanities. This aspect of higher education has been a major difference between the European and American contexts. The American academic system not only employs more Muslim scholars than the European, but is generally more open to them in the first place.

Chapter 9

Al-Qaeda: A True Global Movement

Olivier Roy

In Europe, the popular perception of jihadi terrorism has long been one of commandos coming from the Middle East to attack the West in reaction to the conflicts that set aflame the region. Yet an analysis of terrorists operating in the West shows clearly that most of them are long established in Western countries. They are either born in the West (Zacharias Moussaoui) or have come at a young age (Daoudi), or in some exceptional cases, came as a student (Mohammed Atta). All of them are integrated, Westernised and educated. They do not have any particular social background that would explain their radicalisation because of poverty or exclusion. Most of all, almost all of them became 'born again' in the West, even though in the case of Pakistanis, some in a later stage attend religious studies. The source of radicalisation is the West and not the jihad or the conflicts in the Middle East. None became a radical after attending religious studies completed in Muslim countries. Finally, for almost each one of them, the time between their return to religion and their transit to radicalisation has been very short, which shows that they are as much interested in political radicalisation as in religion.

Al-Qaeda is not at the centre of the conflicts in the Middle East. It is an organisation at the 'margin' – 'margin' in every sense of the word. We have said it repeatedly: the favoured jihadis for al-Qaeda are the ones who went to Afghanistan, Bosnia, Chechnya and Kashmir. It is there that militants have formed and shaped the personal networks that make the strength of the organisation. Of course, the Palestinian question is constantly mentioned, but in the same way as the others. Very few militants went to the Israeli–Palestinian theatre of operations (two to my knowledge, assuming they were members of al-Qaeda), whereas the militants of the extreme left (from the 'Baader-Meinhof Group' to the 'Japanese Red Army'), made it their priority. Likewise, while small groups such as Abu Nidal privileged Jewish or Israeli targets, al-Qaeda favours 'global targets' (big cities, public transport), which reflects its desire to appear as a global threat for the West and not as an agent for settling regional or communitarian scores by which the average Westerner does not feel concerned.

On the other hand, young men that team up with al-Qaeda or the ongoing jihad's do so because of a rupture; rupture with the family, the environment, the country of origin or the host country. None of the members of al-Qaeda that were recruited in Europe went to fight in their family's country of origin (with the exception of some Pakistanis). All of them adopted an extreme version of salafism in rupture with the more traditional Islam of their relatives. Nearly all of them led a very Westernised life before undergoing a brutal return to a stricter religious practice. The transit to acts of violence follows very rapidly after the return to religion or the conversion. It is interesting to note that every time a terrorist is killed or arrested, the reaction of the neighbourhood or the relatives is one of disbelief (contrary to what we observe for the Palestinian or Chechen authors of suicide bombings). Almost all terrorists are in fact 'born again' in the West and rediscover Islam within the framework of a mosque, or more and more under the influence of a local 'guru', like Farid Benyettou, street preacher, arrested in January 2005 at the age of 23, who had recruited a group of young men in the suburb of Curial in the 19th arrondissement of Paris to fight in Iraq.

The 'margin' referred to above is not class-bound: we find people from every social and economic background in the al-Qaeda network (even if some are not formally a member of the organisation). We are not necessarily dealing with young, unemployed, embittered persons and victims of racism. Shahzad Tanweer, one of the authors of the suicide-bombing in London in July 2005, came from a wealthy family. Many also originate from mixed couples, as Jamal Loiseau, killed in Afghanistan in 2001, Hakil Chraibi, 23 years old, a student of Montpellier that went to Fallujah in 2006, Mejjati, one of the leaders of the network of the attack in Madrid in 2004 and many others. The 'margin' can also be geographical: as already noted, there are very few Arabs of the Middle East among the al-Qaeda militants of the second generation, recruited in the West.

The first generation (bin Laden and Zawahiri) came to Afghanistan between 1984 and 1992, in general directly from countries in the Middle East. They were mainly Arabs, but included some Pakistanis, Iraqi Kurds and a handful of Indonesians. They fought against the Soviets until their withdrawal in 1989: during the ensuing civil war among the Afghan mujahedeen, they sided with the most radical (Hizb-I Islami of Hekmatyar), but encountered difficulties to find their place in Afghanistan. Many of them returned to their country of origin, where they joined or founded radical Islamist movements (like the Algerian GIA and Ansar Al Islam in Iraq Kurdistan). Some who could not return found asylum in the West before finding a new sanctuary in Afghanistan, under the Taliban rule (1996–2001). The second generation is made up of Western Muslims, either immigrants, students, refugees or converts, who during the 1990s found their way to different jihads (Bosnia, Chechnya and so on) and ended up in Afghanistan, in the training camps under al-Qaeda control. After 2001 the road to Afghanistan was cut, but contacts were maintained or re-established between the Western cells and al-Qaeda networks in Pakistan. Nowadays, the West may be a geographical margin, as far as the Middle East is concerned, but is the real ground of recruitment. Interestingly enough, we find few recruits with a true Arab Middle East background. We do find some Syrians (Imad-eddin Yarkas, known as Abou Dahdah, one of the leaders of the Madrid cell, but he is married to a Spaniard and resides in Spain). The Moroccans and Pakistanis of the second generation are overrepresented in Europe. More intriguing is the number of people originating from East Africa. Among the authors of the failed attack on the London Underground on 27 July 2005 was the Ethiopian Osman Hussain. The others were Somalis, Eritreans and Ghanaians. In one other case, Binyam Mohammed, an Ethiopian living in London, was arrested for complicity with José Padilla. Not to mention, as we will see, the converts. In short, the map of recruitment of al-Qaeda does not correspond in anyway to the crisis zone of the Middle East. When Mohammed Bouyeri killed Théo van Gogh in Amsterdam, the message that he left did not mention the presence of Dutch troops in Afghanistan or Iraq. It mentioned only the 'blasphemy' committed by van Gogh towards Islam.

The Role of Converts

Above all, in almost each al-Qaeda group and assimilated faction acting outside the Middle East, we find converts in large numbers, frequently occupying key positions (something unique in the annals of radical Jihadi movements). Between 10 and 25 per cent of the activists are converts.[1] The spokesperson of al-Qaeda today in Pakistan is an American, Adam Yahiye Gadahn (real name Pearlman), from a well known family in California. In pro-al-Qaeda networks in the United States we also find a certain number of black converts (James Ujaama, Kevin Lamar James, Levar Haney Washington, Gregory Vernon Patterson). In London, among the four terrorists of the attacks of 7 July 2005 we have Germaine Lindsay, of Jamaican origin. Another, Andrew Rowe, was arrested in the Eurostar with traces of explosives (condemned on 25 September 2005). He apparently frequented another known convert, the Frenchman Lionel Dumont in Malaysia. Still in London, Eisa al-Hindi (real name Dhiran Barot) is an ex-Hindu, Kenya-born, British citizen, who went to Afghanistan and then to Malaysia where he married and was arrested for planning an attack on financial sites in New York: the whole of al-Qaeda is in this journey. Finally, three other converts, Don Stewart White, son of a former conservative politician, Brian Young (Omar Islam) and Ibrahim Savant, borne as Oliver Savant in 1980 (the last two are of West Indian origin), were arrested in London in August 2006, accused of participating in a plot to blow up airplanes.

In Holland, the 'Hofstad group', of whom Mohammed Bouyeri, the assassin of Theo van Gogh, is a member, was composed of several converts (plus one daughter of a Dutch convert): the brothers Jason and Jermaine Walters, son of an American black officer and a Dutch woman (Jason was nicknamed Abu Muhajid Amriki, because converts often take the name of their country of origin), and Martine van der Oeven, a former police officer. It was van Gogh's assassination that blew up Dutch multiculturalism, while the group was clearly 'post-cultural': It did not express the radical vanguard of an ethncio-cultural group, but a mixing of uprooted and de-culturated people with various racial or ethnic backgrounds.

We will recall here the already known converts: the British Richard Reid, the Spanish Luis José Galan (known as Yusuf Galan, arrested at the end of 2001 in Spain), the French Christophe Caze, Jean-Marc Grandvisir, Jérôme Courtailler, Johan Bonte, Lionel Dumont, Willie Brigitte (judged in 2007) and the German Christian Ganczarski (involved in the bombing of Jerba, 2002). Many converts originated from the West Indies. They found in the jihadi environment a fraternity without

---

1 The number of 8 per cent is given by Robert Leiken, 'Bearers of Global Jihad', Nixon Center, 2006. But if we count black Americans (many of whom are converts), then we can reach at least 10 per cent. The number of 25 per cent concerns the Beghal network, tried in 2006.

racism. They were trained to battle the former colonial powers. Finally they acquired in al-Qaeda positions of responsibility that they would never have elsewhere. In addition, we find two modes of conversion among the Europeans of al-Qaeda: those who followed a personal path and converted in a mosque and those who followed their 'friends', often in the context of petty crime.

An exemplary case of conversion is the one of the Belgian Muriel Degauque (who committed a suicide attack in Iraq in the company of her husband in 2005), because she emphasises a recent evolution: the arrival of a generation of women in al-Qaeda, rather misogynist until now. This shift indicates that the converts bring also another form of 'deculturation'. There are more converts in al-Qaeda operating in the West than people originating from the Middle East *sensu strictu* (besides North Africa). This large number of converts, once again by any common measure of comparison with other Islamist organisations, signals different things: 1) al-Qaeda is an extraterritorial movement that does not express in any way a traditional culture of the Middle East or a reaction to the Israeli–Palestinian conflict; 2) al-Qaeda recruits people that probably would have joined extreme left (or right) groups 30 years earlier; 3) there is a frequent link between petty crime (drugs) and radicalisation, just as the extreme left groups also had their criminal side (consider the itinerary of Pierre Goldman in France).

Movement, Rather than Organisation

Al-Qaeda is not a centralised, hierarchical, Leninist type of organisation. It now consists of bottom-up networks. These networks are both international and founded on strict personal relations between its members. They unite globalisation and the *esprit de corps* of a small homogenous group of people that know each other well. It is this solidarity of former international combatants, veterans of the same camps and combats, that makes the network flexible and reliable. As was well analysed by Marc Sageman (Sageman 2004b), we find this *esprit de corps* at the two ends of the journey of initiation towards the Afghan or any other jihad. It is indeed among a small group of 'friends' that one radicalises (in a suburb, neighbourhood or mosque) and that one takes the decision to leave. In Afghanistan (or Bosnia or Chechnya) one encounters other 'brothers', Malaysians, Filipinos or Pakistanis, who will eventually join in their country. The members of the network often behave in spite of any logic of real clandestinity. They share apartments and bank accounts, they are the best man of their friends, and so on. The strength comes from the group, but not from the clandestinity.

The typical schema appears to be one of a group of friends under the influence of a leader, who joined the jihad earlier. For many young people who have an identity problem and followed the path of self-destruction (drugs/trafficking), it is uplifting to identify with international jihad. This contradicts another widespread image that suicide attacks are a specific element of Islam, whereas these days numerous young people commit suicide in the West. It is this same phenomenon that we find when young Americans start to shoot with an AK-47 in their school, kill people and afterwards commit suicide and actually stage their death. This is the product of exacerbated individualism. But with al-Qaeda and the jihad, the young recruits in pursuit of a cause, Muslims by origin or conversion, find a 'true' cause. That explains why prison is also a place of recruitment, as there one achieves maximum exclusion and solitude. The headquarters, the cells at the base, the transnational networks and the chain of command of al-Qaeda are thus basically personal relations, forged either in Afghanistan or at the local level, and transmute into a transnational and extraterritorial dimension (travel, multiple nationalities, and so on). Comradeship plays a very important role, sometimes coupled with matrimonial relationships that are absolutely not 'traditional'. One marries the sister of a friend, but not the woman chosen by one's parents, what often implies a modern couple relationship, as the wife of the murderer of Massoud underlies (El Aroud 2003). In the cell responsible for the attack on the subway in Madrid, Serhane Fakhet in 2002 married the sister of Mustapha Maymouni. In France, Jamel Beghal married the half-sister of Johan Bonte. Beyond the cells that are connected to the centre, there are forms of 'franchising'. It suffices that some local actors take possession of the al-Qaeda logo and concept, without being inevitably connected to the centre, in order for the al-Qaeda organisation to claim an action that it did not organise. This technique of franchising shows to which degree al-Qaeda is indeed a modern organisation: decentralised, flexible, able to delegate and playing with its image.

Finally, one last question about the reversibility of these networks. We have seen that young westerners went to countries to fight the jihad and came back to Europe to commit terrorist acts. But these networks can function both ways, without us being able to talk about a point of departure and a final point. A typical case is the one of radical Pakistani networks. We witness an 'al-Qaedisation' of radical Pakistanis that leave the regional environment to which they confined themselves (Afghanistan and Kashmir), in particular through the Pakistani community in Great Britain (for whom radicalisation is *in situ* and not taking place under the influence of Pakistan). To be an ideological state (the Nation of the Muslims) and not a territorial nation-state is something that is registered in the logic of Pakistan. Rachid Rauf, 25 years old, British national, involved in the terror attempt on Heathrow in August 2006, is related by marriage to the leader of the jihadi group Jaish-e-Mohammed (The Army of Mohammed), a group associated for a long time with Lashkar-i Taiba. There were some precedents: Omar Sheikh, the assassin of Richard Pearl, came from Great Britain and Willie Brigitte, the converted French, was send to Australia by Lashkar-i Taiba in 2003. The same problem exists for France with the Salafist Group for Call and Combat, located in the Sahel (South of Algeria and Mali), and renamed 'al-Qaeda in North Africa'. They may also recruit in the West. In fact, in these two cases, it would be a major error to consider these networks as coming from abroad. They are extraterritorial and recruit indifferently at the same time. Some terrorists in Europe in their 'born again' phase went through organisations not involved in terrorism, like the tabligh, a pious movement, or the Hizb ut-Tahir movement, based in London, and the nebulous movement of Mouhajiroun, once close to Hizb ut-Tahir. These last two are based essentially in Europe and from now on without any doubt constitute a passageway to radicalisation.

Conclusions

Al-Qaeda is not a by-product of the conflicts in the Middle East. It attracts young militants with little connections to the Middle East. Are these patterns susceptible to change? The fighting in Iraq and the tensions in Lebanon might generate a new wave of young radicals, this time from the Middle East. But they will probably be attracted and recruited along the same patterns than their Western fellows: uprooting and de-territorialisation. The crisis of the Arab nation-states, the slow shifting of Arab nationalism to a Sunni pan-Islamism, in the wake of the growing Shia–Sunni tension in the Middle East, will fuel the trend towards the de-culturation of Arab Islam to the benefit of the present form of salafism, so successful among second generation European Muslims. Second or third generation Palestinian refugees in Lebanon, who lost any dream of returning but are not integrated into the Lebanese society, Yemeni or Saudi volunteers flocking to Iraq, migrant workers in the Gulf: the process of globalisation will bring together individuals from various backgrounds in the fold of al-Qaeda networks, or of anything that could claim to follow al-Qaeda's trademark.

Chapter 10

Dutch Extremist Islamism: Van Gogh's Murderer and His Ideas

Rudolph Peters

Is there a special relationship between Islam and terrorism? Many would argue that there is, pointing at the many acts of terrorism committed in the name of Islam. But that only proves that Islamic doctrines, like those of other religions, can be interpreted to justify such acts of violence, not that there is an intrinsic relationship between them. In this article I will argue that those who want to invoke such justifications must actively construct them by choosing between different existing interpretations or proposing new ones. My assumption is not that religion is unimportant in this context, but rather, as Jessica Stern also has demonstrated, that feelings of alienation and humiliation are the primary motivation for contemplating the use of terror. Religion then plays a role in drawing the boundaries between 'us' and 'them' and thus in defining the enemy. Moreover it can provide powerful incentives for entering violent struggles and convincing arguments to be used for recruitment.

In this chapter I will show how Mohammed Bouyeri, who killed the Dutch film-maker and publicist Theo van Gogh on 2 November 2004 and is now serving a life sentence, gradually constructed an Islamic ideology that legitimised the use of violence in Dutch society. By analysing the ideas of Mohammed Bouyeri, I will show how he used and recombined existing interpretations and created a form of extremist Islamism containing elements commonly associated with radicalism and extremism, regardless of whether these are formulated in religious or in secular terms. These elements are the rejection of the world order, since it is allegedly dominated by the forces of evil, the feeling that one's own group is under acute threat, and the idea of a utopia that can be realised, against all odds, by a small and devoted vanguard prepared to use violence in order to defeat the forces of evil. But before sketching Bouyeri's ideological development, I will give a brief general survey of the Islamic doctrines that are used by militants to justify their actions and those that enhance the fighting spirits.

Islamic Doctrines Associated with Violence

Islam, like other religions, has a Janus face: it contains many different and even contradictory sacred texts and interpretations and, in addition, doctrines that are not uniform and monolithic, but can, in concrete contexts, be used to deliver widely divergent messages. Among the Islamic texts and doctrines there are those that preach peace and tolerance, but also those that can justify violence and inculcate militants with a contempt for death and zeal for engaging in violent struggles. There are three doctrines or concepts that are associated with violent actions. The first, not surprisingly, is the doctrine of jihad, the second, the concept of martyrdom, and the third, the apocalyptic notion that the End of Time is near. These notions can have very different meanings and impacts and they obtain their final and definitive content when used in a specific context.

Jihad is a term occurring frequently in the Quran. Its basic meaning is effort, but in the Quran it is usually employed to denote fighting against non-Muslims. Together with canonical stories about the Prophet Mohammed (*hadith*), these Quranic verses are at the basis of the legal doctrine of warfare, which was elaborated in the first centuries of Islam. It contains two crucial notions: the obligation to expand the territory of Islam, that is, the territory governed by an Islamic government and, secondly, the duty to defend that territory against outside aggression. The first obligation is a collective one, of which the whole community is discharged if a sufficient number of men carry it out. Its minimum, if the power relationship does not allow conquest, is sending out an Islamic military patrol into enemy lands to keep the idea of jihad alive. The other duty is an individual one, incumbent on all able-bodied men in the region under attack and, if necessary, the adjacent provinces and, ultimately, all Muslim territory. This is in a nutshell the legal doctrine found in the classical works of Islamic jurisprudence. However, there are also other ways of conceptualising jihad. Certain pious groups saw jihad primarily as a struggle against one's own evil inclinations, or pointed out that jihad was not necessarily waged by the sword, but could also be carried out by the pen and the mouth. These doctrines were not mutually exclusive but could be used by the same person in the appropriate contexts.

By the end of the nineteenth century, Islamic scholars in India and Egypt embarked on a project of reinterpretation of Islam. One of the objects of their endeavours was the legal doctrine of jihad. By redefining the relationship between the various Quranic verses and reading them in a different light, they came to the conclusion that the Quran does not enjoin warfare between Muslims and non-Muslims but, instead, promotes a peaceful coexistence, unless there is a serious *casus belli*, such as an attack on Muslim territory. This notion, that is jihad is conceived as a purely defensive warfare, has been adopted widely in the Islamic world, especially among political and intellectual elites.

Thus, the word jihad refers to very different concepts. But even if we focus on the classical legal doctrine, we find that the ways the rules can be applied are not clearly defined. Take, for instance, the definition of the enemy: in principle, the non-Muslims who are not protected by the Islamic state. If certain groups define being a Muslim in a different way, the boundaries between Muslims and non-Muslims shift and include or exclude certain groups. Certain radical Islamists regard Muslim rulers who do not fully implement the Shari`a as unbelievers or rather apostates, since they have abandoned Islam. As a consequence, they are then seen as persons who have lost their right of protection and may lawfully be killed. This is called *takfir*, declaring that someone who considers himself a Muslim is an unbeliever (*kafir*). It is controversial whether this is allowed at all, but militant Islamists who follow a strict definition of being a Muslim, do apply *takfir*. Another example of the indefiniteness of the jihad doctrine is the legitimisation of defensive warfare: what precisely constitutes aggression that makes jihad an individual duty? The fact that a government of alleged apostates rules part of the Muslim world? The assistance given by a non-Muslim army to one Muslim state in its warfare against another? Osama bin Laden for instance regarded as an act of aggression the stationing of US troops in Saudi Arabia in the First Gulf War, although the Saudi government had requested their presence. Militant interpretations of the jihad doctrine focus on defensive jihad presented as an individual religious obligation. Not taking part in it is then seen as a grave sin. These and similar applications of the jihad doctrine depend on the interpretation of the doctrine and on the appreciation of the facts to which the doctrine must be applied.

Once warfare or violence has been justified by a specific interpretation of the jihad doctrine, the notion of martyrdom can provide further incentives to participate in that struggle. It is a concept firmly rooted in the text of the Quran, where it is frequently referred to. According to widespread Islamic belief, warriors killed in jihad are rendered free of sin and go directly to Paradise, where they will dwell close to God's throne. However, the doctrine of martyrdom also has its controversies. It is, for instance, disputed whether a person who actively seeks it can be regarded as a martyr. The debates on this issue that date back to the early centuries of Islam, have acquired a new relevance in view of the phenomenon of suicide attacks.

A third concept that is germane to our topic is the idea that the End of Times is approaching. There exists a large body of Islamic eschatological writings, many of them going back to the first centuries of Islam. According to these accounts, the final stage of the apocalypse is marked by a deterioration of the conditions in the world: injustice, oppression and famine will spread. This is followed by a cosmic struggle between the forces of evil and those of Islam in which the latter will be victorious. This victory will inaugurate a golden era lasting a specific but disputed number of years (forty, seventy or thousand) until the Hour comes. As in other religions, expectations about the coming of the millennium can have strong political consequences. Understanding and presenting a certain struggle as the apocalyptic battle is a powerful motivation for engaging in it. One cannot lose: the final victory is certain and if one is killed, the ultimate bliss of martyrdom will be the reward. It is also a strong argument that can be used for recruitment. On the other hand, apocalyptic expectations can be used to make people accept oppression and injustice by persuading them that these conditions are only temporary as they belong to a stage in the history of salvation immediately preceding the millennium.

The bottom-line is that such doctrines and ideas are ambiguous and vague and need users to give them a specific meaning and content. What such users do is either select their ideas from a range of already existing interpretations and understandings, or create new meanings. These may be combined to create a radical or extremist political-religious ideology.

Mohammed Bouyeri and the Hofstad Group

When, immediately after the murder of Theo van Gogh, Mohammed Bouyeri was arrested, the police found out that he belonged to a group of young Muslims who, for some time, had been under surveillance by the Dutch Intelligence and Security Service (AIVD). Since they were first spotted in The Hague, the AIVD had dubbed them the Hofstad group (*Hofstadgroep* in Dutch), Hofstad (court city) being one of the epithets of The Hague. Later it became clear that most of its members, including Bouyeri, lived in Amsterdam. They were, with the exception of one or two converts to Islam, all of Moroccan descent and born or raised in the Netherlands. Some of them were old friends of Bouyeri's with whom he had grown up in his Amsterdam neighbourhood. Bouyeri, whom the AIVD first considered an insignificant follower of the group, later turned out to be its main ideologue. The group did not form a tight organisation; its members used to gather on an irregular basis in Bouyeri's living room, where they discussed religion and exchanged digital documents with religious and radical Islamist content. The police investigation did not reveal any direct organisational links with international Islamist terrorist groups. The Hofstad group, therefore, is an example of home-grown Islamic extremism. However, during the initial stages of the radicalisation period, a certain Abu Khaled Redouan el-Issa, a former Syrian army officer who had applied for political asylum in Germany, played a role. El-Issa spoke at informal living-room meetings throughout the Netherlands and introduced groups of Muslims to the thoughts of the founding fathers of Islamic radicalism, such as Sayyid Qutb (1906–66) and Abu al-A`lâ al-Mawdûdî (1903–79). Among the groups he initiated into these ideas were Bouyeri and his friends.

At the time of the arrests of Bouyeri and other Hofstad group members the police seized their computers. The contents of the hard disks and other data carriers were copied into a special forensic program that allowed searching, bookmarking and copying without changes in the original. Within this enormous amount of data, I could identify about 60 texts produced by Bouyeri, either because they were signed with his sobriquets Abu Zubair or Sayf al-Dîn al-Muwahhid (The Sword of Religion, the monotheist), or because the document properties pointed to his computer. The type of texts varies. Some were Dutch translations of Islamist pamphlets or treatises, often preceded by a short introduction by Bouyeri. Other texts were written entirely by him. With one exception, the source texts of the translations were in English. It seems that Bouyeri's knowledge of Arabic was not sufficient for translating complicated religious treatises. The texts he produced were distributed among the other members of the group and some of them were published on the internet. Bouyeri was the ideological leader of the group and his texts were, it seems, used for ideological training. Apart from his texts, the computers contained enormous libraries of religious written material, most of it in Arabic, as well as pictures and short video movies. Most of the latter were related to the oppression of Muslims in, for example, Palestine/Israel, Chechnya, Iraq and Afghanistan, and their armed struggles against oppression. The videos were probably used for recruitment, in order to convince potential members of the plight of Muslims all over the world and the need to do something about it.

An inventory of the documents found on his and other computers shows that he and the group were ideologically heavily indebted to the Egyptian Sayyid Qutb and the Indian/Pakistani Abu al-A`lâ al-Mawdûdî. Moreover, large amounts of more recent salafi material, especially from radical Saudi religious scholars and from authors who had fought in Afghanistan, were found. However, many of these documents were in Arabic, and it is impossible to assess their real influence. Among Bouyeri's translations we find a few texts originally written by radical Saudi scholars and by Afghan jihad veterans. However, the impact of one figure stands out: Abu Hamza al-Misri (b. *c.*1957), the militant imam and preacher of the Finsbury Mosque in London. Born in Egypt, he immigrated to England in 1979. In the early 1980s he fought with the Mujahidin in Afghanistan where he lost his hands and an eye. Bouyeri translated quite a few of his writings, via English versions, into Dutch.

The Construction of a Dutch Extremist Islamist

On the basis of the document properties of Bouyeri's texts I could establish the chronological order in which they were produced. This enables us to follow the process of radicalisation which they went through. Within this process we can distinguish four stages:

- Explicit rejection of Western values and norms (starting February 2003)
- Rejection of Western democracy and law (as of October 2003)
- Global call for jihad against democracy (March 2004)
- Justification of violent actions and the writing of threatening letters (summer 2004)

The Quest for the Truth

The beginnings of Bouyeri's radicalisation can be traced back to 2001. In the summer of that year he had served a prison sentence for assault and battery. Later he said that in prison he had started to read the Quran. His need for a new spiritual orientation was given additional impetus with the death of his mother in December of that year. In the testament drawn up by him shortly before he killed van Gogh, he mentioned that after his mother's death in December 2001 he set out on a 'quest for the truth'. That his ideas and behaviour changed during the following year is well documented by testimonies of friends and colleagues. He became more serious and religious. In his work – he had dropped out of college and found a part-time job as assistant-manager of a community centre in the neighbourhood where he lived – he began to take Islamic injunctions more seriously: he refused to order alcoholic drinks for receptions and parties and to organise activities where men and women would mingle.

Against the ensuing criticism, he defended himself in a short article, published in the centre's magazine in February 2003, entitled: 'Islam and integration'. These I consider the first steps on the road that he was to follow to the end. Whereas the Dutch public debate at that time was dominated by the question of whether Islam is compatible with integration into Dutch society, Bouyeri turned the question on its head by positing that the only true integration was integration into Islam: 'The verb integrating means ... becoming part of a larger whole. This includes for me the Islamic concept of submission (body and soul) to the Unique Power who is the Creator of the larger whole that we call universe and of which man is part.' This, he argued, imposes on him the duty of following Islamic prescriptions, even if these are in conflict with prevailing views in society. At that moment, however, it was not yet clear for him what Islam was. Among the documents written by him in the spring and summer of 2003 we find texts showing that he was experimenting with character-building through acts of piety and with numerological readings of the Quran. However, during that same spring, fundamentalist notions became more prominent. This was the result of two events. The first was the authorities declining his proposal for a club for Moroccan youth. Assisted by the community centre where he was employed, he had applied for government funding but his application was rejected. This must have adversely affected his trust in the Dutch political system and Dutch society in general. The other event was that his contacts with the Syrian preacher Abu Khaled el-Issa intensified. Bouyeri and his friends had met him in one of the Amsterdam mosques in the previous autumn, but El-Issa began to visit and teach them sometime during the spring of 2003. In the summer of that year documents were distributed among the members of the group consisting only of Quranic verses in Arabic with their Dutch translation and arranged around certain themes such as monotheism, unbelief, idolatry and jihad. Since most of these were stored in directories referring to Abu Khaled el-Issa, it is plausible that these were used for sessions with him. It seems that he familiarised them thoroughly with the ideas of Sayyid Qutb and Mawdûdî.

Although not all of their ideas are identical, their foundations are very similar. It is the notion that God has not only created the universe and humanity, but has also revealed rules for mankind to live by. God, in this perspective, is not only creator and the object of veneration but also lawgiver. Now, monotheism (*tawhîd*) implies that besides God no creator can be recognised and that nothing or no one may be worshipped apart from Him. The novel element is, however, that according to these ideas, no human being may legislate, because laying down the law is God's prerogative. States must not enact their own laws but implement the Shari`a, God's law. Muslim rulers who refuse to do so commit acts of polytheism (*shirk*) and are, therefore, apostates who deserve the death penalty. A legal system based on man-made laws lacks legitimacy and cannot be recognised. Democracy must therefore be rejected, as, seen from this perspective, it implies slavery and oppression. It is a political system of domination of men over other men, instead of the domination of God over men. Moreover it is founded on the idea that mankind may create its own laws instead of accepting God's law. Institutions and political and legal systems that violate the principles of monotheism, as well as persons of authority who rule by man-made laws and not according to the Shari`a, are called *tâghût*, idols, because they arrogate privileges and positions that belong to God only. Obeying them is denying God His right to be obeyed. Accepting democracy and a legal system based on man-made laws is dubbed *shirk al-hâkimiyya*, that is, polytheism by recognising the sovereignty of humans and human institutions, thereby violating

God's prerogatives. These ideas deriving from a strict interpretation of the concept of monotheism (*tawhîd*) are perfectly suitable for delegitimising the political status quo and justify the struggle to topple the government.

Rejecting the Tâghût (October 2003)

Abu Khaled's lessons were not lost on Bouyeri and he must have been an eager learner. By October 2003 he felt sufficiently confident to produce a text entitled *Democratie en islam* (Democracy and Islam) on the obligation to reject democracy. It is an introduction to the translation of two anonymous English texts that he downloaded from the internet and that argue that democracy is forbidden in Islam and that participating in it by voting or standing for elected bodies is an act of unbelief. In the introduction, addressed to his brethren and sisters, he writes:

> The democratic system is bleeding to death; its putrid face becomes clearer by the day. We live in a world where the supporters of this system set themselves up as the masters of all other inhabitants of the earth. They claim the exclusive right to subject others. The foremost of all democratic countries is the pernicious America, the motherland and model of the democratic system. Although it becomes clearer by the day that democracy is only a smoke curtain to exploit other people as slaves, there are still those who cannot free themselves from the intellectual slavery [and think] that this system is indeed the best that has been created for humanity (better than the Shari`a).

In this passage we see that there is an identification of democracy with the West and especially with the United States. This, we find in his other writings too. Democracy and the West are often used interchangeably and criticism of Western or US international politics is also addressed to democracy as a political system. It is evident that Abu Khaled's teachings had borne fruit by then. Bouyeri had been put on track and from the autumn of 2003 he continued to develop his ideas himself, aided by the internet. Throughout the autumn of 2003 and the spring of 2004 he translated documents gathered from the internet, all of them dealing with the rejection of democratic governments, with the view that resorting to tribunals not based on the Shari`a entails apostasy and insisting on the urgency of establishing a political and legal order based on the Shari`a. A new element is a document on 'loyalty and distance' (Arabic: *al-walâ'wa-l-barâ'a*). This is the principle that Muslims must only consort with and give their loyalty to other Muslims and that they must keep their distance from non-Muslims. Since the definition of who is a Muslim used by this group is rather narrow, this principle imposes sectarian isolation from mainstream Muslims. In the introductions to his translations, Bouyeri repeatedly speaks about the struggle between the true Islam and its enemies:

> Since the turning point in our history, better known as 9/11, a struggle like the one between David and Goliath has broken out between the followers of Truth and those of Falsehood. … We see nowadays that every day the struggle comes closer to us. [Take for instance] the supervised sermons of imams preaching in the service of malicious tyrants. In doing so they give the truth a totally different meaning and present the followers of Truth in a bad light.

Join the Caravan of Martyrs (March 2004)

The logical consequence of seeing reality in terms of a struggle between truth and falsehood was of course a call for participation in that struggle. The first summon to jihad dates from March 2004 and is found in a pamphlet entitled 'To catch a wolf'. It is an emotional piece of about 3,000 words written in great anger. Its style is slovenly and it contains passages that are not entirely intelligible. But although the wording is confused at times and the text lacks coherence, it is not the ranting and raving of a deranged person. Its overall message is clear: Islam is under attack by the West and this attack must be resisted. The state of the Muslim community is described in almost apocalyptic terms:

> The earth is trembling, the sky is weeping and the wind is raging frenetically. So much injustice, so much misery, so much pain, so many tears, so much Muslim blood being shed daily. It is difficult not to be distressed and dejected when swamped by so many terrible images and reports about our brothers and sisters all over the world.

This is in the first place due to Western aggression, aiming at the total destruction of Islam:

> There are dark satanic forces that have sown their seed of evil everywhere in the world. This seed has been sown in the Islamic world in the times of colonialism and has since then taken root. Since the fall of the Ottoman Empire and the Islamic caliphate the enemies of Islam have been active in gradually carrying out their plans aiming at the total destruction of Islam. The Islamic Ummah, once so powerful and proud, has become no more than a dead drunk and frustrated nation, begging at the doorsteps of the West for a piece of bread. Its honour has no more value than that of a barking mongrel on which passers-by take it out by spitting their gall at it.

The West is not only blamed for defeating the Muslim world but also for the injustice of the unequal distribution of wealth in the world. Addressing the Western leaders, Bouyeri asks rhetorically:

> How did it happen that your bank vaults are full of gold although there are no goldmines in your countries? How did it happen that a rich continent like Africa is poverty-stricken? How did it happen that all those guns, landmines, tanks and other destructive weaponry produced in your democratic countries, have found their way to these poor victims?

The sorry state of the Muslims, however, is not only to be blamed on the West. Part of the decay is the fault of Muslim leaders who have betrayed their community to its enemies:

> The Islamic Ummah seems to be visited by a cancerous growth that has disseminated all over the body. We are on the edge of an abyss and it seems that it is only a matter of time before we smash ourselves up. We are a frustrated nation betrayed by the so-called leaders of this Ummah, leaders who have sold themselves as cheap whores to the West and allow the spirits and souls of Muslim youth to be poisoned by the poison of *kufr* (unbelief).

The title of the document, 'To catch a wolf', refers to an Inuit technique in which they plant a sharp knife covered with layers of frozen blood in the snow. When a wolf passes he smells the blood, traces the knife and starts licking it, thereby cutting his tongue without noticing it. He then continues to lick his own warm blood and bleeds to death. This is related to a message concerning the nature of democracy: the democratic leaders ('the democratic vampires') try to reduce their subjects to a state of languor and inertia, making it easier to exploit them. This, they do by offering them goodies like coffee shops (where, in the Netherlands, soft drugs are lawfully sold), discos, bars and gambling halls, where they become enslaved to their own lusts and desires and lose the will to resist. These goodies are likened to the bloody knife planted in the snow: enjoying them draws the strength from a person and is ultimately fatal.

Bouyeri then seems to suggest that there is a relationship between these goodies, intended to undermine the strength of the people, and the final downfall of the United States, although the passage is not fully clear. It can be read as a message of hope, like the Marxist prophecies of the final downfall of capitalism, but also as an argument for the strength of the elite, whose position is not affected by the ruin of society:

> If we take America, the Mother of all Democracies, as an example and compare the social statistics (crime, violence) with those of other countries then we must conclude that this country is sick to the core. It is only a matter of time before the social order becomes one big chaos. The laughing third parties in this big monopoly game are the democratic vampires. They fortify their bodies by injecting innocent blood into their veins because of their unquenchable thirst for it.

The last message is that a small group of responsible Muslims has emerged in the Netherlands, 'because Dutch politics stimulate its citizens (especially the immigrants = Muslims) to participate in [discussions on] social questions and to take responsibility'. In these words we hear echoes of Bouyeri's former life, when he was active in social work in the community. This small group has assumed 'social responsibility, not only for the Netherlands but for the whole world and taken upon themselves the task of liberating the world from democratic slavery'. Its aim is to establish the domination of Islam and they call on other Muslims to join the jihad. In the last paragraph he addresses Muslim youths and shouts (witness the capitalisation which is Bouyeri's):

> WAKE UP! LOOK AROUND! MUSLIMS ARE BEING SLAUGHTERED AND YOU CANNOT DO ANYTHING BECAUSE YOU ARE BLEEDING TO DEATH. Free yourself! Leave the coffee shop, leave the bar, and leave that street corner. Answer the call of LA ILAHA ILLA ALLAH. Join the Caravan of Martyrs. Wake up from your stupor, rise and shake off the dust of humiliation. Rise and answer to the summons for jihad.

'... Your Blood and Properties have become Halal' (Summer 2004)

During the spring of 2004 members of the Hofstad group must have discussed what kind of actions they could carry out to help Islam. There also must have been suggestions for violent action in the Netherlands. However, on this point there was an ideological problem that had to be resolved. The texts that Bouyeri downloaded from the internet and that inspired him related mainly to the situation in the Islamic world. Even Abu Hamza el-Misri, who was a British citizen and active in London, was hardly concerned with the situation in England, but rather with the Muslim world and could therefore rely on the theories formulated by Qutb and Mawdûdî. Their writings referred to the Muslim world and they argued that Muslim leaders had abandoned true Islam and become apostates. That was their principal justification for a revolutionary struggle. This doctrine, however, did not make sense in the Dutch context. Of course, the country was governed by non-Muslims, but not by apostates. And that made an enormous difference.

According to Shari`a principles generally accepted among pious Muslim immigrants, the relationship of Muslims and the countries where they live is governed by the notion of a treaty or contract. According to the classical doctrine of the Shari`a, non-Muslims living in the Dâr al-harb, the Abode of War, that is, outside the boundaries of the Islamic state and not in a country with which the Islamic state has concluded a treaty, are not protected by the Shari`a. They may be killed, enslaved or robbed with impunity. However, if they enter Muslim territory with a pledge of security (*amân*) granted by officials or by any adult male Muslim, their lives, property and freedom are protected by law, on the condition that they respect the laws of the land. Comparable rules apply if a Muslim enters the Dâr al-Harb with the express permission of the local non-Muslim authorities. If they grant him protection under the local laws, the Shari`a obligates him to respect these laws. Contemporary Muslims equate visa and residence permits with such permission and assert that Muslims legally residing in non-Muslim countries are bound by the local laws.

This doctrine posed problems to Bouyeri's ideas of calling for jihad in the Netherlands. We have no information on whether this was discussed in the group, but it is likely that it was. They were wont to judge their behaviour by Islamic standards and discuss whether certain acts or ways of dressing were forbidden or permitted. There can be no doubt that lawfulness of the use of violence must have been debated. Two solutions were found, as we can ascertain from the documents produced during the summer of 2004. One was the use of violence against individuals, not within the framework of warfare and jihad, but by way of punishment for alleged crimes against Islam. The reasoning behind this must have been that in the absence of a real Islamic state and Shari`a courts, true Muslims were entitled or even obliged to punish individuals who committed serious offences. The other solution was to regard the 'treaty' of the Dutch state with Muslim residents as abolished on the ground that the Dutch government had violated it by supporting the United States and Israel in their warfare against Islam and by sending troops to Iraq.

There are three translated documents laying the groundwork for violence. They provided justifications and encouragement for violent actions. One text, incidentally the only one directly translated from the Arabic, probably with the help of others, is a fatwa by Ibn Taymiyya (d. 1328), stating that it is mandatory to execute persons insulting the Prophet Mohammed. For Ibn Taymiyya this meant that such persons were to be sentenced to death after a trial and a substantiation of the facts. Bouyeri, however, as we know from the ensuing events, misunderstood this and took it as an obligation for individual Muslims to take the law in their own hands. The other document is a recent fatwa issued in November 2002 by a certain Hâmid al-ʿAlî, a radical Muslim scholar from Kuwait, arguing that Yasser Arafat was an apostate because he was in favour of a secularist state in Palestine. The last document is a text listing the blessings of martyrdom and entitled 'The battlefield: the safest place on earth'. Its author, Amîr Sulaymân, argues that he participated in jihad not because his faith is so strong, but rather because it is weak: death on the battlefield will save him from consequences of his sins and secure for him a privileged position in paradise.

During that summer Bouyeri produced seven open letters, most of which were published on the internet. Three of them addressed groups of Muslims collectively: a letter to 'the mendacious ʿulama [religious scholars] and imams', summoning them to mend their ways and to convert to true Islam; one addressing Muslim youth and requesting them to set out on a quest for true Islam; and the third depicting in lively terms the torture inflicted by Americans on Iraqi Muslims – reports on the Abu Ghraib prison had been publicised earlier that year – and summoning the entire Muslim Ummah to jihad against its enemies. Of the other four, three contained threats against Dutch individuals and one against the Dutch population collectively.

Of the open letters to individuals, the most notorious is the one addressing Ayaan Hirsi Ali, at that time a Dutch MP of Somalian Muslim origin (and now Resident Fellow at the American Enterprise Institute). Bouyeri had skewered a copy of it on van Gogh's dead body after he had murdered him. Hirsi Ali had become one of the most vociferous critics of Islam in the public debate and had publicly announced that she was no longer Muslim. The letter is somewhat confused. In the opening paragraphs Bouyeri blames Hirsi Ali not only for apostatising but also for joining the ranks of the 'soldiers of evil'. On the other hand he alleges that she is an instrument in the hands of a clique of Jewish (and allegedly Jewish) politicians and quotes the Talmud 'proving' that non-Jews are not regarded as human and must be killed. These quotations come from an American anti-Semitic pamphlet downloaded by Bouyeri from a fundamentalist Islamic site, which had copied it from an anti-Semitic American site. The letter to Hirsi Ali has a curious end. It does not directly threaten her with death but challenges her to commit suicide. The reasoning behind this is the following: if she really does not believe anymore, she can show in that way that she is not afraid of all horrors that according to the Quran are awaiting the unbelievers in the hereafter. Since the letter was found on van Gogh's body it was understood as a death threat against her. On 29 August of that year (actually, after the letter had been written) a short documentary called 'Submission' produced by her and van Gogh had been shown on Dutch television. This movie was felt by many Dutch Muslims as an outrage against Islam.

Another letter was directed against Ahmed Aboutaleb, an Amsterdam alderman of Moroccan descent. He was criticised for being a 'secular Muslim (*kafir*)', which immediately reminds us of the fatwa of Hâmid al-ʿAlî condemning Arafat for his secular political ideas. The letter concludes with the following warning: 'This letter has been drafted in order to warn you and the other minions of the unbelievers for the horrible consequences of their behaviour and to inform you about your status in Islam.' Given that with 'status in Islam' Bouyeri meant that Aboutaleb was an apostate, the conclusion that this was a threatening letter is fully justified. The last letter to an individual was addressed to the MP Geert Wilders, who was known for his Islamophobic views. Since he used to dye his hair blond, Bouyeri and his group assumed that he was a homosexual and told him that he should be thrown from the Euro mast, a 185 metre tower in Rotterdam by way of Shari`a punishment.

The last and most threatening letter was the open letter to the Dutch people. In it Bouyeri expounds that a war is going on between the forces of evil, that is, the coalition led by the United States, and Islam. In this war millions of Muslims have been brutally slaughtered and raped. The Dutch government, the letter goes on, dominated by Zionist Jews, supports Israel in its struggle against Islam and has joined the coalition forces. Since government policy is based on election, the non-Muslim Dutch have become lawful targets: their lives and properties have become *halâl*:

> The dark clouds of death assemble over your country. Prepare yourselves for that for which one cannot prepare oneself. The death and torture of our brothers and sisters must be redeemed with your own blood. You have become targets everywhere: in trams, buses, trains, shopping malls etc. It won't take more than a fraction of a second and you'll be in the midst of dead persons. The unbearable stench of death will upset your stomach. You will taste the pain of loss and mutilation. ... Life will become Hell for you and you will not find rest until our brothers and sisters have it.

Here ends the process of radicalisation of Mohammed Bouyeri. The next thing he did was to put his ideas into practice by murdering van Gogh.

Conclusions

In the introduction I listed four more-or-less universal characteristics of extremist ideologies. They are:

- The rejection of the world order dominated by the forces of evil;
- The feeling that one's own group is under acute threat;
- The idea of a utopia that is within reach;
- The notion of a small and devoted pure vanguard that is instrumental in bringing about the promised utopia by a violent struggle against the forces of evil.

Let us see to what extent the self constructed Islam of Bouyeri includes these elements. The rejection of the global order is one of the most conspicuous traits in Bouyeri's text. The forces of evil are democracy (or the West), led by the United States who wage a cosmic struggle against the forces of the good, that is Islam. Moreover, democracy as a political system is unlawful according to Bouyeri's Islam, being based on the domination of man over man and not of God over man. The Dutch government and the Dutch people are part of the forces of evil. The government sent troops to Iraq and many politicians and journalists have started a media war against Islam. The Islamic camp, globally, is weakened because many of its political and religious leaders have abandoned the true religion and made common cause with the enemy. Although Bouyeri nowhere explicitly refers to the End of Time, the urgency of the struggle against the forces of darkness is repeatedly emphasised, often in terms that are almost apocalyptic. He claims that the struggle has now become different and that Muslims are attacked everywhere:

> The struggle against the Truth has been fought as long as humanity has existed, but in this time and age it has been fiercer and more massive than ever before. The army of the satanic forces has its monsters everywhere ready to seize people who summon to the uncompromised truth and bury them alive in their brutal dungeons.

However, the realisation of the ideal, a state based on the Shari`a, is near:

> It is but a matter of time before the knights of Allah will march to the Binnenhof in The Hague [the centre of Dutch politics] and raise the flag of TAWHID on the central square. They will (Insha'Allah) rename the parliament to Shari`a tribunal and the chairman's gavel will confirm Shari`a judgments. From the Prime Minister's turret will sound the words LA ILAHA ILLA ALLAH and these words will be carried by the wind and be joined by other words of glory to God. The laudations will reach our Master on His Throne and the Islamic Ummah will prostrate as if in one body before the Lord of the Worlds.

Bouyeri does not give details about how this utopia can be established. However, it is clear that in his view it will be the working of a small group of true and devoted Muslims who have sought and found true Islam. They must wage jihad against the powers of Satan so that after their defeat the Shari`a state can be established. That true Islam will be victorious is certain for Bouyeri. But that requires violent action. However, those undertaking it cannot lose: if they are killed they will enter Paradise, if they live, they will see the utopia of the Shari`a state.

PART 4
Radicalisation in Western Europe:
The Answers

(De-)Escalating Radicalisation: The Debate within Muslim and Immigrant Communities

Tarik Fraihi

A terrorist is someone who loses each debate because reasonable arguments are to be used, and thus chooses unreasonable means. Islamist terrorists, and jihadis in particular, are politically marginal militants that try to carry through their political ideals by means of violence and terror. Their action is not rooted in Islam, but in political interpretations of very specific – mainly salafi – sources of Islam. With the attacks in Madrid and London, jihadi activism has become prominent in Europe too. Networks of jihadis are active throughout Europe. The Netherlands and Belgium are no exception. In the Netherlands, the movie director Theo van Gogh was murdered by a member of a jihadi group known as the 'Hofstad group'. In Belgium, extremists have been arrested and suspected of membership of a jihadi group, Groupe islamique combattant marocain (GICM). The suspected members had connections with and granted lodging to persons involved in the attacks in Madrid, Casablanca and Rabat.

The terrorists' profile is noteworthy. The attacks in London were committed by Britons with Pakistani roots. The members of the Hofstad group were almost all born in the Netherlands. The attacks in Madrid were committed by Moroccan immigrants. Four arrested GICM-members were born and grew up in a small Belgian village and had no relevant history. Radicalisation often concerns intelligent young people, role models, who instead eventually turn to armed jihad.

Radicalisation among young Muslims in Europe is not a new phenomenon and partially coincides with developments in the larger Islamic world, and the Arab-Muslim world in particular. Here, secular socialist and nationalist opposition was eliminated in the 1970s and Islamic and Islamist movements had free play. Around the same time, European Islam gradually started to affirm itself too, incited by dawa groups such as the tabligh movement and the Muslim Brotherhood. They preached a radical, puritanical and intolerant vision of society. The rise of Islamism in the 1970s and 1980s – with milestones such as the Iranian revolution and the assassination of the Egyptian president Sadat – alarmed a number of regimes. Repression followed and a lot of militants fled to the West. Their arrival gave additional traction to the dawa groups in Europe. Their determination to re-convert Muslims in Europe increased through the use of the networks and structures of the dawa organisations. Afghan veterans especially played an important role in the dissemination of Islamist ideology. When the pro-communist regime in Kabul disappeared, many foreign mujahedeen scattered all over the world. A majority among them settled in Europe, specifically in London, Paris and Brussels, and started to support action for the struggles in Palestine, Algeria, Bosnia and Chechnya. These Afghan veterans passed on their military expertise and knowledge to a new generation of jihadis, often young radicalised Muslims, born and raised in Europe.

But the phenomenon of Islamist extremism in Europe cannot be understood if one only takes into consideration the developments in the countries of origin. A whole range of factors – among them the failed integration of new immigrant communities within European societies – motivates some young Muslims to radicalise. This radicalisation is a marginal phenomenon, but at the same time it is an alarming evolution. Several factors play an important role in the radicalisation process, including in particular: the end of the Cold War and the rhetoric of the clash of civilisations, the rise of conservatism in the West and the difficult integration of large groups of immigrants. All three have a strong influence on how radical Muslims think.

Rhetoric of the Clash of Civilisations

During the Cold War the world order appeared relatively simple. The world was divided into two opposing ideological camps: the capitalist West and the communist East. Both tried to extend their influence in the world so as to enhance their dominant position. With the fall of the Berlin Wall, the struggle between East and West came to an end. The Soviet Union imploded. The defeat of the bureaucratised regimes in the East created new opportunities for free trade, investment and production, as well as new consumer markets. The West's triumph was complete. The victory of capitalism confirmed the ideological supremacy of the West. Communism was bankrupt and George H. Bush announced a 'new world order'. The new world order however never came into being; instead the world was confronted with global disorder, with international terrorism omnipresent.

International terrorism and the war against terror – with al-Qaeda as the most well-known and most notorious element – have already created thousands of victims. In a number of countries a permanent feeling of insecurity permeates society. Against this background, the jihadis especially take aim at the so-called winners of the Cold War, the United States and their allies that are the symbols of today's powers that be. However, this 'war' between George W. Bush and Osama bin Laden is not portrayed as a political or ideological conflict, but as a cultural, ethnic and religious confrontation. From a confrontation between ideologies, the world has entered a period dominated by the clash of civilisations. The enemy of the free West no longer carries a chapka, but a turban. Islamic faith is said to be irreconcilable with Western values and standards. Islamic culture is being depicted as backward and aggressive.

This shift from ideological fault lines to cultural and religious dividing lines carries a function however. He who consciously or unconsciously presents Islam as a danger to the West, or presents the West as a danger to Islam, contributes to create an artificial enemy, since reality is being twisted. George W. Bush and Osama bin Laden have much in common. The American rhetoric concerning the war against an 'Axis of Evil' shows striking resemblances with bin Laden's discourse, similarly depicting a war between 'Islam' and 'the big Satan'. Reinforcing one's own political standing is the main driving force behind such caricatures. By dividing and classifying whole populations according to good and evil, discriminations, assassinations and wars become justified – for both sides. The 'Other' is reduced to a dangerous and contemptible enemy who must be excluded and eliminated. The hostile 'Other' takes an archetypical, inhumane form. They both divide the world in 'us' and 'them'. Their own righteousness is emphasised in opposition to the evil of the other. False images of the other become stronger and the hostility between Muslims and non-Muslims increases.

Most terrorists, who nowadays commit attacks against the United States and their allies, are indeed generally Muslims. But not all Muslims are terrorists. Muslims who carry out such acts of terror are extremist adherents of an ideology based upon a religion. Islamism is the name of this ideology, and the religion upon which it pretends to be based is Islam. Islamism represents a wide variety of moderate (the AKP in Turkey) and radical (Hezbollah in Lebanon) tendencies, which all refer to Islam in their political practice and theory. The Islamist extremists use violence and terror out of a political and strategic conviction. This fanatical Islam has something of a religious fascism, since the worship of the leader, martyrdom and superiority are central issues – as in fascist ideologies.

The Rise of Conservatism

Europe has witnessed a conservative revival, shaped and influenced by political topics such as immigration, Islam, delinquency and the many stereotypes about the position of women in the Islamic world. The extreme-right and populist right-wing political parties in Europe present themselves as the true defenders of Western values and norms. Muslims are considered a threat to these Western achievements and way of life. This war logic erodes democratic standards, since it leads to attempts at limiting Muslims' constitutional rights and freedoms. These modern Jacobins seem to think that democracy is to be saved by reducing democracy. They want to guarantee the freedom of speech for themselves by silencing their new enemy's freedom of expression. In their discourse two statements are omnipresent. First, an often heard argument states that 'Not all cultures are equal' – referring to the inferiority of Islamic civilisation. Such statements hardly contribute to any sensible debate. It is a generalisation that induces polarisation and conflict instead of enabling dialogue. Such sweeping arguments ignore, for instance, the many differences within Islamic culture and, more important, the many similarities between Western and Islamic cultures. Everything is reduced to simple categories which depart from the complexities of reality.

A second argument derives from the view that equates integration with a 'civilisation process' of specific groups of immigrants. Immigrants should 'develop' and 'modernise' themselves. In one word, they must change. Integration is considered as assimilation into a Western mould. From that point of view, other cultural groups must undergo an evolution to the higher, Western development stage. This is Eurocentrism at its most acute. Such an interpretation is socially unacceptable, since it furthers the polarisation between Muslims and non-Muslims. Integration instead has to start from the idea that both non-Muslims and Muslims are equal citizens and are part of one and the same society. Integration cannot be but a reciprocal process. It is a common endeavour of Muslims and non-Muslims alike. He who puts all responsibility upon the shoulders of one specific group is heading in the wrong direction. Such a unilateral approach to social problems paves the way to greater polarisation between diasporic communities and the society in which they live. Integration is not a problem for immigrants alone, but a concern for society as a whole.

Laborious Integration

Despite of actions undertaken, several European states are not succeeding in realising an equal participation of immigrants and their children in society. The socio-economic situation of the average immigrants remains simply dramatic. In the Flemish northern part of Belgium, only 21 per cent of non-European youngsters start higher education, whereas the total average of all students who go into higher education lies at 52 per cent. Thirty-eight per cent of non-European immigrants do not have a diploma of secondary education, and only 16 per cent have a diploma of professional secondary education. This means that 54 per cent of young people of non-European origin do not have a diploma that gives them access to higher education, whereas the total average of all pupils in Flanders that has no access to higher education stands at 27 per cent. The inflow of non-European immigrants' children into higher education is thus simply a disaster.

The situation in high schools and universities is barely any better. The average percentage of students who succeed at the universities lies between 45 to 47 per cent, but for non-European students it is a mere 15 per cent. This means that ultimately only 1.5 per cent of non-European students receive a university degree. Whereas half (49 per cent) of all Flemish students obtain a higher education diploma, only 17 per cent of non-European students do. On the labour market the position of diasporic communities is strikingly similar. While the employment level in Flanders fluctuates around 60 per cent, for non-European immigrant communities it hovers around 30 per cent. Non-European immigrants thus score very high in the total population of unemployed. The number of unemployed immigrants has more than doubled in the last ten years, from 7.5 per cent of the total number of unemployed, to 20.9 per cent. The unequal participation of immigrants in the labour market is not only linked with their lower levels of education, but is also partly the result of discrimination. Different surveys in Flanders show that 39.2 per cent of the employers discriminate against applicants of foreign origin. But the permanent inflow of newcomers with poor language skills also ensures an increasing number of jobseekers in diasporic communities. Of the male Moroccan and Turkish jobseekers of age 26–27 years almost 37 per cent are newcomers. This increases to 62 per cent for jobseekers between 34 and 37 years of age.

In most of Europe the situation is hardly better. In some regions the figures are even worse than those quoted above. The big European cities especially continue to wrestle with enduring problems in their districts and suburbs that are the source of many frustrations. Sometimes they surface, as they did in the riots of 2005 in the French banlieues. After the death of two young men hiding from the police in an electricity cabin, riots erupted throughout France. Only after three weeks and a state of emergency did the violence in the country abate. According to all observers and assessments, these riots clearly had no ethnic or religious grounds. Many ethnic and religious backgrounds were involved, but all persons involved shared the same precarious socio-economic situation.

The Radicalisation of Muslims in Europe

Radicalisation is a process in which an individual's convictions and willingness to seek for deep and serious changes in the society increase. Radicalism and radicalisation are not necessarily negative. Moreover, different forms of radicalisation exist. One form of radicalisation is the rise of radical political Islam. Political Islam is a house with many doors and rooms. It is a common denominator for a wide array of political orientations that all pretend to be grounded in Islam as a religion. But political Islam is heterogeneous and has many different, sometimes even contrary tendencies. Militants of political Islam are eager to confuse ideology with religion, judging this to be advantageous to their cause. Indeed, each criticism on political Islam as an ideology then becomes a criticism on Islam as a religion.

Political Islam only plays a minor role within the Muslim communities in Europe. The most radical brands of political Islam also use the rhetoric of a clash of civilisations. According to them, the West started a crusade against Islam. After the 9/11 attacks the number of radical political Islamic groups has clearly increased. But it still remains marginal when compared to moderate political strands within the same communities. The greater the political participation of Muslims in the traditional political parties, the less successful political Islamist groups become.

A second form of radicalisation is radical Islamic puritanism, the tendency to return to a 'pure' Islam, distancing oneself from outside influences and society. A search for a 'pure' Islam should not be seen as problematic as such. However, if the aspiration towards 'purity' in one's own religion and personal life goes hand in hand with intolerance and with disrespect for others (including people of the same faith) then it becomes a problem. Whereas most Muslim-democratic political groups seek a modern-day alternative to the Western political, legal and economic system, the 'puritans' consider such groups as 'infected' by Western influences. Modernity is presented as a Western invention and an instrument to oppress Muslims worldwide. These puritanical groups apply themselves mainly to dawa, or missionary work. They do not claim to be political, nor are they violent. Nevertheless, they create an intellectual and mental framework for extreme puritanical, intolerant and anti-western thoughts and attitudes. They strongly emphasise the re-Islamisation of the Muslim minorities in the West and preach an extreme segregation from Western societies. In contrast to political groups, however, puritanical dawa groups are poorly organised and do not possess a strict, hierarchical structure. Frequently they are diffuse networks, based on the thinking of specific individuals, imams or itinerant preachers. Their influence on especially young Muslims, who wrestle with an identity crisis, can be large through the use of the Internet and other modern technologies such as satellite dishes. The recipes they offer are simplistic, but in some cases this proves to be very attractive. They pretend that it is possible to be a good Muslim by banishing everything that is non-Islamic from one's lifestyle. A good Muslim has to follow strict puritanical rules concerning clothing, personal hygiene, manners of eating and conduct between men and women. They spread ultra-conservative ideas and present these as the only correct interpretation and reproduction of Islam. Although there is an increasingly conservative reflex in a large part of the Muslim communities in Europe, the conservatism and puritanism of these radical groups is nevertheless certainly not representative of Muslim communities as a whole.

A third form of radicalisation is visible in the 'ethnicisation' of being a Muslim in the West. Islam as a religion is not of the essence in this case, but being a Muslim and showing solidarity with the Ummah is. 'Ethnicisation' indicates an increasing solidarity with an imaginary community that is seen as a nation and in which the group's identity is based especially on a negative interpretation of the Other, being the non-Muslim. It is a form of Muslim communitarism which considers the oppression of Muslims worldwide to be at stake. The difficulties of integrating harmoniously in society have made them identify themselves exclusively as Muslims, emphasising socio-cultural rather than socio-economic rights. It is mainly a rising middle class that claims its place in the public space and political arena.

How to Handle the Radicalisation of Muslims?

The radicalisation of, especially, young Muslims in Europe is without doubt occurring. But radical groups still remain a marginal minority within the Muslim communities. Opinion makers and politicians should refrain from making frantic assessments about this radicalisation process. Some common sense would not go amiss. The situation is perhaps disturbing, but certainly not alarming.

The ability of Muslim communities to resist the radicalisation of certain segments within their midst is rather limited. This has to do with a range of factors. The more isolated Muslims become, the more their capacity to oppose this process will be hampered and the greater will be their inclination to remain silent about it, at least in the public arena. The fact that they feel a need to be on the defensive prevents them from openly criticising the different forms of radicalisation in their midst. In Muslim communities, however, there is a clear and largely shared aversion for violence. But frequently the radicalism of certain groups is not felt to be a problem – and rightly so, since not every form of radicalism is negative by definition. The fragile social position of Muslims does not contribute to their capacity to resist radicalisation. Individuals or groups that oppose radical Muslims are frequently considered as traitors and generally will not feel supported. But those who clearly show that they react against certain forms of radicalism out of a concern for the well-being of the Muslim community will encounter a certain amount of approval. Still, it remains a difficult balancing act. This should come as no surprise: when polarisation is widespread, nuanced positions usually are not welcomed.

Offering a counterweight to the different forms of radicalisation is not an easy undertaking. Undoubtedly, cooperating with moderate Muslims is extremely important. They must be supported and stimulated so they can uphold another voice. The dissemination of radical ideas must be stopped, not by simply repressing them, but by giving moderate alternatives a voice. Radical ideologies must receive a moderate and not-dogmatic answer. The 'disarmament' of the radical discourse must be done by experts, both within and outside the communities. The existing organisations and initiatives, as well as the authorities, media and educational institutions can play a meaningful role in disarming the radical discourse by promoting the circulation of democratic and moderate ideas.

As part of a de-radicalisation strategy, it is important to help in shaping the identity of young Muslims. The evolution should be resisted whereby individuals are forced to discard their hybrid identity for a rigid one. The promotion of self-criticism as far as one's own responsibility is concerned is to be emphasised as part of the creation of such a multi-faceted identity. It is also important to stimulate positive role models. Media, public institutions and others can play a role in upholding such role models.

Another aspect of such a strategy concerns the political and state authorities. Measures promoting integration, financing initiatives, measures related to immigration legislation, consultation with all communities involved (paying attention to the position of representation, commitment and integrity of the partners), repressive measures against unlawful activities, even possible cooperation with Muslim states from where radical-Islamist activities emerge and, last but not least, an endeavour to find a sustainable and equitable solution for international hotbeds like the Middle East, are all worth pursuing for their own sake, but also as part of an effort to stem radicalisation.

But all these efforts have little chance of success if the dramatic socio-economic situation of large groups of Muslims is not tackled. This obstructs integration. The fragile socio-economical position of Muslims in Europe often makes them more sensitive for radical discourses. Of course, there is no causal link between a bad economic situation and radicalisation, but the socio-economical factor nevertheless remains a basic problem. It creates frustrations that enable radicals to recruit.

The often young and radical participants in networks have nothing to do with international terrorist organisations. They are not 'recruited'. We are confronted with spontaneous forms of organisation. Young Muslims, from diverse ethnic origins, fall under the spell of radical Islam by what they hear, see and read, thanks to television, satellite dishes and the internet. They absorb this information and interpret it incorrectly, so that the door to extremism and violence is opened. They are often supported by girls and young women, especially converted Muslim women. Puberty and social frustration make young Muslims ripe for radicalisation. Normal juvenile identity-related uncertainty is reinforced because they do not feel at ease – a feeling that is reinforced by frustration and dissatisfaction about the situation in which they find themselves.

Radical alternatives of Islam offer them something to hold on to, something they have perhaps been searching for. These youngsters are attracted by fundamentalist messages. They bump into it on internet sites, in chat rooms and through online preachers. These internet media persuade, bind and instruct. Not only the government, but also the Muslim communities must invest more in these young Muslims. They have to find a better connection with the society they live in. Only on these conditions, will the chance to counter radicalisation be real. By reaching out a hand to young Muslims, we can prevent them from derailing. Furthermore, by offering them the correct interpretation of Islam and by teaching them the skills to improve their chances in daily life, we can prevent them from falling into the hands of a radical Islamism – and jihadi terrorism.

Muslim communities and diasporic communities with a Muslim background are not monoliths. Emphasising diversity will contribute to reducing the polarisation between Muslims and non-Muslims. This polarisation is the largest impediment to de-radicalisation. But we have to acknowledge also that no quick-fix solution to radicalisation exists – and that the (de)radicalisation of Muslims remains mainly the work of Muslims themselves.

Chapter 12

De-radicalisation and the Role of Police Forces

Glenn Audenaert

Before analysing what role police forces could or should play in a process of de-escalating radicalisation, it is essential to start from the traditional tasks police forces perform within any given society. Police forces all over the Western world may differ on a number of points, but they all have a common characteristic: their core business. This consists in upholding the law, preventing crime, assuring public tranquillity and helping and protecting the citizen. As we will show, this definition itself is already a source of ambiguity with regard to jihadi terrorism and the radicalisation challenge in Europe.

Terrorism is defined by law as a serious crime and subsequently treated as a clear and present danger by governments all over the world. Radicalisation and subsequent expression of extreme opinions, on the other hand, are to be considered as an exercise of the constitutionally guaranteed freedom of speech and/or as an expression of the freedom of religion – and thus to be tolerated. Outlining how (Belgian) police forces take on the first challenge is fairly straightforward. But the latter challenge confronts us with a more complicated situation, since it entails simultaneously conducting a high-performance law enforcement policy and contributing to de-radicalisation. Although both tasks seem incompatible at first glance, they most certainly are not. One could even go as far as stating that in today's environment it is not possible to be successful in the first without being equally active and participant in the second. To do so, this chapter will start with a brief survey of the recent law enforcement history of Belgium as a case study, to show how a severe crisis forced the Belgian police forces to a process of introspection and self-criticism that eventually led to a whole new police apparatus that redefined its mission and position within society as a whole.

Reengineering the Police Landscape to Contemporary Standards and Expectations

The international law enforcement community will certainly recall the institutional crisis Belgium experienced in the aftermath of the inquiry about the paedophile Marc Dutroux. The parliamentary commission that was established at the time came to the harsh conclusion that the police forces had manifestly failed in their mission. Moreover, the police, so it was established, operated in such a counterproductive and competitive mode, that they had been unable to prevent at least two of the murders. It is needless to say that these conclusions were deemed unacceptable by public opinion and the government alike. A number of academics, but also members of the police forces themselves, had been calling for years for a shake-up and a reorganisation of the Belgian police landscape, realising the utterly counterproductive nature of this engrained internal competition, but to no avail. The Dutroux drama proved to be the much-needed catharsis that permitted an overhaul of the traditional bureaucratic conservatism within the police and state apparatus. Radical changes resulted in a modern and up-to-date police force, able and willing to tackle the challenges of our times.

Until that period, Belgian police forces were amongst the last remaining institutes of a Napoleonic centralised state that in reality, subsequent to a number of domestic institutional reforms that had started in the 1970s, no longer existed. Only the real core businesses of a national state, such as justice, home affairs, budget, social security and defence, remained federal competences, whereas the largest part of governmental competences were devolved to Regions and Communities being more realistic components of Belgium's multicultural society. Reformers seized the opportunity to reshape the law enforcement apparatus in the spirit of the treaty of Amsterdam (1997) and reengineered it to be synchronised with the federal character of the Belgian state. Indeed, in the post-Amsterdam European Union, military organised police forces, or police forces with general competence but belonging to the armed forces, were no longer deemed suited. As is still the case in a number of member states, Belgium too possessed military police forces, called the Gendarmerie. This corps had played an essential role in domestic peacekeeping and law enforcement ever since the independence of the country. Although the corps was demilitarised in the beginning of the 1990s, as a structure it still remained a remnant of a Napoleonic era. The same can be said about the judiciary police, which was a solely repressive police force at the disposal of the crown prosecution service – hardly in respect of the separation of institutional powers. In this regard, the process of reengineering the police landscape had to recalibrate the forces in presence, putting emphasis on the importance of local communities – the cornerstone of any society – and avoiding an overlap with the federal (that is, the national) level. The new overall philosophy for the reform of the law enforcement apparatus was the formation of a nation-wide, high-quality service, highly participant and clearly focused on the population's needs and expectations. This encapsulates the very essence of what might and should be the role of police forces in de-radicalisation. Today, the 40,000 active police officers in Belgium fulfil their tasks within a quadruple bipolar dynamic:

- Upholding public tranquillity and law enforcement;
- Community policing and intelligence-led policing;
- First-line police care and specialised police care;
- Tolerant on petty crime[1] and applying special investigation techniques with regard to serious crime.

---

1 A nationwide criminal policy of tolerance towards first offenders of non-violent minor misdemeanours.

At first sight, one might draw the obvious conclusion that the fight against jihadi terrorism lies within the realm of law enforcement, intelligence-led policing, specialised police care and special investigation techniques – and de-radicalisation would then rather be characterised by a number of strategies and activities deployed within the remaining complementary fields, such as upholding public tranquillity, community policing, first-line police care and tolerant on petty crime. Although law-enforcement forces are only one of the many stakeholders in this multidisciplinary problem, there exists a clear cause-and-effect relationship between the way one defines and combats jihadi terrorism and radicalisation on the one hand, and eventual successes and the degree to which we contribute to the de-radicalisation of those segments of the population that are most concerned – in particular our immigrant communities with a Muslim background – on the other hand. It is all inherently linked to vision, professionalism, commitment, expertise, equipment and, last but not least, transparency.

As a service provider, police forces are managed through a 'strategic cycle': management of activities and operational goals, human resources management, and the management of means, the continuous learning process, and the customer perspective. Essential to the success of this cycle in a law enforcement environment is the establishment of an accurate picture of the overall jihadi threat. The more precise the general representation of the threat, the more accurate the action plan will be, subsequently enhancing the focus of the operational goals, and the greater the impact will be on jihadi terrorism. The quality of this picture depends for its part largely on the theoretical knowledge of the phenomenon in general, but even more on the ability to collect adequate, accurate and to-the-point information in this domain. To obtain, preserve and enhance this crucial information position, a number of critical success factors need to be secured on a permanent basis:

- All the stakeholders in the law enforcement apparatus need to scrupulously respect the limits of their legally defined competences. When matters are local in scope, the local police should remain in charge. The same goes for federal (that is, national) matters. Only when respecting that principle will the federal level be able to dispose of the necessary *quantitative capacity* to invest pro-actively, that is to say, to be able to secure the crucial information position with regard to groups or authors in the planning phase of a terror plot.
- To acquire an adequate information position, a law enforcement agency, such as the police, needs to develop a well-functioning network of codified informants. Subsequently, to stimulate this endeavour and to monitor the critical steps to take, one not only needs the right manager, in order to recruit and supervise the different sources that provide the much-needed useful information on a regularly basis, but one also needs the right contact officers. To manage the intelligence cycle with regard to the analysis, evaluation and exploitation of the information thus obtained, we furthermore need the right operational and strategic analysts. The second critical success factor is therefore the presence of sufficient *qualitative capacity*.
- The Belgian legislator provided the law enforcement apparatus with a particularly advanced legal system in the field of pro-active work in general

and interaction with informants in particular, offering a number of guarantees with regard to principles such as legality, subsidiarity, opportunity and feasibility. But it remains a tricky matter. It is therefore essential that the chief constable, as overall person in charge, remains highly attentive and functions as the guardian of *integrity*, implementing a policy of zero tolerance with regard to deviant behaviour and intolerance.

- It is obvious that in these matters, the competent law enforcement agency depends of a number of participant *partnerships*. It is insufficient only to collaborate with the usual partners such as the crown prosecution services, the office of the attorney general, the federal attorney, the intelligence services, the local police forces, the customs or the internal revenue service. Partnerships with less usual partners, such as other governmental departments (education) or foreign contacts, are just as essential. Police forces moreover need also to remain in constant and close relationship with the society they serve. Establishing such a relationship in the perspective of a partnership to collect intelligence data that will enhance our information position requires a strategy that is *authentic, transparent, open minded, legal and trustworthy*.

It should be considered obvious that any policy against jihadi terrorism can only be successful if and when supported by the entire community it affects, and specially the Muslim communities. To increase the performance of our anti-terrorist unit and thus its information position, the number of working service level agreements, the strong relationship with the political as well as with the judicial authorities, an assertive and active marketing policy within a relationship of understanding with the press, are all equally critical success factors for, what I believe to be, the only possible overall effective strategy. Taking into consideration that, within the European context, jihadi ideology and terrorism aims at disrupting our way of life and the values as defined in the European Treaty on Human Rights and in our respective national constitutions, the fight against this challenge should be of the highest priority and total resolve is required.

One should be attentive to the fact that the use of sophisticated investigative techniques may create an important democratic deficit with regard to the constitutional rights of the suspects. Every investigation should thus be the subject of a contradictory debate. But at the same time one has to recognise also that extraordinary situations may justify extraordinary measures – on the very strict condition of course that these are taken by democratic political authorities and that they are subsequently controlled by judicial authorities. History indeed teaches us that a democracy in danger needs more democracy, certainly not less. But it would be a grave error to have an ideological discussion with regard to jihadi terrorism and use the same arguments concerning the means of defence at the disposal of a democratic state as the ones that are used when dealing with international organised crime – or other forms of terrorism for that matter. Contrary to organised crime or other forms of terrorism that wish to change our society in order to serve their objectives or to implement an ideology, jihadi terrorism aims at its total destruction.

Democracy has to be defended by adequate means, adapted to a global economy, an encompassing IT and telecommunication environment, a European Union without internal borders and a global geopolitical situation with domestic security consequences. Although this does not mean or justify a never-ending inflation of rules of engagement, we need, however, while defending ourselves against the threat of jihadi terrorism, to adapt our strategy to the means the jihadis have at their disposal and are able and willing to use. So, in conclusion, with regard to jihadi terrorism and the underlying ideology of Islamist extremism, it is and will undoubtedly remain for the foreseeable future 'us versus them'.

A Trilateral Exercise

Only when and if the law enforcement community has a clear understanding of how and why radicalisation occurs and, subsequently, can shift to terrorism, police forces can play a significant part in the process of de-radicalisation. Ultimately, this rests upon an appropriate evaluation of who is 'us' and who is 'them'. Security has to be provided and guaranteed by the government. But it is a collective responsibility. Therefore, one has every right to expect police forces and the law enforcement community to guarantee the same level of services all over the territory. This, however, does not imply they can be present everywhere and at all times, nor that they are able to provide an adequate answer or response for each and every security issue at hand. To try to do so, the need to establish an ongoing dialogue with all stakeholders remains crucial and decisive. In the quest to understand Islamist extremism and jihadi terrorism we need to find an answer to the following questions: Can we identify the root causes of the radicalisation process? Can we subsequently understand its dynamics? Can we understand and/or explain the evolution from radicalisation to actual jihadi terrorism? And, finally, can we locate radicalisation and/or terrorism and subsequently anticipate it?

Undoubtedly, the primary source of knowledge is the Muslim communities themselves, as well as academia. We therefore need to engage a sustainable co-operation between these different actors based upon understanding, confidence and respect for each others' role, responsibility and expertise. It is my conviction that it is up to the law enforcement community, as a representative of the government, to launch such an initiative. Due to the historical and sometimes understandable negative perceptions of police forces, a certain apprehension for such an initiative from the Muslim communities and the academic world is plausible. In order to establish a fertile basis of understanding, police forces need to define and develop a long-term strategy towards co-operation with these partners, based on the same principles that govern our fight against terrorism. We need to invest sufficient and adequate means and people. We have to collaborate as partners. And we need to gain the respect of these partners through a genuine and constant attitude, characterised by integrity, legality, transparency, understanding, authenticity and loyalty.

This proposal may appear self-evident and logical, but in reality a lot remains to be done before a fertile environment for such a permanent endeavour is to be realised. As a matter of fact, there persists a good amount of scepticism and mistrust amongst the three prospective partners. But with the aim being to create a 'win-win' situation for all the actors involved, and security being the core business and responsibility of police forces, it is up to the law enforcement community to take the initiative. If one wants such a trilateral endeavour to succeed, police forces need to convince the Muslim communities and academia that they are serious about a number of issues:

- The law enforcement community has to make it crystal clear that they have no problem whatsoever with the free exercise of Islam – or with any religion for that matter – since this a basic constitutional right.
- Police forces and law enforcement agencies are clearly aware that only a very tiny minority at the margins of the Muslim communities is seized by Islamist extremism.
- Extreme opinions and radicalism belong to the domain of constitutional rights of free speech. Subsequently, where it is undeniable that every terrorist once was an extremist, it does not necessarily work the other way.
- An overwhelming majority within the Muslim communities rejects acts of terrorism and shares the same goal as all citizens, to live a life of happiness.
- We acknowledge that the social and economic situation of large parts of the immigrant communities with a Muslim background can be a source of frustration, especially in the light of problematic access to education, labour and housing.
- Police forces and the law enforcement community in general are neither blind nor deaf with regard to the international geopolitical situation and the way it may affect the Muslim communities.

These are the foundations upon which the initiative of the law enforcement community could be built in order to establish a partnership that could contribute to a de-radicalisation momentum. But as every relationship is based upon reciprocity, it is reasonable to expect that our prospective partners also have to understand and accept a number of assumptions:

- Although we can bring our findings to all of our partners within this partnership, be they governmental or not, international or domestic, we remain only one of the many players in the multidisciplinary endeavour to stimulate the emancipation and integration of the immigrant communities.
- We are by law obliged to fight crime, to gather information and to report to the judicial and administrative authorities. Therefore we are limited in the commitments we can undertake, the liberty of speech and the latitude to make promises.
- Nevertheless and although complementary, there needs to be an impermeable partition between this genuine effort to learn to analyse and understand each other, and the operational gathering of information.

If these terms of understanding can be reached, all kinds of initiatives might gradually become possible, insofar as they have the common objective to identify and subsequently eradicate the domestic root causes that are common to all terrorist groups. The best-placed actors to initiate such partnerships with our Muslim communities are the local police forces, due to their proximity. In Belgium, they started in the early

1990s with a certain amount of actions in the field of community policing, which met with increasing success. But, although they are our first source of information and are being sensitised for the potential danger of growing radicalisation, their first mission remains proximity policing. As a consequence, the federal (that is, national) level needs to join in the endeavour, not for opportunistic reasons, but for reasons of efficiency, authenticity and transparency. Once this dialogue is well-established, a dynamic of mutual learning, informing and – why not – acting, can be started up. As a police officer, I strongly believe that police forces can contribute in a major way to the de-radicalisation of our society, by showing through their actions that they care for the community – and communities – they serve, being especially sensitive to the plight of the most vulnerable groups in our midst. We understand the difficult task of parents and educators and wish to contribute to their effort and to support, if and where needed, their authority through our presence, lectures, information sessions, and so on. A lot is to be done and there is no time to waste.

The Process is of the Essence

Police forces can and should contribute to the endeavour to neutralise de-radicalising tendencies foremost by being as competitive as possible in the execution of their core business: insuring a secure environment and implementing a well-thought-out strategy with regard to radicalisation. This long-term strategy needs to take into account the major security questions and problems of the decade ahead that influence the root causes of radicalisation in our part of the world. Among these we can point to: the exponential growth of the Muslim population worldwide in the next decade; the persistent economical discrepancy between the European Union and the Middle East; a geopolitical situation that probably will not substantially improve in the foreseeable future; the need to assess and address the domestic root causes of radicalisation and terrorism; illegal immigration, which will remain a major topic for the foreseeable future; sophisticated IT and communication technology, globally and generally available; growing polarisation, identity politics and individualism within our societies; fundamental changes in the world economy; and, finally, the evolution of the demographic pyramid that will have major social and economic consequences on our populations.

Within this long-term strategy, the police forces have a specific role to play. As part of the law enforcement community, they can and should be a major player in a multidisciplinary approach involving all public and private stakeholders, taking into account all relevant security issues. In each of their core businesses short-, middle- and long-term strategies need to be conceptualised. Police forces, furthermore, need to focus on their performance and on the sociological environment in which they evolve. They have to be professional organisations with a high level of expertise in the field of radicalisation processes and de-radicalisation strategies. Their performance will depend on their level of expertise, their intelligence management and the availability of modern technology. Finally, police forces need to integrate their action into the entire security community as well as in the overall dynamic of the society they serve. The involvement of police forces in a strategy to de-radicalise society will not be met by success immediately. Participating in this process is of the essence, however. Moreover, the endeavour is not without risk. Nothing happens without taking risks and without taking risks nothing will happen. Police officers have a responsibility and a stake. As the song goes, we shall not sit down in silence, nor will we live in fear.

Chapter 13

The EU Response to Radicalisation and Recruitment to Terrorism

Gilles de Kerchove and Ran van Reedt Dortland

European efforts to study radicalisation and recruitment and formulate an appropriate government response to the problem are not new. Spain and the United Kingdom have long examined and addressed radicalisation and recruitment in the context of their fight against ETA and the IRA. Since the 1990s, in quite a number of European countries, teachers and social workers, as well as police and security services, have observed and reported radicalisation processes among disaffected immigrant communities, in particular Muslims for more than a decade. For instance, in 1998 the Dutch security service issued a carefully worded warning on the phenomenon of radicalisation among Muslim communities, which was controversial at the time but has been vindicated by subsequent events. The French security services have released important studies of the phenomenon. One of their recent publications sketches a worrying picture of radicalisation in the French penitentiary system, characterised by agitation among extremist detainees for special religious privileges and pressure on fellow inmates to support their demands.

Over the last decade, the EU Member States most affected by terrorism have benefited from these studies in pioneering policies to prevent and counter radicalisation and recruitment. Other EU countries, such as the new Member States in Central Europe, have not been confronted with terrorism to any extent. They are, however, keen to learn from the experience of Western Europe in order to prevent the emergence of similar problems at home. Following 9/11, Member States adopted a range of measures that were already in discussion for some time in order to enhance police and judiciary cooperation. Crucially important amongst these measures were the elaboration of a common definition of terrorist offences and the adoption of the European Arrest Warrant, facilitating the intra-EU cooperation on terrorism and the prosecution of suspected terrorists.

In the wake of the terrorist attacks in Madrid, European cooperation went a step further. For the first time the EU and its Member States addressed the factors conducive to the spread of terrorism. At the EU level, the first impetus for action against the factors that underlie the emergence of terrorism thus came relatively recently. The EU provides a platform for European governments to reach a common understanding of the phenomenon and of ways to tackle it. Common measures at the European Union level also supplement national policies and ensure that national governments demonstrate their unity and resolve in combating radicalisation and recruitment. In its Declaration on Combating Terrorism (25 March 2004), the

European Council committed itself to addressing the factors that contribute to radicalisation and recruitment. Further discussion in the EU on this matter led to the adoption of an EU Strategy for Combating Radicalisation and Recruitment in December 2005 (EU doc.14781/1/05). The European Commission made an important contribution to the development of the Strategy through its communication to the Parliament and the Council on 'Terrorist Recruitment: Addressing the Factors Contributing to Violent Radicalisation'.[1] The Strategy for Combating Radicalisation and Recruitment effectively implements one of the four strands of the EU Counterterrorism Strategy[2] which outlines the strategic framework for all counterterrorism efforts undertaken by the European Union ('prevent'; the other strands are 'pursue', 'prepare' and 'respond'). The development of the EU Strategy for Combating Radicalisation and Recruitment has been a challenge. Debate about the security aspects of counterterrorism is often of a practical nature and focuses on the best ways to achieve generally agreed objectives. In the case of the prevention of terrorism, not all experts agree on the objectives. What degree of 'integration' of ethnic and religious minorities is required to prevent the development of parallel societies? And what does 'integration' mean exactly? Should governments address the specific needs and problems of certain communities, or are they best advised to concentrate on a general integration policy? A lack of unanimity among experts is reflected in the wide variation in national approaches to the problem, rooted in the different cultures and traditions of Member States. The contrast between the French ('republican') and British ('multicultural') models of integration, and differing traditions concerning the separation between religion and state, are often cited in this context. Therefore, the debate on radicalisation and recruitment is often of a more political nature. It is a measure of the determination of the Member States to cooperate in the prevention of terrorism that they managed to overcome their differences and forge a collective approach.

Since its inception, the Strategy for Combating Radicalisation and Recruitment has given much greater prominence to the fight against these factors at the EU level. The Strategy has inspired a series of important new initiatives. The fight against radicalisation and recruitment is now at the heart of EU counterterrorism policy, where it belongs.

The EU Strategy for Combating Radicalisation and Recruitment: Underlying Principles

The Strategy for Combating Radicalisation and Recruitment is comprehensive, covering a range of policies across the three pillars of the Union. Most measures and policies in the Strategy are to be carried out at the national level by the Member States individually. In line with the principle of subsidiarity, the EU defines general principles and objectives and helps Member States to identify best practices. It also contains recommendations for collective measures at the EU level and guidelines

---

1 COM (2005) 313 final.

2 The EU Counter-Terrorism Strategy, doc. 14469/4/05; see also the EU Action Plan on Combating Terrorism, doc. 5771/1/06 and the report on its implementation, doc. 9589/06.

for policies in the framework of the Common Foreign and Security Policy. Implementation of the Strategy thus requires a collective effort by EU institutions and Member States. In the Strategy, the Council makes a clear choice to concentrate on the main threat with which Europe is confronted today: the type of terrorism inspired by an extremist interpretation of political Islamism. A careful choice of words is very important here. Terrorism is a method to pursue political objectives; as such, it is not confined to one belief system or political persuasion. The EU recognises that it has been confronted with various kinds of terrorism in its history and that it can use its past experiences in its current counterterrorism policies. Violent jihadis do not represent ordinary Muslims. On the contrary: while terrorists kill indiscriminately, Muslim majority countries and their populations are among the primary victims of the current wave of terrorism. Any identification of terrorism with one religion or culture is therefore false. It is also counterproductive, because it corroborates the message of the extremists, whose justification for the use of violence hinges on the notion of an existential clash between civilisations and religions.

In order to reduce effectively the threat of terrorism, the EU seeks partnerships. Internally, the EU seeks the active support of all citizens, of whatever social, cultural or religious background, in the fight against terrorism. And in pursuing its counterterrorism policies externally, the EU is actively seeking and promoting multilateral cooperation. The Union recognises the importance of globalisation in the context of radicalisation. Terrorists do not respect borders or cultural differences but exploit these to plan attacks and make new recruits – today more than ever. European terrorists may have been recruited by propagandists residing in the Gulf region, whilst young men in North Africa may undergo a process of radicalisation under the influence of radical websites hosted in EU countries. The Strategy therefore recognises the importance of cooperation with third countries in the fight against radicalisation and recruitment to terrorism, and it addresses global problems such as the role of the internet in radicalisation processes and emigration and travel movements of terrorist recruiters.

The EU recognises that future measures against radicalisation and recruitment should be informed by the latest state of research. To this end, the European Commission has brought together a group of eminent academic experts to assist the European institutions in developing policies and measures to address the problem.[3] Funds have been made available for specific academic studies.[4] On the basis of expert assessments and input from interlocutors in academia and Muslim communities, the European Union distinguishes three types of measures to tackle radicalisation and recruitment. First, the EU strives to disrupt the activities of the networks and individuals who draw people into terrorism. Second, the Union sets out to foster voices of mainstream opinion who challenge extremist ideologies. And third, by promoting security, justice, democracy and opportunity for all, the EU works to tackle the climate in which terrorist propagandists and recruiters thrive.

---

3 Commission Decision of 19 April 2006 setting up a group of experts to provide policy advice to the Commission on fighting violent radicalisation, OJ L 111 of 25.4.2006, p. 9.

4 A call for proposals (published in OJ C 21 of 30.1.2007, p. 6) identifies seven themes under which specific projects can be financed.

Countering the Factors that Facilitate Incitement to Terrorism and Terrorist Recruitment

Unsurprisingly perhaps, given their mostly apolitical nature, measures to disrupt the activities of terrorist recruiters proved the easiest to agree on. EU policies in this area focus on monitoring and penalising preparations for recruitment. In the legal field, United Nations Security Council Resolution 1624 (2005) and the Council of Europe Convention on the Prevention of Terrorism provide a framework for the prohibition of incitement to terrorism. The European Commission is currently examining the need for adaptation of important legal instruments, such as the Framework Decision on Combating Terrorism,[5] the Television without Borders Directive (1997) and the E-Commerce Directive (2000), so as to take into account the prevention of incitement as well as the dissemination of information on bomb making. Member States are looking into the possibilities of enhanced exchange of information on the expulsion of religious leaders involved in incitement and recruitment.

Another important focus is the development of community policing. Monitoring of radicalisation and recruitment is often a very local matter. Teachers, community workers and police officers are often the first to be aware of recruitment activities and of feelings of frustration and alienation that may spark a radicalisation process. Community policing plays a particularly important role in detecting radicalisation and provides local communities with possibilities to address the problem at an early stage. EU Member States are therefore committed to ensure that sufficient attention is given to community policing. The EU has also started work on the prevention of radicalisation among prison inmates through an exchange of information and best practices. Particular attention is given to the role of religious leaders in penitentiary facilities, prisoner rehabilitation programmes, and the detention circumstances of detainees[6] who are likely to spread extremist views.

Security services and academic experts are increasingly worried about incitement and recruitment on the internet. To address this problem, the European Union intends to create conditions for exchange of information in order to ensure that national authorities dispose of all relevant information. Auto-regulation among internet providers, which is already applied in the cases of racism and child pornography, could also be helpful.

---

5 OJ L 164 of 22.6.2002, p. 3.

6 In France, the case of Khaled Kelkal, responsible for the wave of terrorist attacks in 1995, has been widely studied and may be seen as emblematic. While serving a prison sentence for petty crime, Kelkal became friends with a fellow inmate who espoused an extremist form of political Islamism. He became much more religious, studied Arabic and religion, and became militant himself. After his release from prison Kelkal was recruited by the GIA and tasked to commit the highly publicised murder of the imam of the Paris Mosque. In the months prior to his premature death during a shoot-out with the police, he was also involved in the bombing of the metro station Saint-Michel and other terrorist attacks.

Reducing the Appeal of Extremist Ideologies

In order to attract new recruits, terrorists distort conflicts around the world as supposed proof of an existential struggle between the West and Islam. It is not always easy for governments to confront these views directly. Muslim voices, inside and outside of the European Union, speak with much greater authority on this subject. The EU therefore has a clear interest in empowering voices of mainstream Muslim opinion. It does so within the borders of the Union and it reaches out to Muslims in third countries through dialogue and technical assistance programmes.

Respected religious and political leaders of Muslim communities are often best placed to challenge the message of extremists who invoke Islam to spread hatred and justify the use of violence. Yet vocal government support for these important voices may sometimes discredit them in the eyes of their followers and thus prove counterproductive. The EU and Member States' governments are keenly aware of this challenge and are working to facilitate an internal debate within Muslim communities from a modest position in the background, if their support is welcome and required. They also recognise that they need to be genuinely prepared to listen to potential grievances if their commitment is to be taken seriously, and fight all forms of discrimination and racism. The EU is determined to make sure that it does not inadvertently bolster extremist ideologies through a lack of clear communication on counterterrorism and other policies that may influence radicalisation processes. The European Union and its Member States are therefore paying attention to the consistency of their message and to the way in which it is worded. They are also examining new ways to deliver their message to audiences that are difficult to reach.

The Union participates in inter-cultural dialogue meetings in various parts of the world and facilitates such meetings in Europe. The Anna Lindh Foundation, an institution established in the framework of the Barcelona Process, is promoting inter-cultural dialogue with the EU's southern neighbours in North Africa and the Middle East. The decision to make 2008 the European Year of the Intercultural Dialogue will give a further impetus to EU efforts to reach out to others and breach cultural dividing lines. Work in this field is not always straightforward. Some counter-terrorist practitioners question the value of inter-cultural dialogue for counterterrorism purposes, as it tends to bring together moderate leaders who are largely immune to extremist ideologies. In addition, the fight against terrorism is not always the best vantage point for outreach activities, because sometimes it may be construed as a purely Western agenda that disregards the interests of the developing world. As engagement with Muslim communities within and outside the EU serves many important policy objectives, not just counterterrorism, organisations in European civil society, not governments, are often best able to lead in this field. The EU is convinced that inter-cultural dialogue can assist moderate leaders in their efforts to stem the tide of extremism and prevent future misunderstandings.

Legitimacy is an essential condition for effective counterterrorism policy. Respect for human rights, fundamental freedoms and the rule of law is an integral part of the EU's over-arching counterterrorism strategy. These values are particularly important in the context of the prevention of radicalisation. Terrorist recruiters exploit violations of human rights to attract new followers and to stigmatise human rights and fundamental freedoms as hypocritical. The European Union is determined not to compromise democratic values in the fight against terrorism. It refrains from deploying the arbitrary violence used by the terrorists themselves, thereby denying them a potential propaganda tool. Effective counterterrorism measures and the protection of human rights are not conflicting but mutually reinforcing objectives. While the EU and the United States have developed close cooperation in the fight against terrorism, the former has made clear its serious concerns about the use of secret detention facilities by the latter. In its relations with other partners, too, the Union systematically discusses the issue of human rights in relation to counterterrorism.

The United Nations, the only truly global forum for the fight against terrorism, has a key role in mobilising the international community and in providing the international legal framework for counterterrorism. The adoption of a Global Counterterrorism Strategy, similar to the Strategy of the EU, is an important development, demonstrating the unity and determination of all states in combating terrorism. The EU will work to implement the Strategy and is ready to help others to do the same. In its external relations, the Union continues to promote universal adherence to, and full implementation of, all 16 UN Conventions and Protocols related to acts of terrorism. Conclusion of a Comprehensive UN Convention on International Terrorism, which has been under negotiation for many years, remains an EU priority. Such a convention should contain a clear definition of terrorism and an unequivocal condemnation of terrorism in all its forms and manifestations. The Comprehensive Convention would complement the existing 16 'sectorial' UN Conventions and Protocols that address specific aspects of the fight against terrorism (such as airport and aircraft security, the prohibition of terrorist bombings, the financing of terrorism, and so on).

Combating the Structural Factors Contributing to Radicalisation and Recruitment

The structural factors contributing to radicalisation and recruitment include perceived or real injustices, bad governance, political repression, and a lack of education and economic or political opportunities (see ICG 2006a). The fight against these factors is inextricably entwined with efforts to reduce the appeal of extremist ideologies. While terrorist recruiters exploit structural factors to spread their extremist ideology, these factors also generate the frustration and alienation that make some people receptive to their message. That is why the European Union remains determined to preserve and protect its democratic values domestically and to promote these in its external relations.

The fight against the structural factors contributing to radicalisation and recruitment is perhaps the most important objective of the Strategy for Combating Radicalisation and Recruitment, even if its results are the most difficult to measure.

Many policies in this field, such as the fight against racism and discrimination,[7] efforts to create employment for young people, and projects to stimulate integration, have been in place for a long time in all EU Member States. These policies have not necessarily been introduced to tackle the conditions in society that may give rise to terrorism. The Strategy for Combating Radicalisation and Recruitment serves an additional reminder of their relevance.

Within the Union, the Commission is engaged in a number of important programmes to raise awareness of the importance of democratic values, human rights and citizenship issues among young people. The Erasmus Mundus Programme enables students and scholars from third countries to participate in courses within the EU. Externally, through its assistance programmes managed by the European Commission, the EU helps more than 80 countries across the globe to develop good governance and enhance the capacity and quality of their judiciary, prosecutors, police, customs and border management. The Commission also supports a great number of third countries in the structural development of their higher education systems. In addition, the Union is currently developing new programmes for specific assistance in the field of counterterrorism and intends to include initiatives that address the factors underlying the emergence of terrorism. The EU has recently adopted the Stability Instrument, which enables the EU to spend Community funding in new policy areas and contains specific provisions for the fight against terrorism. The Union's contribution to a lasting peace in conflict zones also deserves to be mentioned in this context. EU military missions from Aceh to Bosnia deprive terrorists of a recruiting base by bringing stability and democracy to areas ravaged by war and arbitrary rule.

Conclusion

The EU response to radicalisation and recruitment is realistic and practical. The EU does not claim to have all the answers and is willing to listen and take into account the views of academic experts and its own citizens, in particular those most affected by terrorism and by the government policies launched to counter it. The European Union is aware that it needs to cooperate with others to prevent radicalisation and recruitment. Many measures to prevent radicalisation and to combat incitement and recruitment are not put in place at the EU level, but at the national or local level. And the EU works together with third countries in order to enhance the effectiveness of these measures. In the knowledge that its democratic values constitute its most valuable asset in the fight against terrorism, the European Union is determined to protect and promote these in order to achieve long-term success in the prevention of radicalisation and recruitment.

---

7 See the 2006 *Report of the European Monitoring Centre on Racism and Xenophobia: Muslims in the EU. Discrimination and Islamophobia*, p. 114.

Zeitgeist and (De-)Radicalisation[1]

Rik Coolsaet and Tanguy Struye de Swielande

> It takes more than the speeches of bin Laden to turn an
> Islamist into a terrorist. It takes years of feeling abused.
>
> – Rachid, a 31-year-old Algerian, living illegally in London (2003)[2]

Large parts of the world population fear terrorism. Yet at the same time this fear seems to be receding somewhat. In January 2007, in the annual CEO poll at the eve of the World Economic Forum in Davos, terrorism ranked only 11th as a major threat – down from 5th place in 2004 and 1st place in 2003. During the meeting itself, the issue largely dropped off the agenda, as the focus turned to climate change. This slipping of terrorism as a major concern is a trend that has gone on for several years, notwithstanding major terrorist attacks that have occurred since 9/11. This changing atmosphere might help in decoupling two issues that for far too long have become closely intertwined in people's mind in Europe: integration and terrorism. Especially since the 2001 attacks, integration, multiculturalism and national cohesion were increasingly viewed from a national security perspective, thus confusing issues whose origins, dynamics and remedies fall within different categories.

The riots in the French suburbs in 2005 offer a case in point. Almost immediately after the first riots broke out, speculation arose about manipulation by Islamist radicals. Even after the French Renseignements Généraux confirmed that the involvement of Islamists was nil, some media have continued to refer to the rioters as 'Muslim', thus obfuscating the social and political causes driving these events. The sloppy use of the word 'Muslim' is characteristic for the debate about radicalisation and terrorism in Europe. Many tend to privilege the use of the word 'Muslim' to denominate communities originating from predominately Muslim countries. Contrary to widespread popular belief, however, there is no such thing as 'the' Muslim community. In fact, what non-Muslims see as a community is in reality a complex body full of contradictions and divergences along ethnic, ideological and generational lines and not keen on presenting themselves as one single entity or, being secular, do not see themselves as members of a religious community (Roy 2005, 143). Many differences, fundamental and secondary, exist. Discussion rages widely on social and religious issues, exactly as is the case within society itself. As

---

1 We would like to thank Dr John Horgan, Director of International Center for the Study of Terrorism at Penn State, for his timely remarks on the draft of this epilogue.

2 Quoted in *The Observer*, 9 March 2003.

Jocelyne Cesari has researched, the identity of individuals within these communities is defined as well by the society they now live in, by the fact that they originate from recent immigration, by their social and economic situation, their ethnic and national origins and – indeed also – by Islam. They have multiple identities, just like everybody else.

The Lebanese-born French essayist Amin Maalouf offers a nice case in point. He noticed that his friends constantly questioned him about what he really was 'deep in his soul', Frenchman or Lebanese. Since he apparently failed to convince them that he was both and that both parts could not be detached one from another, he explored the issue in depth in his timely *In the Name of Identity: Violence and the Need to Belong*. One's identity, he spells out, is a shifting composite of a great number of different, often conflicting, allegiances and attachments, including one's allegiances to one's family, neighbourhood, village and country, to one's religious, ethnic, linguistic and racial group, to one's profession, favourite soccer team or political movement.

Lumping all these differences and specificities together into one overarching characteristic and thus transforming distinct communities into a single 'ethnic' community – 'Muslims' – privileges what is only one aspect of their identity to the detriment of all others, which are as crucial and important. Doing so, one fails to notice the very real *national* differences between individuals and immigrant communities living in Holland, Belgium or Germany – even if their families originate from exactly the same background. It leads to a religion-based strategy that tries to tackle difficulties and issues that have nothing to do with religion. The French scholar Olivier Roy thus warned for attempts to manage migration issues through imams and city districts through mosques (Roy 2005, 234).

Others, therefore, would by and large prefer to use a somewhat longer definition, such as 'immigrant communities with a Muslim background', as a way of stressing that migratory dynamics might be the crux of the matter, even if specific cultural or religious aspects also play a role. This is more than mere linguistics. The way one perceives reality is usually more important than reality itself, since it is upon 'the opinions about facts – very often quite erroneous opinions – that men act in shaping their conduct and the world around them', Norman Angell, the legendary 1933 Nobel Prize for Peace Laureate, wrote in his autobiography. The issue of radicalisation makes no exception.

Radicalisation: A Context-bound Process *Par Excellence*

Individuals do not become radicals in a vacuum. Being radical, moreover, is not illicit – and even when it goes against the law, it can be legitimate. Most of today's democratic states would not exist lest for some radicals who took it upon themselves to organise the revolt against a foreign yoke or an autocratic regime. The same goes for the anti-abolition societies, the suffragettes (the British radical suffragettes actually engaged in an incendiary bombing campaign in the 1910s, using over 50 devices), Martin Luther King's and Malcolm X's civil rights movement and many other civil society campaigns. As Bernhard Shaw once famously quipped: 'The reasonable man adapts himself to the world; the unreasonable one persists in trying to adapt the world to himself. Therefore, all progress depends on the unreasonable man.' Suffice to swap 'reasonable' for 'radical' and one realises that societies indeed progress thanks to its radicals too.

In any given society there will always exist a certain number of radicals.[3] Their radicalism can take a wide variety of forms and appearances. It can be expressed through a political, religious or social discourse. It can be non-violent or violent, and in the latter case it can be either occasional or systematic. Terrorism belongs to that latter category. Terrorism can indeed be characterised as the systematic recourse to violence by a radical individual or group of radicals. Finally, radicalism sometimes remains limited to individuals or small groups, but sometimes it can gain significant traction, either by capitalising on widespread sympathy, or by being able to draw a significant number of people to join the radicals' ranks.

When significant, the diverse radicalisation processes share a number of common structural features. First and foremost, they surf upon an enabling environment, which is essentially characterised by a widely shared sense of deprivation – real or perceived – by a group of individuals, combined with a sense of inequity. '*It's unfair*' has always proved to be a powerful force in politics and a prime mover for change. When people resent inequity, they are prone to radicalisation. A typical characteristic of such an environment, that is conducive to radicalisation processes, is deeply engrained mutual distrust, offering a favourable framework for depicting the 'adversary' in simple terms, an Us-vs.-Them paradigm.

A second common characteristic of all forms of radicalisation is that it always takes place at the intersection of a personal history and that enabling environment. Not all individuals who share the same fate of deprivation or are living in the same polarised environment, turn to radicalism. Specific personal characteristics or events are needed in order to trigger the process. This can range from a tragic experience, such as the death of a family member, to mundane incidents, as the authorities' refusal to finance a local youth club – as Ruud Peters discovered when analysing Mohammed Bouyeri's personal itinerary. Radicals or terrorists are most certainly not a group of mentally disturbed lunatics, as psychiatrist and psychological research has abundantly made clear – and Noor Huda Ismail vividly depicts as far as members of Jamaah Islamiyah are concerned. Those who engage in terrorist activity are essentially as normal as anyone else, and unremarkable in psychological terms (Horgan 2005, 62).

Whatever the radicalisation process, the course one follows always starts with a trigger, then proceeds fast or slowly, but usually follows the same succession of steps: a growing mental dissociation with society, followed by a 'politicisation' of the individual's views, usually (but not always) implying searching for others with a similar worldview in order to promote one's own agenda (see also Sageman 2004b; Taarnby 2005a). In this process groupthink gradually eliminates alternative views, simplifies reality and dehumanises all who are not subscribing to their extreme views. To illustrate this end result, one can recall that when arrested, Emile Henry, the

---

3 We would like to thank Dr Helmut Gaus, former Chair of the Department of Political Science at Ghent University, for our discussions on this topic.

late-nineteenth-century French anarchist terrorist defended his attacks on innocent people in pubs and restaurants with the argument: 'There is no such thing as an innocent *bourgeois*.'

The Israeli scholar Ehud Sprinzak, who authored a major study on political extremism, has described at length these phases that occur in the social-political field facilitating radicalisation. According to him, a radicalising individual goes trough three successive phases: a crisis of confidence, a conflict of legitimacy and a crisis of legitimacy (Sprinzak 1990, 78–85). A radicalisation process that may have terrorism as its end result is, according to Sprinzak:

> ... the psychopolitical product of a profound process of delegitimation that a large number of people undergo in relation to the established social and political order. Although most of the participants in this process are capable of preserving their sense of reality, a few are not. Totally consumed by their radicalism, they imagine a nonexistent 'fantasy war' with the authorities and expend themselves in the struggle to win it. Ideological terrorism, in the final analysis is the simulated revolution of the isolated few. (Sprinzak 1990, 81)

The third and last common feature of all radicalisation processes is that violence is always the action of a few within the larger group or community whose fate is at stake and whose plight they invoke to try to justify their acts. They form fringe groups that act as self-declared vanguard groups. In all past processes of radicalisations, as Martha Crenshaw indicates in Chapter 3, the number of individuals to choose violence as their privileged method has been extremely small. Violent radicalisation, and especially its systematic form, namely terrorism, is indeed only the far end of a wide array of possible radical attitudes and expressions. One could thus say that it is one of several potential expressions of protest, but one that uses tactics that in a given society are not consider acceptable or 'normal' means of political action.

Besides these common characteristics, each and every mode of radicalisation also has its own specific characteristics. They can vary in form and appearance from explicitly apolitical to violent, from identity-driven to religious, political or social, from an individual option to group mobilisation. Every ideology, belief system or religion can be the face of radicalisation. Today's Islamist radicalisation is the most prominent form of radicalisation. Nevertheless, even if Islamist radicals themselves take this position, Islam is not of the essence.

Growing European Consensus on the Nature of the Threat

In December 2005 the European Council adopted the European Union Counter-Terrorism Strategy. It offered a strategic concept, multidimensional in character, corresponding to the multifaceted reality that terrorism is. It rests upon four pillars, as Gilles de Kerchove and Ran van Reedt Dortland outline in this book. The fact that the very first pillar of its strategy is titled 'Prevent' illustrates a strategic difference between the European fight against terrorism and the US War on Terror. 'Prevent' is here to be understood as 'stemming the radicalisation process by tackling the root causes which can lead to radicalisation and recruitment'. Notwithstanding rare

American voices warning that their country has overreacted to 9/11,[4] to the outsider it looks as if the US administration and the foreign policy establishment at large (CAP 2005) still widely perceive international terrorism as a global Islamist insurgence and a major external threat to be eradicated – quite understandably so in view of the suddenness and magnitude of the 9/11 attacks, but also deliberately sponsored by the US administration for ulterior political motives, as Martha Crenshaw argues.[5]

Europe never wholly shared the perception that the attacks of 9/11 'revealed the outlines of a new world' or 'provided a warning of future dangers of terror networks aided by outlaw regimes and ideologies that incite the murder of the innocent, and weapons of mass destruction that multiply destructive power' (Bush 2005c). Characteristic of the European approach to counter-terrorism has been the constant reminder of the need to address socio-economic and political root causes of terrorism. As of late, within European policy circles the term 'root causes' has become 'politically incorrect', since it gives the impression of condoning terrorism as a legitimate tool for redressing grievances. Now the wording 'conditions conducive to the spread of terrorism' is preferred, but the basic assumptions of the EU counter-terrorism philosophy remain unchanged.

The difficulty for the EU to be effective in fighting terrorism is that its member states remain the primary actors in this domain. The EU as a Union mostly provides only for a framework that adds value to the action of the member states, by strengthening national capabilities, facilitating European cooperation, developing collective capability and promoting international partnership. But in the end, member states remain the ultimate guarantors for intra-European counter-terrorism strategy to bear results. This is all the more so, since the EU gradually zoomed in on the 'radicalisation process' as the main focal point for combating terrorism within Europe. Since mid-2004 European counter-terrorism thinking has rapidly converged around 'radicalisation' as the single most important 'root cause' for terrorism within Europe. The consensus view on terrorism amongst European officials is that jihadi terrorism resembles more or less a patchwork of self-radicalising cells, without any central engine and without any central organisational design, stitched together by occasional and mostly opportunistic links (see also Pillar 2004, 101–13) – just like in a patchwork, without any leader, without any hierarchy, often lacking the operational sophistication of the former al-Qaeda operatives. Terrorism as seen through European eyes is very much viewed as a bottom-up rather than a top-down process. Edwin Bakker and Ruud Peters buttress this consensus, when concluding that no *structural* relationships exist between most European jihadis and al-Qaeda.

Such a patchwork is very similar in character to the left-wing terrorist groups in Europe in the 1970s – or the nineteenth-century anarchists for that matter. There is almost nobody nowadays who sticks to the notion, as was still subscribed to in 2005,

---

4 Recently, the most prominent has undoubtedly been Mueller, J. (2006). Earlier observers making the same argument, include Fred Hiatt, in *Washington Post*, 9 June 2003; Brent Scowcroft, in *New York Observer*, 20 September 2004; Zbigniew Brzezinski, in *Washington Post*, 4 December 2005; Joseph Ellis, in *New York Times*, 28 January 2006.

5 Zbigniew Brzezinski makes exactly this point in an Op-Ed in the *Washington Post* of 25 March 2007.

that 'most of the terrorist threat to Europe originates outside the EU' (Council of the European Union, 2005). This is not to say that no al-Qaeda members remain at large. Most are killed or detained, but some have thus far escaped arrest. Some are trying to regroup, especially in Pakistan, which is now a major pool of new jihadi networks. They represent what Paul Pillar in the first chapter dubs the 'children' of al-Qaeda. Even if these South Asian jihadis have grown somewhat more threatening since 2006, nothing indicates that we are witnessing the 'resurgence' of al-Qaeda, implying the restoration of the ability of Osama bin Laden and Ayman al-Zawahiri to exert any operational control, like they once did. They represent only one out of the many networks, composed of activists that are not being radicalised and recruited by outsiders, but of their own volition. Indeed, the importance of al-Qaeda remnants is dwarfed in the face of the more important dynamics of 'self-radicalisation'. This bottom-up process of self-radicalisation – as opposed to the top-down situation when the al-Qaeda network was still at the height of its power – confronted the European counter-terrorism community and experts with the limits of tackling terrorist recruitment by zooming in on radicalisation, as initially envisaged. This was originally thought to be a rather straightforward tactic. Indeed, identifying particular 'hot spots' where this radicalisation might potentially occur – radical mosques, prisons,[6] schools, neglected city districts and internet chat rooms, and so on – and then disrupting the process by which radicals influenced potential recruits, seemed clear-cut, even if the execution of this strategy would be demanding. However, starting in 2004–2005, European intelligence and police agencies started to observe a growing tendency of self-radicalisation and self-recruitment of individuals. Self-recruitment has now become a more important source of jihadi recruitment than any organised international network of recruiters and takes place outside customary meeting places such as mosques. This then raises the more demanding question – beyond disrupting the message and the messenger – why both message and messenger have become so successful with specific individuals, groups or communities. Ultimately, the most crucial question for European counter-terrorism officials became: why are some individuals and/or groups receptive to radicalisation, ultimately leading some to the systematic use of violence – terrorism? This constitutes the real core issue of jihadi terrorism today.

The Structural Features of Contemporary Radicalisation Processes

Enabling Global Environment

As said above, for radicalisation – a normal feature in politics and society since time eternal – to become significant, an enabling environment is needed that acts as a booster. The most intricate aspect of understanding the radicalisation process is the link between the global and the local. Since individuals do not turn into radicals in

---

    6 The group 'Martyrs pour le Maroc', created by the Algerian Mohammed Achraf, is an example of a network originating from the thousands of North-African inmates in the (Spanish) prisons, detained for minor criminal offences.

a vacuum, what is the exact nature of this link? Put otherwise, even assuming that local root causes are the main driving forces behind jihadi terrorism, what explains that Islamic and Islamist radicalisation today occurs on all continents?

On this there is no consensus among experts, even among the contributors of this volume. To some, Islamic and Islamist radicalisation is essentially a specific, Muslim-related question. Even while acknowledging that exogenous factors most certainly influence this radicalisation process, its driving forces are considered to be specifically located within the Muslim world and communities. Others, including the authors of this epilogue, consider the Islamic and Islamist radicalisation processes to be part of a worldwide phenomenon in which structural features at the global level induce radicalisation within all religious, ethnic and cultural communities. One is tempted to call this by its German name: the Zeitgeist.

International surveys often offer fascinating reading. They bring us as close as one can get to gauging the mood of the world's citizenry. What are the main strands in the mood of today's world citizen? Two features seem to make up the essence of today's global Zeitgeist. One, the world citizen feels at a loss and ill at ease in the complex world surrounding him. Secondly, he resents the state of the world as fundamentally lopsided. The former facilitates polarisation. The latter stimulates radicalisation.

Global Malaise

In a 2006 New York Times/CBS News poll, just 29 per cent of Americans said the country was headed in the right direction. National gloom is not an exclusive American mood however. If there is one feeling today that unites people on all continents, it is their shared uneasiness about the state of affairs, both in their own countries and in the rest of the world. That was one of the findings of an international Pew survey in 2002. The more than 38,000 people interviewed were overwhelmingly dissatisfied with the way things were going in their countries. Solid majorities in nearly every country in every region surveyed said they were unhappy with the state of their nation. Their assessment of the state of the world was even more negative. The reason for so much global malaise is the rapid pace of change, both in world politics and in our daily life. To many, the world is definitely not flat, but rather caught up in a white-water rafting race. In 2004 the Dutch Socio-Cultural Planning Bureau confirmed that a lot of Dutch citizens – and through extrapolation, a lot of people worldwide – shared the feeling that the familiar environment they had been living in was disappearing rapidly. When society changes too fast, feelings of insecurity set in (SCP 2004), and for those who feel insecure, dangers always loom larger than they really are. Chapter 2 in this volume is a case study in point.

What explains the rapid mutation of our familiar surroundings? The Cold War ended and the major ideologies no longer provided for comfort, since they ware unable to give meaning to a rapidly changing world. The technological mutation, in which both information technology and biotechnology will have the same impact as the steam engine and electricity in previous industrial revolutions, pushed the world into a post-industrial era and the individual into uncharted territory. Globalisation brought the world into everybody's living home, but confronted them at the same time with a bewildering complexity of an immense number of local situations. And as times were getting tougher, the polity seemingly withdrew its protective cloak. As described by Joseph Stiglitz, the world began its love affair with deregulation (Stiglitz 2002, 76–89). Governments claimed that citizens were smart enough to make it on their own. As a consequence, people started to feel as if society existed for the economy instead of the other way around.

Today's world is thus more than usually in transition. As a result, people have lost the familiar beacons that had enabled them to construct their identity. Identity provides for a sense of togetherness, for certainties and for self-esteem. Individuals need an identity in order to be able to interact with others. But one's identity is not set in stone. We construct our identity in relation to very specific reference points surrounding us: the world, the state, the society we live in and finally our individual life story. He who loses his identity loses his certainties and his self-esteem. With all identity beacons adrift, people felt alone and abandoned. When faced with chaos and uncertainties, men then grope, just like castaways, for new certainties to hold on to: New Age, cults, spirituality, nationalism and – often – religion. Sometimes these new guiding principles provide for a positive outlook, such as the World Youth Day in Roman Catholicism or the Fethullah Gülen movement within Turkish Islam.

But often they only provide for a dangerous surrogate for the lost beacons of our identity, steering people towards a mental wall dividing the world into a protective 'Us' and a threatening 'Them', according to Tariq Ramadan (Ramadan 2006), leaving no middle ground, no room for nuances or tolerance. The religious revival had already started in the 1970s, but it gained enormous traction in the following decades. In 2004 both the UNDP and the US National Intelligence Council noted that in the years to come religious identity was likely to become an increasingly important factor in how people define themselves. Both reports mentioned the rise of *identity politics*: 'In vastly different contexts and in different ways ... people are mobilizing anew around old grievances along ethnic, religious, racial and cultural lines ...' according to the UNDP. Within all major religions, the NIC noted, the same tendency towards radicalisation exists, producing a whole new generation of activists with the same characteristics: 'A worldview that advocates change of society, a tendency toward making sharp Manichaean distinctions between good and evil, and a religious belief system that connects local conflicts to a larger struggle' (UN 2004).

In the Muslim world, from Sudan to Indonesia, this translated into a salafi renaissance, based upon a literalist reading of scripture and holding out the prospect of a return to the seemingly simple world at the time of the Prophet.[7] After the Shiite revolution by Ayatollah Khomeini in 1979 and the defeat of the Red Army in Afghanistan, Islamism (also called political Islam) made its definite entrance on the international scene. Fringe groups at the margins of the Islamist movements then carried the reasoning all the way down to its extremist end, splitting up the world into Us and Them and disposed to wage jihad, first against the 'near enemy', their lapsed fellow-Muslims, and subsequently against the rest of the world, the 'far enemy'. In immigrant communities in Europe a 'cut and paste' Islam emerged, in

---

7 See also the special issue of *The Muslim World*, (95)3, July 2005.

which individuals appropriated the right to interpret the Quran without the lengthy studies and training that usually were considered essential in order to become an *ulema*, or Islamic scholar.

In the United States, the literalist reading of the Bible was the inspiration for the revival of Christian or Evangelical fundamentalism. In the United States, some born-again Christian extremists went so far as to bomb abortion clinics. Inside and outside the United States, this specific thread in Christianity has become one of the fastest growing religions, especially prosperous in Latin America and Africa. In common with the European 'born-again' Islam, it also does not have a particularly demanding theology, since anyone can become a preacher without the rigours of traditional theological schooling. 'Born-again' interpretation of Islam and Christianity furthermore share a particular force of attraction to uprooted individuals that feel ill at ease in the rapid, modern-day life.

In India, radical Hindu nationalists attempted to redefine the nature of the nation along the Hindu religious identity and in doing so re-appropriated heroes from a distant past, such as Mother India, Rama and Hanuman. The same goes for the Sikhs, Jewish fundamentalists in Israel, such as the Gush Emunim, and Buddhists in Sri Lanka. In Japan the Aum Shinrikyo cult, which claimed to be associated with Buddhism, poisoned commuters on the Tokyo subway system in 1995.

Only Western Europe seemed to stand largely apart from this growing global religiosity – except for immigrant communities with a Muslim background. But here a parallel demon popped up: the seemingly inescapable growth of extreme-right and populist right-wing political parties. What links all of these parties in Europe is what they dub the 'invasion' of our familiar surroundings by the 'immigrant'. Having asserted itself in the 1980s, the extreme right succeeded in growing further during the 1990s, and now appears to have turned into a permanent feature within European political structures. The debate on integration, multiculturalism and the place of Islam in the West has been hardening as a consequence. The global malaise is the common source on which the extreme right in Europe as well as religious revival and the radicalisations around the world feed. All of them have the same recipe on offer: nostalgia for times gone by, simple certainties, distinct scapegoats and simple solutions. They use the same rhetoric: 'Us vs. Them', offering an apparent order in a chaotic world. Political forces, parties and organisations that capitalise on this stand to score. But as a result, societies experienced new forms of polarisation, between newcomers and native citizens, between Muslims and non-Muslims. World politics discovered new clashes between civilisations.

Global Inequity

This global malaise that the 2002 Pew survey highlighted has since become intertwined with another thread in world opinion. During his tenure as World Bank chief James Wolfensohn repeatedly warned that global inequity was to become the major theme of the twenty-first century. In different international surveys, including one commissioned by the German Bertelsmann Stiftung in June 2006 (German Bertelsmann Stiftung 2006), a pervasive sense of global inequity indeed seems to permeate world opinion. In this survey, poverty comes off as the second most important global challenge and poverty reduction is considered the prime objective world powers should pursue. While respondents do not view the United Nations as a world power now, many clearly hope for a more prominent role in the future. In all continents respondents express the hope that their government will distance itself from the United States. This so-called anti-Americanism is no rejection of the values of democracy and freedom America stands for. It would be rather the opposite. To quote the legendary US Senator William Fulbright, when speaking of the United States in the 1960s: people resent the arrogance of power. This mood helps to explain why a left-wing momentum is sweeping Latin America. This same rejection of power inequity propelled Hassan Nasrallah in Lebanon for a brief period after the 2006 Lebanon war to the stature of the new Nasser of an Arab-Islamic national movement – or, for that matter, Osama bin Laden as the new icon of the worldwide T-shirt market. When people resent inequity, they are prone to radicalisation.

Even if Islamist radicalisation is the most prominent form of radicalisation today, radicalisation is certainly not limited to the Muslim world, as the aforementioned 2004 NIC and UNDP reports observed. Sundeep Waslekar, the president of the Mumbai-based *Strategic Foresight Group*, describes the world in a strikingly similar way:

> As we have seen from numerous case studies around the world, exclusion produced by relative deprivation, resulting from social structures and state policies, feeds extremism. The conditions for relative deprivation prevail all over the world, from Muslim immigrants in Western Europe, the poor in the American mid-west to farmers in Colombia and the Philippines. The intellectual project to define terrorism only in relation to the groups in the Middle East turns a blind eye to the growth of terrorism and extremism not only outside the Middle East, in Asia and Latin America, but also in the American and European homelands. (Waslekar 2007, 24–5)

Global malaise and global inequity, together with their corollaries polarisation and radicalisation, constitute the 'rage of our era'. In this, our era resembles the late nineteenth century, when the same global mood brought about a similar wave of terrorism, but couched in political (anarchist) terms. But then and now, the discourse was not the driving force. The state of the world we are living in is.

Intersection of a Personal History and the Enabling Environment

After interviewing a number of radical Islamists in French jails, Fahrad Khosrokhavar concluded that the argument stands that their radicalisation too is often at the intersection of personal experiences and a global political and social situation:

> Every [Islamist] group refers to a major political fact that appears to have been the essential driving force behind its radicalisation, next to certain facts of daily life such as being subjected to humiliation, a sentiment of indignity or personal offence. The conjunction between [the] two procreates the passage to extremism. (Khosrokhavar 2006, 14)

As in all previous radicalisation processes, today's radicalisation, including its terrorist offspring, starts with social bonding, not religion, social bonds being the critical element and preceding ideological commitment (CIEM 2006). Noor Huda Ismail and Edwin Bakker both refer in their chapters to 'kinship ties', or the ties of affinity between the jihadis. A number of home-grown jihadis were already active together in low-level criminal, non-political activities, before even thinking of becoming a jihadi. Jihadis in Europe appear to be more and more the product of self-recruitment. Self-recruitment is largely the result of an individual track of self-radicalisation outside usual meeting places such as mosques. It more often than not involves individuals with college education. Frustration offers the main engine for this process. They feel rejected and abandoned by society. Alain Grignard emphasises, based upon first hand experience, that individuals rebel against a society in which they feel they do not belong. Even though conferences given by itinerant self-proclaimed imams can and do have an influence, the internet,[8] satellite dishes, CDs and chat forums play an increasingly important role in the individual and independent process of radicalisation, without external mentoring. Sometimes, but not always, a 'gatekeeper' or intermediary accompanies this process. These are:

> ... Specific individuals with numerous personal contacts, who through these contacts have the ability to make things happen. ... they know the congregations at the radical Mosques, the former mujahedeen and active terrorists. While not necessarily conducting terrorist operations themselves, they are able to open the gate to the exclusive community of militant Islamism. (Taarnby 2005a, 23)

Violence: A Minority's Path

Contrary to widespread popular belief in the West, large majorities among Muslims worldwide oppose violence in the name of Islam. This should come as no surprise. Terrorism always is the recourse of the few. Moreover, as indicated in Chapter 2, Muslims are the primary victims of jihadi attacks. According to a very rough estimate, produced at Ghent University, the number of victims in Muslim countries is as high as forty times the number of victims in Western countries since the start of jihadi terrorism in the beginning of the 1990s. Every jihadi attack involving the death of Muslims further delegitimates and isolates jihadis within the Ummah they pretend to defend. The jihadi movement is, at best, a fragmented and limited movement at the fringes of the Muslim and immigrant communities with a Muslim background.

> The idea of recreating a universal caliphate is cherished only by the elements on the furthest fringe of political Islam. It is marginal to the large majority of Islamist movements and ineffective as far as the day-to-day political struggles within Muslim countries and Muslim communities are concerned. In Muslim countries, most mainstream Islamist movements operate peacefully within national boundaries. (Ayoob 2005)

Moreover, surveys in countries where significant jihadi attacks have occurred clearly indicate the plummeting appeal of terrorism. Six months after the July 2005 attacks in the London Underground, an ICM poll among British Muslims noted that, while

---

8 The internet also plays an important role in providing instruction and skills needed for combat methods.

radicalisation and a sense of alienation amongst British Muslims had increased and a majority expected a worsening of relations between Muslims and non-Muslims, almost nine out of ten respondents rejected al-Qaeda violence. As for the July 2005 attacks, only one per cent of respondents considered this to be a justified action. In another poll, that indicated a slightly higher number of British Muslims sympathetic to the 7/7 bombers, still only two per cent would be proud if a member of their family would join the ranks of al-Qaeda, while 78 per cent replied that they would be angry.[9] The same phenomenon occurred after the Amman bombings of November 2005. In 2005, before the bombings 25 per cent of Jordanians said they had a lot of confidence in bin Laden to 'do the right thing regarding world affairs', while another 35 per cent said they had some confidence. A year later, almost no Jordanians (less than one per cent) expressed a lot of confidence in bin Laden, and 24 per cent said they have some confidence in him. In most of the Muslim world, support for the al-Qaeda leader has eroded too (Pew 2006a). A 2006 poll in Indonesia indicated that only about nine per cent of Indonesians supported the use of violent attacks such as the 2002 Bali bombings that killed more than 200 civilians, if the attacks are aimed at defending Islam. At the same time, the survey by the Indonesian Survey Institute found more than 80 per cent of the Indonesian population strongly condemned violent tactics used by al-Qaeda and affiliated Indonesian terrorist network Jamaah Islamiyah to establish a separate Islamic state, and favoured peaceful democracy.[10] Jason Burke, the Paris-based European correspondent of the London *Observer* summarised it on the eve of the fifth anniversary of the 2001 attacks as follows:

> ... the truth is that out of a total of 1.6 billion Muslims, very few have joined terrorist organisations. In countries that have suffered violence, such as Saudi Arabia, Jordan and Iraq, there has been a strong counter-reaction to the atrocities of recent years. The number of young men attracted by violence in the UK is larger than it was a decade ago, but is still statistically insignificant. If bin Laden's 'awakening' has started, it is taking a long time. The world's Muslims are not behaving as bin Laden wants them to. They are behaving, still, as individuals. Militancy or, more often a lack of militancy, is still a personal and rational choice.[11]

The Specificity of Islamist Radicalisation Today

As already indicated above, without being the exclusive form of radicalisation and terrorism today, Islamist radicalisation and terrorism clearly is its most prominent variety. The question then arises as to the reasons behind this specific appearance today? Why are we confronted with a wave of terrorism couched in religious terms rather than in extreme-left, extreme-right or nationalistic terms, as in earlier waves of (international) terrorism? One might for example reasonably argue that since the 'enabling environment' is characterised by feelings of alienation and inequity, left-wing terrorism might find fertile ground. Framing the question in these terms is

---

9 ICM poll, February 2006; Populus poll, 7 July 2006.
10 *Jakarta Post*, 20 October 2006.
11 *Guardian*, 10 September 2006.

not fortuitous. Researchers have indeed hinted at sporadic contacts between jihadi extremists and leftist extremists, joining forces around a common anti-imperialist agenda. In her contribution, Jocelyne Cesari too mentions this anti-imperialist feature in Islamist rhetoric. Such contacts, however, are epiphenomena in a contemporary terrorism that is indeed couched in Islamic terms. In a nutshell: rather than being rooted in 'Islam', as many maintain, Islamist radicalisation in general and jihadi terrorism in particular are the product of an accidental concurrence of specific circumstances.

Within the enabling global environment as sketched above there exists within Muslim communities worldwide a very acute sense of marginalisation. Mohammed Ayoob of Michigan State University described the enabling environment as seen through Muslim eyes as follows:

> It is the Muslims' collective memory of subjugation and the current perception of weakness in relation to the West that provides the common denominator among the many divergent manifestations of political Islam. ... The common denominator among Islamists, therefore, is the quest for dignity, a variable often ignored by contemporary political analysts in the West. (Ayoob 2004)

While the West sees a threatening Islam looming, large majorities in Muslim countries are convinced the West has declared war on them and has decided to keep them in a permanent position of subordination. In certain Muslim countries, up to 70 per cent believe that Islam is threatened by the West (Fair and Haqqani 2006). But this widespread feeling of humiliation rests upon a whole array of widely diverging specific local circumstances, that one should carefully take into account, as Hugh Roberts emphasises, to get to grips with the emergence of jihadi groups. These range from decades-old separatist longings in a number of countries with large Muslim minorities, such as southern Thailand or Chechnya; long-term neglect of whole communities, as is the case with the Bedouin in the Sinai; the stalled peace process between Palestinians and Israelis; the social, political and economic deadlock in a number of Arab countries, as highlighted by the successive UNDP Arab Human Development Reports; specific policy orientations in the countries of the Maghreb, as Hugh Roberts explores; and, as far as Europe is concerned, the failing integration of second and third generation youngsters in immigrant communities with a Muslim background.

Nothing creates so fertile a breeding ground for political radicalisation than the feeling of belonging to the camp of the losers and upholding potent and aspirational symbols to identify with. 'Humiliation is the single most underappreciated force in international relations', *New York Times* columnist Thomas Friedman observed when analysing a notorious farewell speech by the departing Malaysian President Mahatir Mohamed, in October 2003. Everyone condemned the anti-Semitic fragments in the address, but failed to notice his lucid diagnosis of the situation within the Muslim world. Mahatir talked about the feelings of humiliation, oppression and hopelessness which are prevalent in the Muslim world today, about the dignity of 1.3 billion Muslims being pushed aside and about the marginalisation of Muslim communities all over the world. Built upon these shared feelings of humiliation, bitterness and besiegement, there now exists an astonishing degree of solidarity amongst Muslim communities worldwide, so international surveys confirm.[12] In his speech at the Council on Foreign Relations in Washington, in May 2004, former Prime Minister of Singapore Goh Chok Tong observed: 'It is a fact that there is a living, vibrant Islamic Ummah or global Islamic community more so today than in any time in modern world history.' The daily plight of the Palestinians and the ongoing war in Iraq further cements these feelings of solidarity among Muslims worldwide. In all polls, interviews and in-depth discussions these situations are seen as major boosters of solidarity among many Muslims, and the ensuing radicalisation among a limited number of them. Rather than making the world safer, the war in Iraq has exacerbated radicalisation and the threat of jihadi terrorism today. The familiar reasoning in policy circles in the United States is that 'we're fighting the terrorists in Iraq and across the world so we do not have to face them here at home' (Bush 2005b). Seen from Europe, most counter-terrorism officials would draw exactly the opposite conclusion: we're fighting in Iraq and the longer that we do so, the more would-be terrorists are being born in our streets.

By attacking the symbols of Western power, Osama bin Laden succeeded in plugging into existing insurgencies, rebellions, local brands of terrorism, disenchanted youngsters and stitching them together in a shared world view of a worldwide oppressed virtual Ummah and a simple, salafi reading of the Quran as the religion of the oppressed. His success in doing so was less depending upon the intrinsic strength of his terrorist network, than on today's global environment that proved to be very conducive to radicalisation, due to its twin characteristics of widespread unease and feelings of inequity.

Amongst the existing transnational value systems, Islam was the only candidate left that offered the aspirational symbols of resistance against inequity and unfairness and that provided extremists a justificatory discourse in a global atmosphere that was conducive to simple representations of the world opposing 'Us' and 'Them'. Extremists hijacked Islam, simplified it to the extreme and turned it into a justification of violence and opposition to injustice. Christianity could never have played this role, since it was the religion of the rich and the powerful of today. Left-wing ideology could not play this role either, due to the demise of ideologies. Thus to some, jihadism has become the religion of resistance, offering a religion-based Utopia within reach – not altogether that different from what Marxism once offered to the oppressed. Then and now, for each and every militant arrested, a new one steps forward. For each attack foiled, a new one is being planned, giving the feeling of a never-ending threat.

The Specific Circumstances in Europe

In Europe too, specific conditions contributed to the emergence of a radicalisation process couched in Islamic terms. The post-9/11 obsession with violent radicalisation

---

12 *Views of a changing world*, Washington, DC, Pew Global Attitudes Project, June 2003; *Muslims in the American Public Square: Shifting political winds & fallout from 9/11, Afghanistan, and Iraq*, Zogby International, conducted in August and September 2004.

and terrorism has obscured the fact that what drives radicalisation within specific segments of European societies has less to do with Islam and religion than with the typical difficulties faced by the children and grandchildren of immigrants in any given migratory wave. Teenagers and teens in immigrant families today face the typical challenge of all second and third generation youngsters in earlier immigrant communities: who am I and where do I belong to as an individual? It is customary in all migratory waves that the quest for identity is much more demanding for youngsters than it was for their parents. They are simultaneously considered an *émigré* in the country of origin of their family, and an *immigré* in their new country (Garton Ash 2006). No longer able to identify with the country of origin of their parents or grandparents, the countries they now live in constitute their sole natural environment for identification. Within this environment, however, they are confronted with a number of real obstacles, in particular discrimination on the job and in the real estate market, and educational deficiencies.[13] As a second generation, usually better educated than their parents, they are more sensitive than their parents to the feeling of being excluded or rejected as second-class citizens by their natural environment.

This tension is a characteristic obstacle for the children and grandchildren of immigrants in all immigration communities, since time eternal. As a rule of thumb it is said that a significant migratory wave requires three generations before being absorbed, both by the immigrants' communities and the receiving society. This time, however, integration might prove to be thornier. For one, the European context is less conducive for integration than traditional immigration countries like the United States or Canada. Europe has indeed long been more a region of emigration than of immigration – even if some countries, like France, experienced huge immigration in the period 1880–1930. When the immigration wave started in the early 1950s, people from Turkey and North Africa were welcomed as 'guest workers'. Everybody, including the immigrants themselves, assumed that one day they would return. In the beginning, racism was less the problem that it became later on, when the birth of the second generation signalled that these communities where here to stay.

Moreover, there is an additional problem that hinders integration following the classic paths of before. Having a job still being the major vehicle for socialisation for individuals, the relative scarcity and especially the higher skills that are now required compared to the post-1950 job market erects higher barriers for today's youngsters in immigrant communities, making upward social mobility a more demanding endeavour. Research in a number of European countries, including France and Belgium, has indeed indicated that unemployment among immigrant communities is many times higher than among the indigenous population.

Within parts of the immigrant communities, despair and discouragement nowadays prevail with regard to their youngsters' chances of overcoming these situations in the foreseeable future. It cannot be excluded that part of today's group of children and grandchildren of immigrants will find themselves trapped in a semi-permanent underclass situation. There are indeed impressionistic indications that, contrary to earlier migratory histories where the third generation in a sense 'concluded'

---

13 In the recent literature on Western Muslims, one can refer to Masci (2004).

the integration itinerary that their grandparents initiated, today's grandchildren of immigrants dispose of less qualifications and language skills than their parents, the immigrants' children.

In this process some of them have discovered religion. They are 'born again' Muslims, stripping the Islamic heritage from its religious, cultural and ethic features and reducing it to mere identity – thus assuming for their part the stamp society puts on them: 'Muslims'. But their father's mosques do not capture their imagination, since the (often foreign) imams do not offer them a message they can identify with. They create their own subculture, withdraw from many social contacts, and sever family ties. As a result, these youngsters have a tendency to become an introverted generation. In their subgroup they find the proximity and the sense of belonging that they think they cannot find elsewhere.

Embracing Islam as their new identity, they resort to a 'cut and paste' Islam, where they interpret the Quran in concordance with their own life experiences and sometimes even as a kind of redemption for their petty criminal behaviour in the past (see also AIVD 2004a). Religious radicalisation is the result of a process of personal re-identification and shows a need of affirming this new identity. One of the most visible signs of this process is the increased presence of Islamic garments in Europe's streets.

This generational phenomenon has been enhanced by the rise of identity politics worldwide. One could argue that the difficulties surrounding integration can as well function as a catalyst for second and third generation youngsters to identify with their environment. But the global environment, as described above, pushes in the opposite direction. Immigration communities with a Muslim background in Europe show signs of both increased religiosity and cultural conservatism – a development not unlike the born-again Christian phenomenon in the United States. Within Muslim communities – but also amongst converts – rigid interpretations of the Islam, both tabligh and salafi, provide for a strict set of rules in times of rapid change and uncertainty. The ready availability and the built-in simplicity of salafi books and texts privilege this specific hard-line strain within Islamic thought and practices, as both Jocelyne Cesari and Tarik Fraihi show.

As in all major social developments, extremists are part and parcel of this generational phenomenon too. Assessing that the speed of change is too slow, they take it upon themselves to hasten the evolution through violence. A tiny minority within the second and third generation of immigrant communities undergo a political radicalisation that should not be confounded with the aforementioned religious radicalisation. Difficult self-identification and frustration on the one hand and their feeling of belonging to a communal group that is sociologically at the lower end of the ladder as all immigrations are upon arriving, on the other hand, form the major engines behind this political radicalisation, facilitated by the stereotypical 'Muslim' stamp put on them by the surrounding society. Individuals radicalise into self-declared local vanguards of the worldwide 'liberation struggle', translated as 'jihad', sometimes under the influence of a charismatic individual. By seemingly acting in community with a worldwide emancipation movement, they develop a sense of self-esteem, feeling in communion with other jihadi 'theatres of war' in the world. One of the jailed Islamists Fahrad Khosrokhavar interviewed clearly expressed this identity vacuum in which he constantly moved:

> 'Between whom I was and who I wanted to be: an ordinary Frenchman, while in fact I was an Algerian.' Trying to behave like a Frenchman, he felt despised. Embracing Islamism, he felt respected: 'They hate us, but they respect us. We are no longer ragtag and bobtail …. They are deeply suspicious of us, but we gained our dignity through the fear we inspire them.' (Khosrokhavar 2006, 136–7)

In Search of a De-Radicalisation Strategy

The processes leading to radicalisation have by now been well researched. We dare to hope that the contributions in this book have made clear that we now have a fairly good understanding of the broad processes at work at the individual, group, community and even global level – even if some aspects are still in need of more thorough exploration, especially the interaction between the global and the local and the action–reaction dynamics of radicalisation, implying that the way authorities and societies react to radicalisation influences its further development, as both Glenn Audenaert and Tarik Fraihi acknowledge.

What has been researched much less is the way out. De-radicalisation has received far less attention than is warranted. Glenn Audenaert argues that we are in need of a major endeavour linking authorities (including police forces), academia and immigrant communities in a joint effort to establish a sort of framework to tackle this major multi-faceted issue. Social exclusion, a sense of alienation and the international dimension: all these factors indeed feed into the mindset of youngsters in immigrant communities. Radicals capitalise on anger and frustration and propose a simple answer to all their ills: terrorism. However, it cannot be sufficiently stressed that this (self-)recruitment track only concerns a very limited number of individuals and that it occurs at the fringes of immigrant and Muslim communities. Tarik Fraihi has pointed out in this book that the de-radicalisation of Muslims is mainly the work of Muslims themselves. But for a number of reasons, he too acknowledges, these communities are unable to cope with this issue solely by themselves. They need a permissive environment that enables them to tilt the balance in their favour. This environment is the responsibility of immigrant communities and their fellow-countrymen alike, individuals as well as authorities.

The principles that underpin de-radicalisation are to be derived from the analysis of what drives radicalisation. The basic assumptions behind a de-radicalisation strategy can thus be summarised as follows: (1) no fixation on Islam, since this is not the main engine behind radicalisation; (2) inclusiveness as the main thread; (3) disruption of messenger and message; (4) a global and integrated approach, involving all the stakeholders. These general principles should guide de-radicalisation efforts at all levels, from global over national to local. Put otherwise, socialisation and reinforcement of cohesion at all levels are the main overarching objectives of any de-radicalisation strategy. But having said so, describing how to move forward can easily result in a depressive picture, due to the sheer complexity of the processes at hand and the many uncertainties surrounding them (Horgan, 2005, 166). One shall readily accept that it is easier to describe what should be done, than actually doing it, since so many parallel tracks have to be followed and so many stakeholders to be involved all at the same time.

A word of caution, though: de-radicalisation as a process is not simply the inverse of radicalisation. People do not move 'backwards', that is, they do not become as they were before they were radicalised. De-radicalisation means different things to different people in the process, and also implies that it may be expressed in many different ways also. De-radicalisation might also suggest a focus on achieving particular objectives – for example, ensuring agreement on the non-targeting of civilians, or use of certain methods. But it does not have the same connotations as initial radicalisation has with respect to the supposed link to involvement in terrorism. As studies on extreme-right individuals have shown, even having dropped violence, some of these individuals are still very radicalised. De-radicalisation might thus best be viewed as a process inducing radicals to express their ideas through accepted political means, in particular by tackling the root causes that fringe groups among the radicals otherwise invoke within their wider community to justify their recourse to violence.

The Global Level

The main root causes behind radicalisation are local. Hugh Roberts clarifies this convincingly in his chapter as far as the Maghreb countries are concerned. But it also helps to explain the feeling amongst EU officials that the aforementioned 2005 European strategy against terrorism and violent radicalisation has difficulties in getting into full swing. The international and intra-European counter-terrorism cooperation has been successful in degrading al-Qaeda as an organisation and in decreasing its ability to conduct massive attacks (US Department of State 2005). By now the era of vertical and hierarchical organised terrorist organisations is largely over. Victory over terrorism, however, will not be achieved as long as the circumstances are not addressed by which specific individuals turn into radicals and, ultimately, terrorists. If radicalisation is the main path towards terrorism and the root causes of radicalisation are mainly local and thus within the competences of the member states with widely diverging political traditions, the EU involvement becomes secondary.

The European Union, however, holds an important key as far as the global environment is concerned that only the Union as a Union can use. The West is resented as representing the rich and powerful of this world. Compared to the United States, Europe still has a slightly better image in world public opinion. It thus carries the greatest responsibility in trying to correct this global resentment that permeates world politics today. No quick fix exists for rectifying this perception gap. No revitalised public diplomacy effort will do. It can only be addressed by restoring a minimal sense of communality at the global level through a long-term effort aimed at the creation of a more just and fair world, built on shared priorities and concerns and founded on institutions, representative of the entire world population and where there is place for the interests and self-esteem of all members. Global governance, that is how Nader Fergany, the lead author of the Arab Human Development Reports, named this perspective at the 2003 international conference in Brussels on the root causes of international terrorism, referred to in the introduction (Fergany 2003). But the 27 members of the European Union lack the internal consistency and thus the ambition to start working on such an overarching inclusive agenda, as outlined in the December 2004 Report by the High Level Panel on Threats, Challenges and Change, the ensuing recommendations by former UN Secretary-General Kofi Annan, issued in March 2005, and their formal endorsement by the world leaders during the Millennium review Summit of September 2005 (UN 2005).

In his aforementioned *Inclusive World* report, Sundeep Waslekar of Strategic Foresight Group warns that without such global collaborative projects the world might enter into an 'age of competitive fundamentalism': 'If many societies and states are governed by extremist forces, an international military confrontation can not be ruled out', he grimly concludes. In his report he suggests a number of ventures, such as a semi-permanent conference on the Middle East, a Western–Islamic Dialogue and Engagement Initiative, an International Historical Study Group on Common Human Civilisation and, finally, an Arab Islamic Renaissance Initiative. Partly for reasons of geographical proximity, partly also because it is the region of origin of a large part of the recent immigrations, Europe has a special interest in the Middle East. For Europe it is of vital importance to neutralise the commonly held view which persists in the Arab world of a West which is only interested in securing its own interests by bolstering authoritarian regimes at the expense of democracy promotion. If this does not happen, the democratisation process in the Middle East – that prudently started more than half a decade ago and received an impulse with the introspection and reflection upon its own responsibilities that started after 9/11 – will again result in anti-Western populism and stimulate the emergence of more intensely anti-Western regimes, so Burhan Ghalioun, director of the Sorbonne's Centre d'Etudes sur l'Orient Contemporain, has warned (Ghalioun 2002).

Even if it seems moribund at times, the main CFSP instrument in this regard still remains the European-Mediterranean Partnership, the so-called Barcelona Process. The dilemma between short term and long term objectives needs to be fully addressed within this framework, by enhancing the dynamics of the European-Mediterranean Partnership, especially in its political, cultural and economic dimensions. A particular way of overcoming this dilemma is the creation of informal channels between European officials and Arab reformers, of liberal and moderate Islamist orientation alike, with the aim of fostering gender empowerment, political freedom, rule of law and civil liberties. In the past, Europe has privileged encounters with liberal reformers. Taking into account that only a very small minority of Islamists are in favour of the violent, confrontational strategy – as endorsed by Osama bin Laden – it might be advisable to take into account broadening the spectrum of potential partners in the region, as some observers have been suggesting as of lately. Most Islamist movements have now accepted democratic norms and principles, while simultaneously adopting a modernist attitude to Islamic law. This tendency is in some measure embodied in the Muslim Brothers, the Moroccan Justice and Development Party (PJD) and the Muslim-democratic Turkish Justice and Development Party (AKP). They accept the state not only as the framework for their main activity but also as legitimate in itself, thus abandoning fundamentalist views which deny legitimacy to the nation by counter-posing to it the Ummah, the supra-national community of believers (ICG 2005).

European engagement with moderate Islamists on democracy promotion in the region is risky for both the EU and the Islamists themselves. Both fear a hidden agenda behind the other's intentions, yet both stand to gain from a systematic dialogue on democracy. As has been argued by El-Din Shahin of the American University in Cairo, an even-handed approach by which Europe is moderately vocal but firm and consistent with the ruling regimes, and as consistent and vocal with their Islamist partners as to the respect of the basic rules of democracy, will elevate democracy promotion to have the same salience as social and economic reform (El-Din Shahin 2005). As a first step in exploring this issue, Dr Ahmed Idrees, the Egyptian-born European Affairs Correspondent of the BBC Arab service in Brussels, has suggested the creation of an *ad hoc* unit of experts on Islamist extremism, at the disposal of both the Council and the Commission. This unit could help European decision-making by monitoring and analysing the trends and causes of religious extremism in the Muslim and Arab world and present policy recommendations for specific measures.

Of particular importance in the West's involvement in the Middle East as part of a de-radicalisation strategy is the peace process between Palestinians and Israelis. The daily pictures from the Middle East, more than those of any other international tragedy, have kept fuelling the perception within the Muslim world of a hostile West. Over the past years this has induced the political conflict between Palestinians and Israelis to be seen as a religious conflict between Muslims on the one hand and Jews, supported by the Christian West, on the other – instead of a nationalistic struggle as was customary before.[14] It has driven a wedge between the West and the Islamic world and has thus developed into an ideal rallying cause for both Islamist recruiters and self-recruited jihadis. Ending the conflict between Palestine and Israel will certainly not suffice to halt jihadi terrorism. A renewed effort and a more balanced attitude on the part of the international community with regard to this conflict are nevertheless essential elements for a strategy aimed at conquering the hearts and minds in the Middle East. International surveys indicate that majorities in different countries surveyed consider the European Union's involvement in world politics as positive. Some observers have concluded from this goodwill towards European global involvement that the EU is uniquely well equipped to function as a bridge between the West and the Muslim world (Mogahed 2006).

The National and Local Level

Most of the de-radicalisation strategy will take place at the local and national level, since the root causes of radicalisation and terrorism are local too. It goes without saying that reducing the radicals' ability to convey their message constitutes one of the first tasks of the authorities in the framework of any de-radicalisation strategy, including through European and international cooperation. Monitoring radical websites, internet forums and radio programmes, checking potential leaders' influence, keeping an eye on potential groups and on what happens in prisons is a

---

14 Maurits Berger in *NRC-Handelsblad*, 27 March 2004.

task only governments can and do pursue – taking into due consideration, as Glenn Audenaert observes, the basic constitutional rights of freedom of speech and freedom of religion.

Prevention is even more important than repression. Much has been written about possible steps to combat discrimination, racism, reciprocal enemy images and stereotypes. None of what follows will thus be very original or novel. Since radicalisation is a multi-level phenomenon, a de-radicalisation strategy will unavoidably be multi-dimensional as well. The complexity of the approach necessitates a long-term engagement by authorities. But often the attention span of governments and authorities is limited, especially if they do not feel pressed by events. As written above, it is easier for an academic to describe what *should* be done, than for officials and governments to actually *do* it. Therefore, the trilateral approach proposed by Glenn Audenaert merits special attention. In what follows, a 'catalogue' of possible tracks and venues is suggested. Some of them are already in place in European countries, but in a fragmentary manner. None are easy to implement.

The numerous suggestions, initiatives and actions that aim at preventing and rolling back radicalisation at the local and national level easily fit into three categories: (1) reducing the receptivity of the radicals' message; (2) offering perspectives; and (3) de-legitimating the radicals' discourse. De-radicalisation cannot be but a common undertaking, with objectives to be pursued by immigrant and Muslim communities, and society as a whole. On the one hand, Tariq Ramadan, Europe's leading Muslim intellectual, is quite explicit when he addresses Western Muslims' self-identification as a people apart and wallowing in what he calls an 'unhealthy victim mentality' and an 'Us-vs.-Them' mind-set. This perception of victimisation and obsession with a minority status must be rejected, according to Ramadan, who further implores Western Muslims to reach out and connect with fellow citizens in their countries of residence, to resist the impulse to withdraw into isolated communities and to get involved in community politics. De-connecting people from their countries of origin without denying them the cultural and religious specificities of these origins, and espousing Western values is undoubtedly happening within immigrant communities as generations go by.[15] It is a positive development that is to be encouraged, instead of being hampered by stereotyping Europeans of foreign origin as outsiders or representing a monolithic Muslim bloc.[16] Instead, there is a necessity to develop a model of citizenship that reflects peoples multiple identities and allegiances and finds strength in its ability to accommodate each of them and to hold them together (Home Office 2005, 9). On the other hand, for this effort within immigrant communities to succeed, there must be a partner on the other side. Many non-Muslims have no clue about the degree to which Muslims feel excluded from society. The mutual distrust and polarisation between Muslim communities and the society in which they live is subsequently growing instead of diminishing.

---

15 ICM Muslim poll, February 2006.

16 The Kuwaiti reformer Dr Ahmad Al-Baghdadi makes a similar point in: <http://www.alseyassah.com/alseyassah/opinion/view.asp?msgID=10097>. Quoted in *Memri*, 12 April 2006.

Reducing Receptivity

First and foremost, the debate about multiculturalism is in dire need of de-escalation, for polarisation only breeds more polarisation. National authorities must take the lead in this. Only when the inherent difficulties of a multicultural society are patiently described and explained will people, Europeans and immigration communities alike, fear its unknowns less. If, on the contrary, the polarisation within Western and, more specifically, European societies is permitted to metastasise, Osama bin Laden will have won by default, since polarisation between Muslims and non-Muslims was uppermost in his mind when authorising the 9/11 attacks (see also AIVD 2004b). A timely first step would be that both media and politicians resist the temptation to explain complex community problems by using sweeping generalisations about cultural backwardness (AIVD 2002). Islam provides a rationale for would-be terrorists, but is not the origin of their acts.

The commonly heard disapproving remarks about Islam as a religion are deeply offensive to all Muslims, even to those holding secular views. Such discourse facilitates the formation of conflicting ethnic-religious fronts pitting Muslims against non-Muslims (Phalet 2004). Amin Maalouf has convincingly argued that language and religion are the most vulnerable and sensitive dimensions of one's identity. When individuals feel attacked in one of these aspects, they start looking for others experiencing the same vexation. The group thus created then easily reverts to the kind of brutal and extremist group behaviour that could be witnessed in Rwanda, Bosnia or Lebanon (Maalouf 1998). Jocelyne Cesari sees the same dynamic at work. The current debate about integration and multiculturalism in many European countries tends to breed a climate which encourages individuals and groups of fanatical and volunteering young men to declare themselves the vanguards of a 'defensive jihad'. By their acts – not that different altogether from the nineteenth-century anarchist terrorist's claim of acting in favour of a marginalised and despised working class – young jihadis see themselves as avengers of an oppressed community. A climate which also offers plenty of opportunities to Islamist recruiters and is propitious to self-recruitment. Authorities and the media need to de-dramatise their common parlance. When confronted with incidents – especially when of a dramatic nature – involving youngsters with an immigrant or Muslim background, it makes a huge difference if the reaction is a 'declaration of war against Muslim radicals/terrorists' or a condemnation of these incidents as unacceptable behaviour of a small group of young thugs, whatever their origin may be.

A case in point that received some attention in the media was the effort by the European Union to make its officials aware that in an emotionally charged political climate, the words that are being used in describing the EU's efforts to tackle terrorism and radicalisation might easily be unnecessarily provocative and thus counterproductive. Peter Clarke, who was referred to in the introduction of this book, thus warned against the sloppy use of words linked to Islam when speaking about jihadi terrorism. Some have ridiculed the EU endeavour to come up with a 'lexicon' as excessive political correctness. However, the issue surrounding unduly stigmatising people is comparable to the American situation where the 'N-word' too is carefully being avoided. As David Ignatius observed: this word reminds us that there is a rage so deep and abiding that it can be triggered by a small comment (Ignatius 2006).

Secondly, authorities have to recognise explicitly that for some segments of our society discrimination unfortunately is still a reality that should be pushed back as much as possible. In most European countries, unemployment within immigrant communities, and especially among youngsters, remains greater than within the general population, as Tarik Fraihi sketched for Belgium. Much-needed talents are wasted when youngsters remain for too long at the sidelines of the job market.

Thirdly, physical segregation needs to be addressed. Authorities must be seen to be making significant efforts to end the sociological apartheid in major cities, through bold social engineering, new housing and neutralising discriminations of all sorts, by whatever political party, structure or individual.[17] European cities always have been characterised by a form of segregation, with low-income districts on the one hand and high-income districts on the other hand, with significant disparities in education and city services. Traditional low-income districts have attracted the bulk of immigrant families in search of affordable housing – which in turn has stimulated an exodus of original inhabitants. The combination of feelings within immigrant communities of being left aside, and amongst the original inhabitants in low-income city districts of being pushed aside, have proven to be a potent boost for reciprocal polarisation, as can be judged from the electoral successes of extreme-right political parties in many European countries.

Fourthly, feelings of insecurity that are felt by both immigration communities and the public at large are to be neutralised. Glenn Audenaert emphasised the importance of community policing in this respect. Local authorities might consider enhancing multicultural awareness programmes for police units operating in specific city districts.

And, finally, paraphrasing the American folk song, the message 'This land is your land … too' is an important one to convey, both within immigrant communities with a Muslim background and Muslim communities in Europe and in European society as a whole. Again, contrary to popular belief and notwithstanding the riots over cartoon portrayals of the Prophet Mohammed, these communities do subscribe to Western values, especially as times go by. Surveys indeed show that Muslims accept Western society and prefer to live according to 'western values' (Pew 2006a). One poll thus concluded:

> However, there is little evidence of a widespread backlash against Muslim immigrants among the general publics in Great Britain, France, Germany, and Spain. Majorities continue to express concerns about rising Islamic identity and extremism, but those worries have not intensified in most of the countries surveyed over the past 12 months; a turbulent period that included the London subway bombings, the French riots, and the Danish cartoon controversy. (Pew 2006a)

---

17 In their elaborate letter to parliament dated 10 November 2004 and dealing with the murder of Theo van Gogh, the Dutch ministers of Justice and Interiors, Messrs Donner and Remkes, also stress the need to connect youngsters from immigrant communities with Dutch society by removing the impediments to social and economic participation.

One should certainly not obscure the fact that cultural and social attitudes differ, sometimes to a great extent. Some aspects, such as homosexuality and same-sex marriages, prove difficult to accept for immigrant communities. Portraying such attitudes as intrinsically 'Islamic', however, draws too rapid a conclusion. European conservatives too are often very reluctant to accept these. One is tempted to predict that if European states succeed in de-escalating the debate on multiculturalism and integration, a cultural landscape will develop, not unlike blue and red America, divided by opposing value systems. One will be culturally traditional, shared by conservative Christians, Muslims and non-believers alike, stressing family values, anti-abortion, anti-gay and (for some) religion. The other will be culturally open-minded, and will find support in all segments of society too.

Offering Perspectives

Probably the main task for authorities lies in the formulation of a common project that is able to bind immigrant and non-migrant communities into a shared sense of communality. 'Equity' probably comes closest to expressing the nature of this endeavour. Equal chances are the main weapon against radicalisation and terrorism. Just like non-Muslims, European Muslim's main concern is finding a job (Pew 2006b). The formation of a (Muslim) middle class will help to provide for a role model and erect a dam against radicalisation (Khosrokhavar 2006, 400). If member states prove incapable of providing newcomers and their children a place in society, the combination of racism, economic exclusion and humiliation, Fahrad Khosrokhavar fears, will continue to swell the ranks of the terrorists.

A significant responsibility lies upon the shoulders of local and national authorities. This includes taking care that local services, including police forces, reflect the diversity of society itself. In some countries, such as in Belgium, the reflection of this diversity at the political level is rather well established. Most representatives, local as well as national, take great care – and pride – in not portraying themselves as 'minority' politicians, but as representatives of all their voters, whatever their ethnic origin. In other European countries, however, immigrant communities do not encounter 'familiar faces' in politics, which contributes to their self-image as foreigners in their own country. Once again, this is not a simple undertaking. Discussions are ongoing in most of the EU member states on the best way forward. Some argue that affirmative action might be an appropriate remedy, as was the case in the United States, where the federal government used affirmative action as a lever to enhance the social position of black Americans. But, notwithstanding the many successes of the civil rights movement since the 1960s, relations between black and white remain a delicate issue in the United States too.

It also implies that special attention should be given to securing the same chances for everybody, whatever their ethnic or social origins might be. Leaving no citizens at the margins of society is to be considered of paramount importance if one cares about social cohesion. Social isolation is indeed the worst thing that can happen. Muslims and children and grandchildren of immigrants have every right to claim and feel that they are legitimate members of society. Intercultural dialogue between community leaders is important, but civil society involvement even more so in order to wipe out prejudices and stereotypes. The diversity within Islam is too often being ignored. Education in particular needs special attention. A sort of 'no child left behind' approach can help in providing all youngsters with the same opportunities, and consequently improve their performances at school. After-school programmes or activities are only some of the actions that might be considered, especially if articulated with the families of the children involved.

Delegitimising Radical Discourse

Delegitimising leaders and ideas is an important undertaking, according to Noor Huda Ismail in Chapter 5. Sociological research has hinted at the fact that when people tend to be active in social and other organisations, they usually are more democratically-minded than people who do not and liaise more easily with the other members of society. The empowerment of self-organisations is part of the endeavour to responsibilise communities, including immigrant communities. Cooperation between local authorities and ethnic, cultural and religious organisations is also part of the same strategy of socialising all groups. Individual exit programmes for radicals might be of some help too. Local leaders, teachers and social workers are best-placed to detect changes in the behaviour of specific youngsters, and can consequently intervene more easily, facilitating the de-radicalisation process in an early stage. Reinsertion or rehabilitation programmes facilitating the reconstruction of the identity have to be available and social workers, psychologists, and so on trained to deal with the problem. Measures taken can best go from local authorities to national authorities and not *vice versa*, because each city has its own realities and problems. Also in this perspective, community policing can prove to be extremely timely.

Many young Muslims in Europe have only a cursory knowledge of Islam. Consequently they are an easy prey for itinerant preachers or self-radicalisation through internet or satellite stations. It is not the government's role to interfere in or steer religious debate, or to promote the 'good' interpretations of Islam – or the 'good' imams and scholars for that matter, which would equate to a kiss of death. What society as a whole can do is contribute to improving the environment, enabling intra-Muslim debates to be able to proceed, by supporting intra-dialogue initiatives, as some groups within the Muslim and immigration communities are attempting to do. In some European countries, immigrant communities are requesting means for launching a major awareness programme, especially directed towards their youngsters, as well as for an increased professionalism of immigrant organisations. Such schemes provide for an opportunity to further the much-needed structured cooperation with immigrant communities, allowing for a possible gradual waning of the polarising mirror images.

Migration flows always create frictions and tensions. Never has the ensuing integration been easy. Now, however, these difficulties have become intertwined with the terrorism issue, the result being that harmonious integration has turned into a Herculean task. Even if there were no terrorism threat, a satisfactory integration of youngsters from minority communities as full members of Western societies would not happen without significant efforts on both sides. But this has now become all the more urgent, since ultimately such an effort will prove to be the only antidote capable of halting the consequences of insidious (self-)radicalisation.

A Ray of Hope – Based upon History

Ultimately, the strategy of terror as a solution to the malaise felt by Muslim and immigration communities will prove to be as much a dead-end as it turned out to be for the anarchist terrorists when they tried to fight the humiliation and marginalisation of the nineteenth-century workers by terrorist tactics.

On the eve of the twentieth century, almost everywhere anarchist terrorism, however, slowly died out. There were two reasons for this. On the one hand, anarchist leaders like Prince Kropotkin realised that terrorist acts could not change things and that the chosen strategy was self-destructive. With each attack the anarchist terrorists drifted further from the working class on whose behalf they claimed to take action. One of the turning points was undoubtedly the aforementioned attacks by Emile Henry in the centre of Paris in 1894. No government buildings or police in sight, only ordinary people going to pubs and theatres and passers-by. Dozens of innocent persons were injured and some were killed. So with each attack the anarchist terrorists turned more and more into the fringe groups they had always been. The anarchists' terrorism was a dead-end. 'They showed us how a Revolution must *not* be made,' Kropotkin said at the end of his life to a fellow-terrorist. At that time he had turned his back on violence, especially on the gratuitous kind Emile Henry had used. Attacks did nothing but provoke an effect opposite to the one sought for: it did not weaken the bourgeois state, on the contrary, with each and every attack the power of police, the military and governments grew. The vicious circle of attacks–repression–attacks turned out to be far more destructive for the anarchists themselves than for the bourgeois society at which their attacks were aimed. A large number of the most devoted anarchists languished in prison. The impact of anarchist terrorism had been minimal.

The second and more important reason for its demise was the emergence of an alternative path to giving the working class a say. The organised labour movement and trade unions offered a far better answer to the desperate marginality of the working classes than the terrorist bombings had ever done. They gave the worker a sense of self-esteem and identity and thus an equal place in society. In sharp contrast with anarchism, it was an influential and legal movement – albeit a very radical one in the eyes of the contemporary observer – thanks to which the individual worker no longer had to face society alone. The legal and constitutional way turned out to be more efficient for enforcing political rights, social reforms and economic improvements than 'propaganda by the deed'. Because of this, anarchist terrorism lost its breeding ground in the constitutional regimes and along with it any hope of legitimacy. It was by this process of gradual evolution that the working class, so feared and despised in those days, slowly gained a fair position in the political and social system and the worker stopped being a second-rate citizen, an outcast.

The same goes for today's jihadi terrorism. Ultimately it will prove to be as self-defeating as its anarchist predecessor experienced. None of the causes that al-

Qaeda inspired radicals and terrorists are said to pursue will be advanced through a strategy of violence. Quite the contrary is true. It will signify these groups' defeat, because it will increasingly isolate the extremists from the communities in whose name they claim to act. But in order for this to become true as swiftly as possible, the perspective of a more inclusive international agenda and action is necessary. Without this, terrorism will keep on smouldering. Only when hope is offered will the breeding ground for violent radicalisation and terrorism dry up.

Bibliography

Abou El Fadl, K.M. (2001), *And God Knows the Soldiers: The Authoritative and Authoritarian in Islamic Discourses* (Lanham, MD: University Press of America).

Abou El Fadl, K.M. (2002), *Conference of the Books: The Search for Beauty in Islam* (New York: University Press of America).

Abun-Nasr, J.M. (1987), *A History of the Maghrib in the Islamic Period* (Cambridge: Cambridge University Press).

Abuza, Z. (2003), *Militant Islam in Southeast Asia Crucible of Terror* (Boulder, CO: Lynne Rienner).

AIVD (2002), *Rekrutering in Nederland voor de jihad*, The Hague, 9 December.

AIVD (2004a), *Saoedische invloeden in Nederland. Verbanden tussen salafitische missie, radicaliseringsprocessen en Islamistisch terrorisme*, The Hague, June.

AIVD (2004b), *De AIVD in verandering*, The Hague, Commissie Bestuurlijke Evaluatie, November.

Aldrich, R. (2005), 'The New Terrorism', *The Independent*, 10 July.

Alexander, Y. and D. Pluchinsky (1992), *Europe's Red Terrorists: The Fighting Communist Organizations* (London: Frank Cass).

Ali, J. (2003), 'Islamic Revivalism: The Case of Tablighi Jamaat', *Journal of Muslim Minority* Affairs, 23(1): 173–81.

AP (2005), 'Indonesia President: Must Stay Vigilant against Terror Attacks', *Agence Presse*, 16 August.

Ayoob, M. (2004), 'Political Islam: Image and Reality', *World Policy Journal*, Fall: 1–14.

Ayoob, M. (2005), 'The Future of Political Islam: The Importance of External Variables', *International Affairs*, 81(5): 951–61.

Bakhtin, M. (1981), *The Dialogic Imagination: Four Essays* (Austin, TX: University Press of Texas).

Beckford, J.A. (ed.) (1988), *New Religious Movement and Rapid Social Changes* (London: Sage/Unesco).

Bell, B.J. (1977), *Terror Out of Zion* (New York: St. Martin's Press).

Benjamin, D. and S. Simon (2000), 'The New Face of Terrorism', *New York Times*, 4 January.

Benjamin, D. and S. Simon (2003), *The Age of Sacred Terror: Radical Islam's War Against America* (New York: Random House).

Bennison, A. (1999/2000), 'Abd al-Qadir, Morocco and the Sharifian model', *Journal of Algerian Studies*, no. 4/5: 1–20.

Bremer, P. (2001), 'A New Strategy for the New Face of Terrorism', *The National Interest*, 23–30.

Bruce, S. (1996), *Religion in the Modern World: From Cathedral to Cults* (Oxford: Oxford University Press).

Burnett, J. and D. Whyte (2005), 'Embedded Expertise and the New Terrorism', *Journal for Crime, Conflict and the Media*, 1(4): 1–18.

Bush, G.W. (2002), Graduation Speech, United States Military Academy, West Point, New York, 1 June.

Bush, G.W. (2005a), Address to the National Endowment for Democracy, 'The Nature of the Enemy We Face and the Strategy for Victory', 6 October.

Bush, G.W. (2005b), Presidents Bush's Remarks at the FBI Academy, 11 July.

Bush, G.W. (2005c), President Bush's Remarks at the National Defense University, March.

CAP (2005), 'The Terrorism Index', *Foreign Policy*, February.

CAP (2007), 'The Terrorism Index', *Foreign Policy*, February.

Central Intelligence Agency (1976), 'Research Study: International and Transnational Terrorism: Diagnosis and Prognosis', April.

Cesari, J. (2004) *When Islam and Democracy Meet: Muslims in Europe and in the United States* (New York: Palgrave Macmillan).

Cesari, J. (2006), *Muslims in Western Europe: Why is the Term Islamophobia More a Predicament Than An Explanation?*, Report to the European Commission, <http://www.euro-islam.info/PDFs/ChallengeProjectReport.pdf%20-4.pdf>.

Cesari, J. and S. McLoughlin (eds) (2005), *European Muslims and the Secular State* (Aldershot: Ashgate).

CIEM (2006), *Trends in Terrorism Series. Militant Jihadism: Radicalisation, Conversion, Recruitment*, vol. 4.

Clarke, R. (2004), *Against All Enemies: Inside America's War on Terror* (New York: Free Press).

Clarke, R.V. and M. Felson (eds) (1993), *Routine Activity and Rational Choice: Advances in Criminological Theory*, vol. 5 (New Brunswick, NJ: Transaction Books).

Coolsaet, R. (2005), *Al-Qaeda: The Myth* (Ghent: Academia Press).

Coolsaet, R. and T. van de Voorde (2004), *International Terrorism: A Longitudinal Statistical Analysis* (Ghent: Ghent University, Department of Political Science).

Coolsaet, R. and T. van de Voorde (2006), *The Evolution of Terrorism in 2005: A Statistical Assessment*, University of Ghent Research Paper, February.

Council of the European Union (2005), 14469/4/05 REV 4, 30 November.

Crenshaw, M. (ed.) (1995) *Terrorism in Context* (University Park, PA: Pennsylvania State University Press).

Cronin, K.A. and J.M. Ludes (eds) (2004), *Attacking Terrorism: Elements of a Grand Strategy* (Washington, DC: Georgetown University Press).

Cullison, A. (2004), 'Inside Al-Qaeda's Hard Drive: A Fortuitous Discovery Reveals Budget Squabbles, Baby Pictures, Office Rivalries—and the Path to 9-11', *The Atlantic Monthly*, 55–70.

Dassetto, F. (ed.) (1997), *Facettes de l'islam belge* (Louvain la Neuve: Academia Bruylants).

DNI (2006), Office of the Director of National Intelligence, Declassified Key Judgments of the National Intelligence Estimate 'Trends in Global Terrorism: Implications for the United States', dated April.

Doran, M. (2002), 'The Pragmatic Fanaticism of Al Qaeda: An Anatomy of Extremism in Middle Eastern Politics', *Political Science Quarterly*, 117(2): 177–90.

Droz, B. and E. Lever (1982), *Histoire de la guerre d'Algérie, 1954–1962* (Paris: Seuil).

Eade, J. and C. Mele (eds) (2001), *Urban Studies: Contemporary and Future Perspectives* (Oxford: Blackwell).

Eickelman, D.F. and J.P. Piscatori (1996), *Muslim Politics* (Princeton, NJ: Princeton University Press).

El Aroud, M. (2003), *Les soldats de Lumière* (published by the author).

El-Din Shahin, E. (2005), *Political Islam: Ready for Engagement?*, Madrid, Fride, Working Paper 3, February.

Etienne, B. (1977), *Algérie: Cultures et Révolution* (Paris: Seuil).

EU (2005), *The EU Strategy for Combating Radicalisation and Recruitment to Terrorism*, doc. 14781/1/05, <http://www.consilium.europa.eu>.

Fair, C. and H. Haqqani (2006), 'Think Again: Islamist Terrorism', *Financial Express*, 6 February.

Falkenrath, R., R.D. Newman and B. Thayer (1998), *America's Achilles' Heel: Nuclear, Biological, and Chemical Terrorism and Covert Attack* (Cambridge, MA: MIT Press).

Fergany, N. (2003), *Preventing Violent Protest Behaviour: An Arab Region Perspective*; *A Role for Europe?*, IRRI-KIIB, Brussels, 'Clingendael', The Hague, Why 9/11?, The Root Causes of International Terrorism, Brussels, 20 November.

Fromkin, D. (1975), 'The Strategy of Terrorism', *Foreign Affairs*, 53(4): 683–98.

Gambetta, D. (ed.) (2005), *Making Sense of Suicide Missions* (Oxford: Oxford University Press).

Garton Ash, T. (2006), 'Islam in Europe', *New York Review of Books*, 53(15), 5 October.

Gellner, E. (1974), 'The Unknown Apollo of Biskra: The Social Base of Algerian Puritanism', *Government and Opposition*, 9: 277–310.

Gellner, E. (1981), *Muslim Society* (Cambridge: Cambridge University Press).

German Bertelsmann Stiftung (2006), *Who Rules the World? World Powers and International Order*, Berlin, Bertelsmann Stiftung, 2 June.

Ghalioun, B. (2002), interview in *Le Monde*, 25 March.

Ghalioun, B. (2004) 'The Persistence of Arab Authoritarianism', *Journal of Democracy*, 15(4).

Giddens, A. (2004), 'The Future of World Society: The New Terrorism', delivered at the London School of Economics, 10 November, available at Columbia International Affairs Online (CIAO).

Gorka, S. (2004), 'Al-Qaeda's Next Generation', *Jamestown Terrorism Monitor*, 2(15).

Gorriti, G. (1999), *The Shining Path: A History of the Millenarian War in Peru* (Chapel Hill, NC: University of North Carolina Press).

Gray, J. (2003), *Al-Qa'eda and What it Means to be Modern* (London: Faber & Faber).

Grignard, A. (1997), 'L'islam radical à travers la littérature de propagande: une introduction', in Dassetto (ed) *Facettes de l'islam belge* (Louvain la Neuve: Academia Bruylants).

Grignard, A. (2001), 'Contribution à l'historique des groupes armés Algériens', *Les Cahiers de l'Orient*, no. 62.

Grignard A. (2005), 'Lutter contre le terrorisme sans diaboliser l'immigré', *Le Soir*, 30 November.

Guelke, A. (1995), *The Age of Terrorism and the International Political System* (London: Tauris Academic Studies).

Halliday, F. (2002), *Two Hours that Shook the World, September 11, Causes and Consequences* (London: Saqi Books).

Haroun, A. (1986), *La Septième Wilaya; la guerre du FLN en France* (Paris: Seuil).

Harrison, A. (1989), *Challenging De Gaulle: The O.A.S. and the Counterrevolution in Algeria, 1954–1962* (New York: Praeger).

Hassan, Nasra (2001), 'Talking to the "Human Bombs"', *The New Yorker*, 19 (19 November).

Holmes, S. (2005), 'Al-Qaeda, September 11, 2001', in Gambetta (ed), *Making Sense of Suicide Missions* (Oxford: Oxford University Press).

Hoffman, B. (1998), *Inside Terrorism* (New York: Columbia University Press).

Hoffman, B. (2006) 'From the War on Terror to Global Counterinsurgency', *Current History*, 105(693).

Home Office (2005), *Preventing Extremism Together, Working Groups*, Home Office Report.

Horgan, J. (2005), *The Psychology of Terrorism* (London: Routledge).

Hourani, A. (1962), *Arabic Thought in the Liberal Age, 1798–1939* (Oxford: Oxford University Press).

Hundaine, K. (2003), 'Becoming a Committed Insider', *Culture and Physiology*, 9: 107–27.

Iannaccone, L.R. (1994), 'Why Strict Churches Are Strong', *American Journal of Sociology*, 99(5).

ICG (2003), 'Jamaah Islamiyah in South East Asia: Damaged but Still Dangerous', *Asia Report*, no. 63, 26 August.

ICG (2004a), 'Islamism in North Africa, I: The Legacies of History', *Middle East/ North Africa Briefing*, no. 12, 20 April.

ICG (2004b), 'Islamism, Violence and Reform in Algeria: Turning the Page', *Middle East/North Africa Report*, no. 29, 30 July.

ICG (2005), 'Understanding Islamism', *Middle East/North Africa Report*, no. 37, 2 March.

ICG (2006a), 'La France face à ses musulmans: émeutes, jihadisme et dépolitisation', *Rapport Europe*, no. 172, 9 March.

ICG (2006b), 'Terrorism in Indonesia: Noordin's Networks', *Asia Report*, no. 114, 5 May.

Ignatius, D. (2006), *Washington Post*, 10 February.

Ismail, N.H. (2005), 'Quest for the Meaning of Life Drives Educated Men to Death', *The Australian*, 12 December.

Jordan, J. and N. Horsburgh (2005), 'Mapping Jihadist Terrorism in Spain', *Studies in Conflict & Terrorism*, 28: 169–91.

Kalyvas, S.N. (2001), 'New and Old Civil Wars: A Valid Distinction', *World Politics*, 54: 99–118.

Kepel, G. (1993), *Le Prophète et Pharaon* (Paris: Seuil).

Kepel, G. (2002), *Jihad: The Trail of Political Islam* (Cambridge, MA: Harvard University Press).

Kepel, G. (2004), *The War for Muslim Minds: Islam and the West* (Cambridge, MA: Harvard University Press).

Kerr, M. (1966), *Islamic Reform: The Political and Legal Theories of Muhammad 'Abduh and Rashid Ridâ* (Cambridge: Cambridge University Press).

Khosrokhavar, F. (2006), *Quand Al-Qaïda parle. Témoignages derrière les barreaux* (Paris: Grasset).

Krueger, A.B. and D.D. Laitin (2005), 'Misunderstanding Terrorism', *Foreign Affairs*, 83(5), September.

Kruger, A.B. and J. Maleckova (2003), 'Education, Poverty and Terrorism: Is there a Causal Connection ?', *Journal of Economic Perspective*, 17(4): 119–44.

Labat, S. (1995), *Les islamistes algériens, entre les urnes et le maquis* (Paris: Seuil).

Laqueur, W. (1986), 'Reflections on Terrorism', *Foreign Affairs*, 65(1).

Laqueur, W. (1999), *The New Terrorism: Fanaticism and the Arms of Mass Destruction* (New York: Oxford University Press).

Lawrence, B. (2005), *Messages to the World: The Statements of Osama Bin Laden* (London: Verso).

Leiken, R. (2005), 'Angry Young Muslims in Europe', *Foreign Affairs*, 84(4).

Lesser, I.O. et al. (1999), *Countering the New Terrorism* (Santa Monica, CA: Rand Corporation).

Lubeck, P. (1999), 'Antonomies of Islamic Movements under Globalisation', *CGIRS Working Paper*, no. 99-1.

Lubeck, P. and B. Britts (2001), 'Muslim Civil Society in Urban Public Spaces: Globalisation, Discursive Shifts and Social Movements', in J. Eade and C. Mele (eds), *Urban Studies: Contemporary and Future Perspectives* (Oxford: Blackwell).

Maalouf, A. (1998), *Les identités meurtrières* (Paris: Grasset).

Marty, M. and R. Appleby (eds) (1994), *Accounting for Fundamentalism: The Dynamic Character of Movements* (Chicago, IL: University of Chicago Press).

Masci, D. (2004), 'An Uncertain Road: Muslims and the Future of Europe', *The Pew Forum on Religion & Public Life*, December.

Merah, A. (1998), *L'Affaire Bouyali* (Alger: Merah Editions).

Merkl, P. (1995), 'West German Left-Wing Terrorism', in Martha Crenshaw (ed.), *Terrorism in Context* (University Park, PA: Pennsylvania State University Press).

Miller, M. (1995), 'The Intellectual Origins of Modern Terrorism in Europe', in Martha Crenshaw (ed.), *Terrorism in Context* (University Park, PA: Pennsylvania State University Press).

Mogahed, D. (2006), 'Understanding Islamic Democracy', *Europe's World*, spring.

Morgan, M.J. (2004), 'The Origins of the New Terrorism', *Parameters*, 34(1): 29–43.

Morgenthau, Tom, 'The New Terrorism', *Newsweek*, 5 July 1993: 18.

Mueller, J. (2006), *Overblown: How Politicians and the Terrorism Industry Inflate National Security Threats, and Why We Believe Them* (New York: Free Press).

Murphy, D. (2006), 'A New Generation of Jihad Seekers', *Christian Science Monitor*, Friday, 18 August.

Nadwi, S. (1964), *Hazrat Maulana Muhammad Ilyas Aur Un Ki Dini Dawa't* (Lucknow: Tanwir).

Nesser P. (2006), 'Jihadism in Western Europe after the Invasion of Iraq: Tracing Motivational Influences from the Iraq War on Jihadist Terrorism in Western Europe', *Studies in Conflict & Terrorism*, 29: 323–42.

NIC (2004), *Mapping the Global Future*, Report of the National Intelligence Council's 2020 Project (Pittsburgh, PA: GPO).

Palmieri-Billig, L. (2003), 'Survey Shows Xenophobia, Anti-Semitism Rising in Italy', *Jerusalem Post*, 1 July.

Pape, R. (2005), *Dying to Win: The Strategic Logic of Suicide Terrorism* (New York: Random House).

Parkin, R. (1997), *Kinship: An Introduction to the Basic Concepts* (Oxford: Blackwell).

Pew (2006a), ICM poll, February 2006, *The Great Divide: How Westerners and Muslims See Each Other*, Washington, DC, Pew Global Attitudes Project, 22 June.

Pew (2006b), *Muslims in Europe: Economic Worries Top Concerns About Religious and Cultural Identity*, Washington, DC, Pew Global Attitudes Project, 6 July.

Phalet, K. (2004), *Moslim in Nederland. Een onderzoek naar de religieuze betrokkenheid van Turken en Marokkanen* (The Hague: Sociaal en Cultureel Planbureau).

Pillar, R. (2004), 'Counterterrorism after al-Qaeda', *Washington Quarterly*, 27(3): 101–13.

Postiglione, G.A. (1983), *Ethnicity and American Social Theory* (New York: University Press of America).

Quillen, C. (2002), 'A Historical Analysis of Mass Casualty Bombers', *Studies in Conflict and Terrorism*, 25(5): 279–302.

Ramadan, T. (2006), 'The Global Ideology of Fear', *New Perspectives Quarterly*, 23(1).

Rapoport, D.C. (2004), 'The Four Waves of Modern Terrorism', in A. Kurth Cronin and J. M. Ludes (eds), *Attacking Terrorism: Elements of a Grand Strategy* (Washington, DC: Georgetown University Press).

Reich, W. (ed.) (1990), *Origins of Terrorism: Psychologies, Ideologies, Theologies, States of Mind* (Baltimore, MD: Johns Hopkins University Press).

Robbins, T. (1988), *Cults Converts and Charisma: The Sociology of New Religious Movement* (London: Sage).

Roberts, H. (1994), 'From Radical Mission to Equivocal Ambition: The Expansion and Manipulation of Algerian Islamism, 1979–1992', in Martin E. Marty and R. Scott Appleby (eds), *Accounting for Fundamentalism: The Dynamic Character of Movements* (Chicago, IL: University of Chicago Press).

Roberts, H. (2003) *The Battlefield: Algeria 1988–2002. Studies in a Broken Polity* (London and New York: Verso).

Rose, G. (1999), 'It Could Happen Here: Facing the New Terrorism', *Foreign Affairs*, 78(2).

Rousselot, Fabrice (2001), 'John Walker, de la Californie aux talibans. L'itinéraire de ce "soldat d'Al-Qaeda" américain déconcerte les Etats-Unis', *Libération*, 17 December.

Roy, O. (2002), *L'Islam mondialisé* (Paris: Seuil).

Roy, O. (2004), *Globalized Islam: The Search for a New Ummah* (New York: Columbia University Press).

Roy, O. (2005), *La laïcité face à l'islam* (Paris: Stock).

Rudolph, S. and J.P. Piscatori (eds) (1997), *Transnational Religion and Fading States* (Boulder, CO: Westview Press).

Sageman, M. (2004a), 'Jihadi Militants Defy Stereotypes, Author Says', *Washington Times*, 5 July.

Sageman, M. (2004b) *Understanding Terror Networks* (Philadelphia, PA: University of Pennsylvania Press).

Schmitt, K. (2003), 'Islamophobia on Rise in Germany: Study', *Islam Online*, 26 December.

SCP (2004), *In het licht van de toekomst* (The Hague: Sociaal en Cultureel Planbureau).

Seale, P. (1992), *Abu Nidal: A Gun for Hire* (New York: Random House).

Sendagorta, F. (2005), 'Jihad in Europe: The Wider Context', *Survival*, (47)3.

Sikand, Y.S. (2002), *The Origins and Development of the Tabligi Jama'at, 1920–2000: A Cross Country Comparative Study* (Hyderabad: Orient Longman).

Simon S. (2003), 'The New Terrorism: Securing the Nation against a Messianic Foe', *The Brookings Review*, 21(1).

Simon, S. and J. Stevenson (2005), 'Thinking outside the Tank', *The National Interest*, 78: 90–98.

Sivan, E. (1985), *Radical Islam* (New Haven, CT and London: Yale University Press).

Smith, C. (2005) 'Raised as Catholic in Belgium, She Died as a Muslim Bomber', *New York Times*, 6 December.

Sprinzak, E. (1990), 'The Psychopolitical Formation of Extreme Left Terrorism in a Democracy: The Case of the Weathermen', in W. Reich (ed.), *Origins of Terrorism: Psychologies, Ideologies, Theologies, States of Mind* (Baltimore, MD: Johns Hopkins University Press).

Stark, R. and W.S. Bainbridge (1985), *The Failure of Religion: Secularization, Revival and Cult Formation* (Berkeley, CA: University California Press).

Stern, J. (1999), *The Ultimate Terrorists* (Cambridge, MA: Harvard University Press).

Stiglitz, J. (2002), 'The Roaring Nineties', *Atlantic Monthly*, October: 76–89.

Swanstorm, N. and E. Bjornehed (2004), 'Conflict Resolution of Terrorists Conflicts in Southeast Asia', *Terrorism and Political Violence*, 16(2): 328–49.

Taarnby, M. (2005a), 'Recruitment of Islamist Terrorists in Europe: Trends and Perspectives', Research Report funded by the Danish Ministry of Justice, January.

Taarnby, M. (2005b), 'Yemen's Committee for Dialogue: Can Jihadists Return to Society?', *Terrorism Monitor*, 3(14).

Taarnby M. (2006), 'Jihad in Denmark: An Overview and Analysis of Jihadi Activity in Denmark (1990–2006)', DIIS Working Paper, no. 2006/35.

Taji-Farouki, S. (1996), *A Fundamental Quest: Hizb al-Tahrir and the Search for the Islamic Caliphate* (London: Grey Seal).

Taylor, M. (1993), 'Rational Choice, Behaviour Analysis and Political Violence', in R.V. Clarke and M. Felson (eds), *Routine Activity and Rational Choice: Advances in Criminological Theory*, vol. 5 (New Brunswick, NJ: Transaction Books).

Taylor, M. and J. Horgan (2006), 'A Conceptual Framework for Addressing Psychological Process in the Development of the Terrorist', *Terrorism and Political Violence*, 18(4).

Taylor, M. and E. Quayle (1993), *Terrorist Lives* (London: Brassey's).

Tucker, D. (2001), 'What is New about the New Terrorism and How Dangerous is It?', *Terrorism and Political Violence*, 14(3): 1–14.

Tucker, J.D. (ed.) (2000), *Toxic Terror: Assessing Terrorist Use of Chemical and Biological Weapons* (Cambridge, MA: MIT Press).

UN (2004), *Human Development Report 2004. Cultural Diversity in Today's Diverse World* (Washington, DC: UNDP).

UN (2005), *In Larger Freedom: Towards Development, Security and Human Rights for All*, New York, United Nations, 21 March 2005 (A/59/2005).

US Department of State (2004), 'Patterns of Global Terrorism 2003', April.

US Department of State (2005), 'Country Reports on Terrorism 2004', Washington, DC, April.

US Department of State (2006), 'Country Reports on Terrorism 2005', Washington, DC, April.

Vidino, L. (2005), *Al Qaeda in Europe: The New Battleground of International Jihad* (United Kingdom: Prometheus Books).

Volpi, F. (2002), Islam *& Democracy: The Failure of Dialogue in Algeria, 1988–2001* (London: Pluto).

Waslekar, S. (2007), *An Inclusive World: In Which the West, Islam and the Rest Have a Stake* (Mumbai: Strategic Foresight).

White House (2006), Office of the Press Secretary, 11 January, 'President Participates in Discussion on the Global War on Terror', Kentucky International Convention Center, Louisville, Kentucky.

White Paper, Ministry of Home Affairs Republic of Singapore (2003), 'The Jemaah Islamiyah Arrest and the Threat of Terrorism', The Singapore Minister of Home Affairs, 7 January.

Wiktorowicz, Q. and J. Kaltner (2003), 'Killing in the Name of Islam: Al-Qaeda's Justification for September 11', *Middle East Policy*, 10(2): 76–92.

Yeo, E. (2006), 'Terror Cells Spread across Indonesia and More Attacks Inevitable: Minister', *Agence France-Presse*, Kuala Lumpur, Malaysia, 5 October.

Zimmerman, D. (2003), *The Transformation of Terrorism* (Zurich: Andreas Wenger).

Zulaika, J. and A.W. Douglas (1996), *Terror and Taboo: The Follies, Fables and Face of Terrorism* (New York and London: Routledge).

Index